DO YOU WANT TO GO TO JAIL TODAY?

Mark

Thanks for all your friendship.

It's always gonna be a pleasure to know you.

Best wishes,

Peter Hall

Do You Want to Go to Jail Today?

Peter Hall

Peter Hall can be reached for questions, comments, and/or public appearances at peterocks212@yahoo.com

This book was printed in the United States of America.

To order additional copies of this book, contact:
Xlibris Corporation
1-888-795-4274
www.Xlibris.com
Orders@Xlibris.com
43926

ABOUT THE AUTHOR

I have been born into upper middle class. I am the last of six children.
I have been afforded the benefits of being the youngest of our clan.
My father is a reputable doctor, and my mother is a registered nurse.
I have had every opportunity of succeeding in this world, but I allowed countless
opportunities to pass me by.
I have attended both public and private educational institutions. I dropped out on several
of them.
I have worked for the best of organizations . . . and the worst.
I have owned my own businesses, but neglected the most important golden rule.
I am an entrepreneur, but failed to follow through.

I have owned many wonderful luxuries in my life.
I have lived in beautiful homes and vacationed at the best resorts. I have also slept under
bridges, in sheds, and other homeless venues.
I have driven the fastest cars and the biggest trucks. Today, my beat up old van is my lifeline.
I have tasted the finest of gourmet foods. I have also begged for food and even scavenged
for your leftovers.
I have dressed in the finest clothes for all the world to see. I have also taken clothes from
the line in your backyard.
I have been seduced by the most exotic women of this world.
I have been in the best of relationships . . . and experienced the worst of betrayal.

There are many events and activities leading up to this fateful day. It was a long time coming.
And when this day finally arrived, it was all gone . . . in the blink of an eye.
It is the end result of a wrong turn . . . and a bad decision.

By reading this book, you may find insight into the way your life is headed.
Look around you . . . I mean, really look around and ask yourself . . . is it *really* so bad
that you would venture into something that begs the question . . . *Do You Want To
Go To Jail Today?*

Peter Hall

Foreword

There are over two million persons in jail today. *I was one of them.* The numbers constantly vary from one day to another as the revolving door of prison continues to scrap up lawbreakers from coast to coast. Most of them, who are released to the free world, will be sent back to some type of jail after being let back into society. In addition to the inmates in jail today, there are over 7 million adults on probation or parole. That's about one in every thirty adults. The numbers are increasing everyday.

But there are a larger number of people to contend with besides just inmates. It is the people who are affected by the turmoil created when a person does go to jail. I'm talking about your mothers, fathers, brothers, sisters, sons, daughters, spouses, and of course, the victims. When you calculate all the persons affected by a prisoner's incarceration, the numbers rises exponentially. It must be in the tens of millions. But as you will discover, the number of people that will continue to care about your whereabouts while you are in jail will fade quickly over a short period of time. For them, life will continue without interruption. *It has to in order to survive.*

Consider this: *before doing the crime that requires you to do the time,* spend some precious moments reflecting on all the persons that will suffer because of your disregard for your own freedom and your lack of concern for the future of all those affected by it. **The tragedy we place upon ourselves by going to jail is a burden to all.**

Do you want to go to jail today brings the reader deep into the mind's eye. **You will bear witness to the horrid conditions and terrible events deep down in the fires that light hell's furnace.** Even deeper, are the torturous scenarios of what you wish your life should've been if you hadn't come to jail today. The "what ifs", and "only ifs" of the *"would'ves, could'ves, should'ves"* are all that you can cling on to for hope and prayer. And you will pray. *For what?* Only you will know. *For who?* I can only guess. And my guess is that you will pray for somebody that gives a damn too. Somebody that cares about you . . . *more than you do.*

Are you alone? Did you come to jail today? Will you be there tomorrow? Does your history wish for a better re-occurrence of events unfolding in your life? Right now, at this very moment, are you in jail because of some unforeseen future that should have been recognized long before the cuffs were placed around your wrists? If you are in jail today, have been in jail before, or are setting yourself up to go to jail, this is the book to read. Jail is the sentence you receive for committing a crime. And the sentence is time. But the *true punishment of your crime will come from the imprisonment of your mind.*

I would like to offer infinite thanks to my sister Elizabeth for providing me with a place for inspiration . . . a room with a view.

For Mom, Dad, and Nick

Special Thanks:
Paul Contro
Chris Reminder
Kristy Wingate

I would like to offer the greatest of thanks to all of the staff of Xlibris Corporation for their time, energy and infinite patience. You guys are the best!

Extra special thanks to ISTOCKPHOTO . . . best photo website on the planet

RUNNING TO STAND STILL

And so she woke up
From where she was lying still
Said we got to do something about where we're going
Step on a steam train
Step out of the driving rain
Maybe run from the darkness in the night . . .

. . . Sweet the sin
But bitter the taste in my mouth
I see seven towers
But I see one way out
You got to cry without weeping
Talk without speaking
Scream without raising your voice . . .
I took the poison from the poison stream,
Then I floated out of here . . .

. . . She runs through the streets
With her eyes painted red
Under black belly of cloud in the rain
In through a doorway she brings me
White gold and pearls stolen from the sea
She is raging
She is raging and the storm blows up in her eyes
She will suffer the needle chill
She is running to stand still

Running To Stand Still
The Joshua Tree
U2

I cannot bear to read this book ever again. It hurts too much. The ups and downs of daily life are nauseating. I am bouncing uncontrollably amidst the confusion of what's being told to me, what's being dealt with, and what's really happening back in the free world. It isn't so much as the time and conditions of my sentence that has me suffering, as it is the disbelief of my own mind running itself into insanity. I am turning on myself over and over. I keep starting from scratch . . . again and again. At the same time, I am enduring countless words and promises of false hope and deception. I have lost any recognition of what is real or not. It is the endless, tormenting, imprisonment within my sentence. Don't make it yours!

Peter Hall

CONTENTS

Daily Diary

Back Cover: Why You Should Be Reading This Book

The Pen Drops

1. This book is a "*Pulp Fiction*" so to speak. **It should be read from beginning to end in order for you to gain any insight to the resolution of things to come.** Many questions remain unanswered. Many answers contain questions within themselves. While on this trail ride into hell, all my prayers of everything a man should ask (and more often beg) for will come to light. All except for one. It will remain unanswered. Only God knows what the outcome of this unfulfilled prayer will be. He's funny that way. He answers all prayers in His own time. He grants nothing on demand and always is on the lookout to make your stay here on earth as comfortable as possible. **Even if it means you have to venture through the darkness of hell to finally come to the Light.**

2. This journey transcends over time to eleven different units within five districts in the state of Texas. **During this time, I have become a broken man stumbling down into the deepest darkest depths of despair. I have reached out to empty hands and a lost heart. I have pleaded to deafened ears. I have caused pain and suffering and anguish beyond the scope of my conscience to even those I am unaware of. I have become an *inmate in the penal system* and have been branded as such for life. My record is public for all those to see and judge. I possess the minimum of rights and have *lost all civil liberties as a free individual*.**

3. Imagine a place where you are not wanted and never cared about as an individual. A place where being yelled at, kicked, and punched, is the constant reminders that you are nothing of anyone in a system that focuses on *denying you everything*. Now, multiply that by an everyday revolving door of over two million inmates across the land.

4. This is a place where the purpose of keeping order is the priority. No one is here to reason, communicate, or listen to what you think is important. Nothing that is important to you is ever considered in this uncaring, and unforgiving place. There is no compassion to interact on any level close to being human. Most behave like guard dogs, barking orders and commands to those not even remotely interested. Looking at them in their fitting roles, I realize the only thing separating these guards from actually being dogs is facial hair. God help us if they ever stop shaving!

5.   This is a place where needing something means getting in line . . . a very long line of time and frustration. *A line that can last for weeks to months, and even years.* Here, someone always needs something and whatever is needed, is needed right now and that *"right now"* keeps getting pushed back. No one remembers what you needed yesterday—not even you! What matters is . . . what's needed now and you're the only one who cares about how you get it. But for now, as it appears, nobody . . . *but **nobody** gives a damn what you need*! So for what ever it is you need, don't expect to get it now. *We are the ambassadors of patience.*

6.   *Come here, and you will have to do whatever it takes to survive the onslaught of character defamation and the degrading of any self-respect you possess as a result of the physical and verbal abuse of the guards.* Now, compound that with the steady challenges of push-n-pull attitudes from the inmates. The strategy here is to play like a chameleon and adapt to the continuous changes going on throughout the system; to blend with the program and go with the flow. *To get in where you fit in!* **This is the penal system**: *jail, lock up, incarceration, it's all the same. Call it whatever you like, but whatever you call it, chances are better than ever . . . that you won't like being in jail today!*

Introduction

1. **To see its cover triggers an instant need to pick it up** . . . *just as you have.* Its title alone casts a shadow of immediate reflection of someone you know, something you've seen or heard, and somewhere you don't ever want to be. This book can save the lives of a million marriages. *It could spare ten million children from decisions of regret and remorse, which can last a lifetime.* If you're going to read it, **read it thoroughly** . . . *then pass it on.*

2. It's not so much about life on the inside of jail that held me captive, as it is about what went on in my head, and the lives around me while I was on tour throughout the Texas prison system.

3. *Nobody wants to go to jail today* and surely nobody is sitting down at the dining table plotting ways to volunteer their services to an inmate program. It's not the vacation of a lifetime that anyone should look toward. Unfortunately, the surprising reality is that an *endless number of people are unknowingly setting themselves up at this very moment for so many different circumstances that will put them there tonight.*

4. Hidden deep within their compromising minds, they gamble the odds with each passing moment. It's happening right now and more often than you'd like to believe . . . and so much more closer than you think. **Each and every day, never-ending streams of lawbreakers are herded into jail like cattle. The result of a wrong turn leading to a chase, a verbal argument turned physical, or a petty theft resulting in a shootout. Simple events becoming unnecessarily complicated.** No insurance, lost tickets unpaid, broken headlights, DWI's, domestic disputes, possession of "whatever", . . . the list is endless. Just look at the back of one of those citations you recently received. The list goes on and the excuses are infinite, but the results are most often always the same: *break the law and you're going to jail today*! It leaves you wondering what the hell happened and why you are sitting in jail while the rest of the world is passing you by.

5. **Somebody is going to jail today**. That's the sad and pathetic news! Its point of discovery is both an end to false security and justification . . . and the very beginning of a tragic and sorrowful truth. **"It" (jail) becomes a place where the past, present,**

and future are simultaneously blended into one constant time zone. Now, within this presence (which is the present situation of being arrested), all future regrets are occurring from a multitude of bad decisions. The feeling is mind-bending. *The sensation triggers numbness.* The steel around your wrists collapses all instances of being able to retrace your steps.

6. The domino effect sets in as the events of the moment leave behind the reasons you didn't think of, or just to choose to ignore. Once arrested, there is no *rewind* or *stop* button to leave enough time to escape. *"What if's"* and *"if only's"* are piling up in your surrender. Alternate routes spin endlessly through the alleys and the intersections of where you should have turned to reach your destination. But now, your only option is to continue on with *play* . . . and now, that means playing the role of an inmate. *Time* will now slide into the *slow, long, play (SLP)*. There is no *fast forward* here to bring you up to speed on the latest developments pertaining to your case. You will not pull the world in around yourself here and if you do, it will push back down on you. Your world of "hurry up and wait" has become nothing more than "wait for what?" . . . Wait for nothing! The intervals crawl and creep through the cracks of time and more often than not, *pause* seems to hold the curse of permanence.

7. **The *good news* is that you can *prevent it and break from the circle of destruction* in your life. Consider the events that will make up your day. What puts you at risk? The drives? The pick-ups? The drops? The fighting? The stealing? The dealing? What's it going to be today that sets you apart from the rest of them that says . . . *"you're under arrest, and you're going to jail today"*!**

8. The law says, *"Don't take it personally"*, but they're lying! You have to take *"it"* personally because if you don't, *"it"* won't matter. That *"it"* is your freedom, and the right to choose the events of sleeping, the luxury of quietness, or the scent of cleanliness. It is a breath of fresh air, the feel of rain upon your face, or the sunshine soaking through your skin. It is the wantingness of saying *"yes"* or the right to express *"no"* within any decision. **The moment any one of these rights are not taken personally, or are taken for granted—you lose them!** And why not? The law diligently sits, plots, researches, and waits with surveillance to capture those who will go downtown where the only surround sound comes from the echoes of hundreds of other inmates loudly replaying their own circumstances. Unfortunately, each one of those speakers has his own story to tell, and is fighting at the gates of hell to tell it to whoever can hear—*even if you're not paying attention.*

9. The choice becomes clear. **Choose the freedom to come home tonight to what you are familiar. No matter the circumstances or the conditions, it's still *freedom*, and that in itself . . . *gives you the right to control your surroundings*. Take it away and it becomes a bitter fight to get it back. Your life is reduced to sympathetic pleading, slave begging, unconditional promises, and infinite apologies to all those affected by your ill-fated decisions.**

10. Today should be . . . or tomorrow will be the day that, before your breakfast, or brushing your teeth, before the kids or the parents, before opening the door and leaving the nest, you will take a deep, long, breath and speak the words . . . *"Do you want to go to jail today"?*

11. Come with me on a ride into hell. However temporary in time or whatever the place of geography, hell has the same similar features no matter where you may reside. From L.A. to Miami, Salt Lake City to Houston, Seattle to Cleveland, the name remains the same. **Jail is a place where you are bound to a confinement against your will for an undetermined amount of time.** *The conditions of restraint and the lack of humanity are what you can refer to that time in jail as hell!*

12. Let me take you into a world of hatred. A breeding ground for the strong preying on the weak. A place where your identity is branded by only what you can give or what can be taken from you. Enter this place, and the chaperones hold you in contempt. Their hatred burns with desire to suppress you—*by any means necessary!* And when it's not necessary, *it's still the necessity!* Surviving this place is for real. The danger is always constant. Its reality is defined as a nightmare, but you keep waking up to the same truth. It's a place where you never really sleep. Your life becomes a daily series of naps and resting periods. You wake to the same burden of prison 2, 3, and even 4 times in a day. This is a constant interruption of your life (or *what remains of it*) and your thoughts. It is a submission of privacy.

13. You are never alone in this place, not with your body, not with your mind. There is no avoidance. You cannot close your eyes and forget where you are. You are an inmate, not even a number to be identified, as you are a bunk number to be called out—*even when there is no bunk!*

The Arrest

1. I knew it as coming but chose to ignore it. And then when it finally came, there was no way to avoid it. It was, to say the least, a public display of humiliation . . . a *PDH,* as I like to call it. I was called out into the street for all the surrounding folks to see me. It was right in front of the place where he knew I'd always be. In the midst of rush hour parties on a Friday night, the 10pm hour had given way to a few concoctions already.

2. The cop and I had been social acquaintances during the pool league which allowed for some conversations of sorts between us, but any friendship compatibility quickly subsided when the team got cut. He is nothing more than a beat cop, but continued to fight at the gates of fame to tell his story to whoever would show even a remote interest. *His story is his pick up line.* I'll never know what compelled him to highlight his evening at my expense. We used to drink, and socialize within the same confinements of bars all along the Historical District.

3. It happened without warning. It always does when being arrested. Why had I become the scapegoat? Did he need the bust bad enough to strip me of my life, as I knew it? He must have known it could've waited till Monday. Instead, he arrested me on a Friday night knowing full well nothing could be done to aid in my release until Monday. In any case, the alternate routes weaved a web of decisions I could have made to avoid this weekend in jail—or so I thought. This day marks the beginning of a trail of endless nightmares. Strap yourself in, for I have just been arrested and I'm going to jail. *Damn!* I did not want to go to jail today.

4. Let's get started. It always takes a very long time to leave a public place when being arrested. Too long actually. It's always exaggerated in order for the arresting officer to showboat his authority, talk to onlookers, wait for sergeants, and prolong the agony of paperwork. Whatever the reason is that you're still there, it is at your expense. Selfishly, everything from this point forward is at your expense while you are in jail and beyond the reaches of freedom. It's called time, and time is costly. How costly you dare to ask? Well . . . you're about to find out. The *costs of loss* run much deeper than your possessions. It takes away your *history*. All that's been acquired through time, energy, money, love, work, patience, and accumulation. It

eats away at the *present*, painstakingly slow and tediously, as you will find out in detail. Tragically, it destroys your *future*, and the future of those dependant and respondent to your dependability. The costs are exponentially staggering when you considered all the *missed opportunities* that will be denied because you went to jail today.

5.   The cuffs are never loose enough on your way to jail. The metal is sharp and you're constantly adjusting yourself in the backseat of the car during the ride. The seats are usually hard plastic with no padding to absorb the active road below. The ride is always longer than you wish for, but right now, there are no wishes to draw upon. What is clear to you at this point is the fact that this squad car you're riding in, seems to be catching every single red light. You can feel the stares a mile away. All of a sudden, you're attracting more curious onlookers than the fire engine running through the intersection. Could it be the instinct to relate the face to the crime and wonder how the bust went down? Of course, this only begs the question of whether you'll be seen on TV tonight. Whatever *they* are thinking, you can bet it is at your expense.

6.   **By now, your head is spinning because already there's too much unfinished business to tend to in that postponed life of yours: calls to make, people to hug, bills you wish you could pay for, doors to lock, lights to turn out, food to eat, addresses to get, phone numbers that accept collect calls, last cigarettes to smoke, hits to take, and drinks to chug.**

7.   *Already, there are too many regrets.* One leading to the other, piling up like the trash that's never taken out in time. And now, you begin to smell the neglect of it all . . . or is that just the stench from the puke and urine, rising up from the floorboard of the cop car? What's the difference? You've just been caught and are charged with a crime and now you're doing time. Forget about that do-list! *You're going to jail today*!

Galveston City Jail

1. I was brought to the city jail where I made my only phone call: The call I had rehearsed a thousand times to myself. She and I were together earlier that day, but I had become agitated with her. I used it as an excuse to use some time alone. We never did get the chance to kiss and hug goodbye that night. My 2-hour break turned into 4 and, just as I had gotten the urge to go back to my family, it happened. From that point *everything* became too late! The phone call was an endless session of "I love you" and "please wait". My son spoke with authority. *"Why daddy why? Why did you leave the house? Will you be home tomorrow? When? What will I do now daddy?"* I tried to give him hope amidst the sobbing, wishful, thinking, but it was in vain.

2. He had just arrived 5 days before to spend the summer. It was supposed to be lazy days ahead; surfing, sandcastles, and ice cream sandwiches. Now, he would be gone. We said goodbye and I knew this would be the last time we would speak while I was in jail. Her phone did not accept collect calls and that was the only way to reach outside parties. As many times as we tried to correct this, the phone company never responded to our requests. I was led into the holding cell.

3. BLAM! There *are* many words to describe the sound of the jailhouse door closing behind you. There *are* also many words to emphasize the abandonment you feel when these doors close in on you. *But these would just be words* on paper and your imagination could not feel the slamming *thud* against your chest. There are no stoppers or bumpers to cushion the door to the frame. It is the weight of the caged door that conotates strength unrelenting! It is the power to keep you in. The guards just exploit it by slamming it . . . *every time!*

4. Looking for a clean place to stand . . . to sit . . . to lie down? Forget it! It's non-existent! This is a hell that's been used and abused for many years before you. Every minute of every hour of every single day. Not one hour or day has passed in 1,5,10,or 25 years (depending on it's start date) that some person or something has not spit, pissed, shit, puked, bled, or scraped along the surface on which you are considering your resting place.

5. There is nothing soft in jail—except your excuses. There are no comfortable chairs to kick back on, no rugs to rub your feet into, or soft toilets to sit down on. Understand

very clearly, this is not your regular waiting area. It is the holding cell used by all who pass through here. It is the bullpen . . . and here, there is no personal home team to guide you through the ropes. Here, it's do nothing and wait. Wait for hours and more often than that, you will wait for days. Oh sure, you can yell, scream and holler for information, but what you're going to get, is nothing but more time, and more time is wasting time. You get no information and the more you demand it, the longer you are ignored. So be prepared to sit for another day . . . or two . . . or even three. It is the not knowing that can be the killer of your spirit to live. Not knowing the when's, whys, what's, or who's. *I swear it's enough to break any man or woman.*

6.   We all live by beginning and ends. The patterns of sleep, work, play, or whatever other activity we engage ourselves in throughout the day. Here, the guards aren't talking and no one's listening to your pleas. My time has begun now. God only knows when it will end. He's got a funny way of *not* telling before its time. With Him, we're always on a need to know basis. For now, only time will tell if I can stand the test of time.

Galveston County Jail—Medical Ward

1. I was fortunate to get through the city system in six hours. Handcuffed and shackled, I was led to a van with the chain gang. We were transferred to the county facility where the waiting begins again. It's Friday night/Saturday morning about 4-5 am. The bullpens have filled to capacity and beyond. All cells are overflowing with drunks, druggies, thieves, violent offenders, sexual predators, and the likes. These are the young, old, rich, and poor. Educated or not, the arresting process will not make concessions based on how well you speak or negotiate. Men or women, *if you break the law, you're going to jail*. Crime does not discriminate! The fruits of another tempt us all. Those of us that follow through and get caught, become a statistic in an unforgiving system. *This becomes the consequence of your life.*

2. The stench here is unbearable, but unavoidable. You can try to filter it out by using your shirt. As you pull up your shirt to mask your face "cowboy style", it becomes untucked at the bottom in the back, only to be met by the cold steel or cement benches. I don't know which is consistently colder, steel or cement. They are both "rock" hard and have never seen the light of day: warmth breeds life and liberty, while the dark and cold encourages sleep and depression—as if there wasn't enough to chew on already. Best chances are that when you come in, it's freezing. Come in the summer wearing short sleeves and cut offs, and you'll be huddled in a fetal position till your back is strained. If your shirt can be stretched at all, you can tuck your arms in the sleeves so you can wrap your arms around your own body. *Do it* . . . for it is the only comfort you'll receive while in jail.

3. That night, I had gone in with two broken ribs from something unrelated. This compounded my need for something soft to remedy me. Though I had no idea at the time, *soft and comfortable*, were two conditions I would not experience for several months. As my first night came to a close, the events unfolded in my mind. It will become etched in my memory forever. Morning approached.

4. On the way up, my clothes were taken into property. I was stripped to the bone along with 20 other inmates. We picked out our scrubs, sandals, a towel *(torn)*, a blanket *(dirty)*, a piece of soap, a two-inch toothbrush, and toothpaste. Then it was off to the medical ward.

5. Now, by definition of a medical ward, I had assumed it would be the place that treats boils, spider bites, broken bones, knife wounds, busted lips, and the like. It also treats and detains the depressed and drug induced freaks of the streets. You know the ones; those multi-tasked characters that can introduce all 6 of their personalities to you in one long sentence. *Never a dull moment!*

6. The steel doors opened to reveal three sections making up a horseshoe shape of single cells. Two steel doors with a small viewing window separate two sections. The front one is visible to the medical desk and patrol hallway. This front section was full, but I could see that the back sections have empty cells available. "Oh God . . . please don't . . . *please don't put me back there.* Not with them!" I silently begged. I could hear screaming and hollering. The echo was deafening to my ears. *Intolerable.* I soon realized none of them were communicating to each other, but rather only to themselves. That meant the self-inflicted arguments *would never stop* until the point of exhaustion overcame each of them, and it would never happen at the same time. An endless day lay ahead. I didn't know it at the time, but the truth would be in my favor—*this time!*

7. Before being released upstairs from the holding cells, I had been interviewed by a residing nurse. Somewhere within the barrage of questions concerning my health, history, and habits, the concern of suicide had been strategically placed on the list to ask. The swelling of my eyes and the tears drenching her questionnaire were ample proof in the pudding. There was no lying and she picked up on my condition. Nothing else was said. It was understood . . . I was to be watched. So it is now ordered for me to stay up front near the medical door . . . visible to the staff. There were no available cells in this front section. I was directed to the floor at the back behind the metal picnic table area right along side of the back cell. It was occupied. I beat the single width mattress to a pulp before laying my sheet over it. Spiders, especially recluses, were notorious for nesting in them. All of the mats had been ripped and torn open from angry abusers. The smell of urine was soaked into the fabric. I remember the stench being stronger than a pesticide. I looked at the floor around me. Food and bathroom waste littered the floor from days gone by. The only ones cleaning were sugar ants. I lay down upon the hard mattress on the floor and closed my eyes. *The weight of this burden crushes my soul.* My spirit slips away into the darkness. My identity becomes unknown. I am an inmate.

8. I could not have been "semi out" out for too long because the cell in front was still pouring out the same steady stream of snore echoing loudly against the brick walls. Those of us that can survive being awake for another 8 hours on a 15-minute nap will suffer the most. I, being one of them, would endure endless days and nights listening to snoring, shouting, and spitting. I swear I must have been dreaming of getting splashed by on-coming traffic as I stood to the side of the road. No such luck. "Crazy-eights", the most notorious of inmates, was slamming soaked toilet paper rolls just above my head, splattering chunks of soggy spray onto my face and body. "Kitty Corner" was in full swing and already I am ready for "time out".

And so it begins, the first of hundreds of antagonizing events and situations I will have to endure throughout my unwanted stay in jail. Some life altering, many life threatening. Unbelievably, a few actually brought forth humor and even laughter, but it was always at the expense of another. There is no conscience here.

9.   This is the medical ward. It is a place where I witnessed addicts coming down and crashing hard! There are people here that have been going and going on their dope binges for days and easily weeks without coming down. Then, in a flash, they are *hauled off to jail*. Suddenly cut off from the supply, stripped, and wrapped in a suicide blanket 10 inches from the shitter and left to recover. The conditions would get much worse before any type of recovery could be heard or recognized. Excretions, vomit, grunts, and growls, fill the air. Inmates with 5 or 6 different personalities conversing; each voice within his own language. Some were on the horizon, while others camped beyond our solar system. For me, the *process of detox* became synonymous with exorcism! *It's all the same when you are trying to expel the filth spewing from the gutters of that septic tank in the middle of your face!* Here, I bear witness to the true meaning of "a cleansing of the body and soul".

Galveston County Jail—General Population

1. Ten days and what seems like ten different lifetimes later, I am being transferred to general population. It's a small cellblock housing only seven other inmates; a couple of white boys, some black gangsters, and an Asian kid. A bland routine had already set into the drudgery of my life. Exhaustion gave way to the relentless pursuit of alertness. It had become difficult to keep my guard up.

2. My son was sent back to Florida to his mother on the second day of my incarceration. He had visited me the day after I had checked into this nightmare motel. Then he was shipped out on a plane. He was supposed to have spent the summer with us. I guess my wife decided not to take responsibility for his well being without my support. How quickly she runs from any consideration on my behalf. I sobbed uncontrollably. Before he left on that day, we spoke through the glass. To see, but not be able to touch. To scream, but not be heard. Everybody was yelling through the glass partition. It is *chaos*! How can I pour out my heart of regret and remorse through the metal screen? I knew he was going back to his mother now, and it would be months or even years before we would see or speak to each other again. *This visitation caused more hurt than it ever could to heal the painful loss of my son.* I etched his face into my mind and swore *I'd see him again.*

3. The heavy door opened and I dragged my mat onto my second altar of hell. I chose the top end bunk at the far end of the cellblock. The same darkness that filled the long nights, continued on during the day. There is no change in the lighting to distinguish time. Now comes *the most horrific experience of my life*. It is here, I am subjected to witness tragic, human, suffering. A testimony to the existence of Satan's work. It is here, amidst the screams of torture, I become truly afraid in my life. Streams of perspiration begin to drain off my grimy body. Shivers of chills keep me frozen in time. What is unfolding is being recorded in my memory for all time. *It will be with me for all my life. It will never leave me.*

4. Up until now, my belief in the faith of God was for what I needed, and any doubts I had, stemmed from why I didn't have it. I had grown up in the Catholic Church believing in God (mostly the fear of God's punishment), but have been *"backsliding"* for as long as I can remember. I did, however, find much satisfaction in the

philosophical discussions of theology during my last year in a Catholic University. I remember one night as I was writing a paper for this class; I stumbled onto an evolution of thought drawn from many personal observations. I realized that we, as humans, are more apt to find the security in the imagination of God when at two extremes within the chaos of our lives: when we have everything, and when we endure nothing. The *"haves"* and the *"have-nots"*. When the world is ours, and when the world is yours. Let's consider for a moment when the entire preserved world is ours; *love, money, fame, wife, kids, careers, and security* in general. It is all that can be considered worldly. How many of us can attribute all of our worldly matters and possessions to the life of God? How many of us have truly become one with God by walking with Him, praising Him, and honoring Him as a true Christian believer? How many of us understand the significance of His sacrifice by dying on the cross for us? At what point do we realize that all of the worldly worthlessness means nothing without the presence of God? Those with everything find the love of God everyday to bring new significance in their lives.

5. And now there are the rest of us. Those of us who are on the spiral downward heading toward the drop off. The deep, dark, secrets of our despairing life. Here, in the pitiful sorrow and self-regrets, among the *"have-nots"*, you reach for something less than you deserve. And then it comes. The downpour of emotions. The outcry of a wasted life immersed in self-reflection. These are the tears of Noah's Flood. *The would've, could've, and should'ves, piled high into the sky.* I wish I could reach back into time for them, but my arms aren't high enough. Instead, all that can be felt is a life gone by scraping upon the ocean floor. I can get no lower. It is dark. *Pitch black.* There is nothing to focus upon. Nothing to grasp. My eyes are open, but I have no concept of to whom or where to turn. There is no concentration. I am thinking about it. But what is it? I have no idea. I am entranced!

6. It happened about 3:30 am that morning. It is quiet, except for the usual snoring. I had just finished reading the end of *Star Trek* with Caption Kirk. It is my first of many books I will read to escape the realities of this terrible place. Through the bars and the chain-linked fence in the other cell beside me, I could hear the conversations of two inmates conversing in the background. It was a good-natured talk, mostly filled with joking and laughter. It could, by all practical standards, have been your everyday, regular, conversation between two buddies at a bar. Maybe two guys from work talking about the weekend past, or an up and coming event. But it didn't last long! The tone quickly changed when the steel door opened and slammed shut again, pushing the neighboring cell deep into the darkness of evil. I immediately heard the shuffling of inmates from the closest wall next to me quickly fade to the to the farthest point away from where I was laying on my bunk. The two men approached someone lying in the bunk in the cell next to me. There was silence . . . and then it came. The flurry of fists pounded into the body of a victim. Immediately, the screams began as the thundering fists shot out like a spray of bullets smashing his face, ribs, and back. It was a beating that was going to last. I could see shadows

dancing around in the dungeon of terror. The screams turned to pleads to God. He *begged for mercy* as the life was beaten out of him. As unconsciousness set in, any articulation of sound became grunts. The hits slowed and then, finally stopped. I looked through the mesh to see what was left of him. There was blood everywhere; on the bed, floor, and all over him. And now begins the interrogation of this event. It was hard to comprehend the actual conversation over the sobs and moaning. From what I could make out, he was being asked to give specifics of his deeds that landed him in here. During the details of his crime, the bouncers became enraged and let loose a beating of multiple levels. *Rape followed*, leaving him to defecate all over himself. The stench of feces rose into the air liking a burning pasture. The smell soaked through my skin. Masturbation secretions covered his face. Others in the cell were enticed to join in the mayhem, but no one offered their services. The victim had become a useless mass of rotten flesh left for dead. But he didn't die. They didn't want him too. They kept him alive. They also kept him hidden for a day before being found.

7. I saw him a couple of days later. He could not see out of one eye, and gaping wounds were numerous. The places where his head had been smashed against the steel plates on the wall showed the rivet indentations on his face. One side of his face had collapsed. Someone spoke to him and he muttered something of God being the final judge in his life. Even in all his suffering, he was brought back to jail to serve his time. *He had molested two young teenager girls.* He is a sexual predator and paid the initiation fee of it that night. He will pay many times more before he dies. Eventually, he will be transferred to a correctional facility. Most likely, he will be killed by the system *before* his 80 years runs out!

8. **And so it is here, in the darkness, surrounded by cold, metal bars and hot, tempered inmates, I struggle to make sense of it all. *This is not the life I had planned.* It is not the expectations of my parents, for me to live a life of imprisonment. And pathetically, it is not the way to maintain any type of relationship with my wife and children.**

9. My hand brushed up against the pages of a book hidden underneath the mattress. It was tattered, torn, and stained, but still illuminated in the dark; a kind of blue sky, metallic with raised dramatic features of gold trim. I stared at the beautiful woman shrouded in a flowing garment. Her hair, though beautifully brushed, was waving in the wind. I looked at it for a long time really not caring about it's content, but only that it was easy to look at. As I began to read the words in the pages, *a faint sensation of warmth began to compliment the flicker of light inside* my body. There was nothing to focus on, just something to think about. After a while, not really knowing how long it had been, I realized the deafening silence within the cellblock. Except for the usual, distant, screams way down the corridor (medical ward), everything within my immediate surroundings was calm. *I felt very lonely that night.* My back remained against the wall for the rest of the night. I brought my knees to my chin, and held my fists together. I prepared for the worst. My eyes

never left the door. I prayed for all my life never to walk without God again. Who wouldn't after seeing such violence? So here and now, while I remain to be a lonely man missing my family, in the midst of life altering threats and tragedy, after being stripped of everything that is decent, *I make the decision to never be alone without God in my life to protect me.*

10. I'm looking around the cellblock and realize I have confused calmness with terror. *Everybody in here is frozen with fear.* I could tell each was giving thanks to "whatever" they believed in for being on *this* side of the bars and meshed fencing. From that point onward, no one is my cellblock slept or rested at night. We silently agreed to each other never to close our eyes in the dark. I was transferred four days later to Houston County Jail. *Enter . . . the coals below hell's fire!*

Harris County Jail

1. I *thought* I had prepared myself for the next 1-2 days during the check-in process. I was gravely mistaken. This was to be my 2nd rodeo of going through the hoops, which were required before having any chance of getting released. In anticipation of this "hurry up and wait" while getting booked into jail, I had my wife bring me socks, tennis shoes, and a shirt . . . all white. This had been done back in Galveston, so I could at least be processed into the system with them. It's better than barefoot, bareback, and free ballin'! My only other possession is my newly found tattered book. It's all I had to *"keep the faith"*. I am surrounded by hundreds of others, but still I am feeling so very alone in my life to deal with the circumstances at hand. I am lonely, but continued to nurture the belief that I was not alone. I tried to believe the strength of my strong family support would bridge that gap. **What I failed to realize is that we, here in prison, are not war heroes. Nor, are we in a far off land, imprisoned by terrorists. And finally, we are not on a noble global mission to save the children of a foreign country. No, we are none of these. We are, however, in jail today and there's a pretty good chance our wives, girlfriends, families, and friends are out having a drink *not* in your favor.** And if they're not doing that, then maybe they are trying to figure out what the hell they're supposed to do, now that you have involuntarily abandoned them to go to jail today.

2. Let's talk about phone calls: Phone calls to your parents, wives, children, friends, and whoever else within the extended family must endure your pleas while listening to your problems. The problems that you most likely brought upon yourself. And now, you expect them to take collect calls all through the night to keep you company. Make no mistake about it . . . whatever your conversation, however you feel, and whomever you're angry at; be careful how you speak to the other end of that phone! Amidst the crying, regrets, and promises of a better tomorrow, you have to grasp a hold of this reality: whatever the other side of that phone was doing *before* the phone call, they've probably gone right back to doing it *after* the call. If your intended recipient is watching T.V., then they are going right back to watching the program after you hang up. Were they washing dishes? Of course they'll go back to finish the job. Someone making love to your woman? The old "now . . .

where were we" is back in session. And all of this is coming into play at about the time of "click" when the phone hangs up. **Just remember, you're the one in jail today—not them! They still have a life and the hardest part for you will be to let them live it!** *So take a deep breath . . . and hang up the phone!*

3. I was transported to Harris County on July 2nd, the weekend of the big freedom celebration. Now as I understand it to be, this facility belongs to the 4th largest city in the good ole' USA. *Can you just try to comprehend the population explosion within the confinements* of these walls during such a time? It is well known in these parts, the streets are cleared of wrongdoers and the indigent in the days before to keep the streets safer for the party. We are racked and stacked exponentially. There are no health codes here. It is hard rules, harder floors, and the hardest hitting guards that you care to come to know in your lifetime. The foulness of bodies lay carelessly about. The stench of feet soaked in days of sweat fill the air. *Alcoholics, dopers, acid trippers, brawlers, thieves, car jackers, predators, and the like, are all meshed together.* All these crimes and more are shared by a wide array of college boys to professional bums, and all points in between; lawyers to maintenance, plumbers to bus drivers, doctors to teachers, and gangsters to bitches, all make up the party weekend here in Harris County. There are no considerations when it comes to being arrested on the street. *Everyone is discriminated upon.* I knew what was coming. I was headed for a wreck with absolutely no way of stopping it. *Enter . . . the bullpens!*

4. I mingled with hundreds of others while waiting to be prodded into the next holding cell. It was nothing more than a human oven. The heat and humidity is unbearable; a baker's oven. The thickness of the hot, still, air is suffocating. The ribbons hanging from the vent remain motionless. The human stench is nauseating. Sounds of exhaustion, moans, whaling, and screams, all echoed off the walls. There is nothing to muffle the noise against the brick enclosures. Every conversation seemed to be amplified to its extremity. The continuous sound barriers exploded in my head.

5. I kept looking up hoping to see the Zyclon Pellets being dropped into the holding cell. A few deep breaths and it would all be over. I drew upon the images of their strength, courage, and bravery to endure this fraction of a moment in time. It made me weak to know that their suffering ran deeper and longer than what I could ever comprehend. A snap shot of a history of which I have great respect for, and admiration to those who endured . . . and those that died trying to live. This has the likes of a modern day extermination camp. They will always be in my prayers. I wanted to deny the guards any further satisfaction of my own suffering. *I wished for it time and time again.* The pellets never did come down that shoot above my head . . . nor did the air, except when the metal door would slide to a grind to let someone in the bullpen.

6. Those of us lucky enough to be near the door found ourselves laying our faces flat upon the filthy floor with our noses and mouths flush to the slight crack under the door. As the door would open to let a new inmate in, we would scatter to let him

pass through. And then before the door closed, we would quickly return to our places to suck up the small stream of cool breeze, which edged through the one-inch opening. The effort was futile. The air quickly dispersed in the sauna like conditions. *This foulness of human waste, marinated with heat and noise will alone, be the deterrent that keeps me wishing for freedom.* Pile that on top of *regrets, remorse's, anger, injuries, fights, arguments,* and finally . . . the lack of knowing when you'll move forward to the next pen; the wait to hear my name so I can move one more step closer to freedom. I needed something. *Anything!* Give me something to let me know I'm going to make it through this ordeal. My blood type, an address, a toenail, it didn't matter . . . *"Please call my name"* . . . for anything. Something to let me know my paper work didn't fall behind the desk. Just keep me moving on to the next stage of suffering so I can crawl on to the other side of this wall.

7. Of course, my hopes were to be moved to a better place each time, but that's just not possible in jail. There is no better location in jail. It's just another location of a worse place.

8. And now it comes to pass after a full day and a full night of waiting in a boxcar packed and loaded with wasted wrongdoers, we are moved to the strip center. Once again, I shed my clothes for the required scrub attire. *"Take any color you like . . . as along as it's orange"*. The wait continues; 5 hours to get an x-ray, then another 8 hours to be reviewed. This was nothing more than being asked a few questions and listening to a rundown of my criminal history. Waiting . . . . waiting . . . waiting. Two days later, I finally arrive upstairs away from the blistering conditions of heat, sweat, and stench. I am suffering from dehydration and heat exhaustion. My head is pounding intensely. I was looking forward to a mattress, blanket, and a bunk, but the 4th of July weekend tells me that's not happening. There were no mattresses or bunks to find. I did well in just getting a dirty blanket full of holes. This overflowing pod would be my home for the next few weeks.

9. It is early morning hours now as I look for a place to lie down on the floor. Everyone is in their bunk and those that don't have one are lying about on the hard cement. I found a place in the aisle between the rows of bunks. It was that, or sleep next to the shitters. It makes no difference, because all of it is filthy. The torn blanket wrapped around my body twice did nothing to fend off the freezing, cold, concrete ground. There were too many holes in it. I estimated the room to be below 60 degrees. The floor is colder as it has absorbed the constant freezing temperatures. My body became numb within moments of laying on it. I constantly struggled to turn in my blanket to ease the sting of coldness against my bare skin. I couldn't believe the difference in temperature up here. I had gone from two days of hot, sweltering, heat to this hell frozen over. It's amazing how much pain 10 feet of altitude can bring forth.

10. Every 3-4 days is laundry time to change out scrubs. They are picked up in the early morning hours. Inmates lined up and stripped. Those with shirts, boxers, and socks were able to keep them. Mine had been taken during an earlier change out. Those without went naked for the next 5-6 hours. As no such luck would have it,

35

tonight happened to be that night. So now I must shed my scrubs and hit the floor, basically bare ass and all.

11. The lights came on for me to see the conditions of my fifth altar of hell. I see 24 numbered bunks, several mattresses on the floor, and many more inmates on the bare surface. I'm counting at least 40 inmates crammed into a pod designed and equipped for 24. Our clothes were thrown into the pile by the doorway and taken away by trustees. Many went back to their bunks while others found their naked bodies against the concrete slab—I included! I wondered if the blanket would support the weight of a noose around my neck. I had no sheet to tear and fold for optimum results. I looked around for rafters and beams. They must have known every other man's thought, because there were none to be found. *"If I could just hang off the rail of a bunk, then maybe . . .* No, I'd probably wake someone up and be stopped just as brain damage set in. Then I couldn't finish the job!" *Maybe nobody would care.* After all, this is jail. A place where care is not a consideration.

12. Men slept wherever they could. Some with their heads two feet from the commode, which by the way, doubles as a sink. I had not had a drink of water since my arrival two days ago. *My head was pounding for relief.* I would wait for the juice cups. However, I would not make it until breakfast (4:30am) before being "juiced" by the neighborhood recluse. It swelled massively in the up and coming days.

13. I wept uncontrollably at different times all through the day—*every day!* I struggled to hide the depression that set deep within my soul. **It consumed my every waking hour. I wanted to go home each and every second of the day. I prayed for death in the middle of the day . . . and even more so at night. Time had made it more difficult than I could bear, and I just couldn't bear it anymore.** *"There's no rest for the wicked,"* I say. And here, in this hellish nightmare, the wickedness *never* sleeps!

14. There are no windows. We are housed in a pod within an atrium of this massive complex. If it were banging bombs outside, we would never know it. It's difficult to imagine life without weather; not seeing the sky or feeling the warmth of the sun. Some inmates have been here for months without a breath of fresh air. The only hints of time inching forward are the differences of meals served. Breakfast's bag meals and tray dinners separate it.

15. **How do I occupy time in a vacuum? It is the difference of . . . well, everything. Sleeping to pass the time is easy. The rest of our time awake is to enter into a conscientious effort of occupying time; eat, sleep, read, write, workout . . .** *rinse and repeat*! **"Oh wait", I forgot to mention argue, fight, curse, lie, cheat, and steal. What else could you expect among 50 men?**

16. "Chow . . . wake em' up for chow!" This will remain to be to be my reminder for years to come, each time I sit down for a meal. We line up for breakfast bags and lunch/dinner trays. There are never enough table spaces for everyone, so someone's always on the floor. Every meal becomes barter town. Traders are always yelling during the meal; giving up this . . . or taking that! "Milk for a sweet thing" or "juice

for cereal". The meals are terrible here and there's never enough. I developed a terrible case of constipation. The pressure became unbearable. I silently screamed each time I tried to pass stool. Of course, to complicate my private theater of pain boils set into my backside cheeks. They grew to golf ball size and became rock hard, and black as blue. I could not sit on any type of surface. Nor could I lie on my back or right side.

17. Medical appointments were treated slowly. They were meant to deter you from making any more appointments in the future. It's only a five-minute walk upstairs to the medical ward; however, once you get there, expect to jump through a series of hoops. Most inmates that leave their pod to go to the medical ward do not return for 6-8 hours. Many times, it's longer. We wait in a holding cell for hours on end to be seen. *Everything here is about waiting.* It takes days, weeks, and even months, to get any type of requests answered. Many times you are just denied justification to be seen. Don't expect to see the actual doctor until death is on your doorstep, and if you are unfortunate enough to be there, most staff members curse at you (loudly and under their breath) for providing them with the opportunity of a job to administer aid in such a place. Expect to spend hours in cold, nasty, and unsanitary conditions, only to be met by rude and crude attitudes. I was laughed at openly as I explained my dilemma.

18. **So, here I am now, locked in a pod with 40 other men, within these institutional walls. Men who quite possibly carry every conceivable virus and/or sexually transmitted disease known to man.** Maybe even some that aren't recognized yet. Showering is not comprehendible without shoes and if you do decide to jump into the area without them, expect things to start growing from within your toes the very next day. The sour sting in your nostrils reminds you that most urinate while rinsing. The water line refuses to subside. When it's time for you to sit on the toilet, be sure to "clean the rooftop and lay down some tile", which means: be sure to wipe off the cold, metal seat and layer it with toilet paper. Even then, you'll have to contend with the flies and gnats as they hover between your legs under the rim.

19. I had put in for a transfer to a place where I could function properly. A place where I could be given some type of responsibility to others *and myself*; food service, maintenance, or some other trustee position.

20. Some time during the third week, I was uprooted from my bunk in the middle of the night. Is it time to go home? Has a miracle just happened? Is my family waiting for me downstairs? *"Please . . . let me go! I promise to be good now, and change my ways."* **If only it could be that simple. But if it was, how on earth would we ever be able to learn the hardest lessons in life?** My name was called for "ATW" which means *all the way . . . out!* Where the "out" will lead me to I have no idea, but if it's away from here, I'm doing better than yesterday. I've got 5 minutes to grab all possessions of papers, commissary, sheets, towels, and my mattress and haul ass to the door. *5 minutes top . . .* before they come in and start throwing all my shit out the door.

21. Deep inside, I knew I couldn't be leaving. *I hadn't even seen the judge yet!* I was supposed to have seen the judge just a week after arriving in this pod, but that morning, she was noted as being in a "bad mood", so my attorney rescheduled me to be seen at a later time . . . *a month later!* I can't believe my ears of making this my dwelling for another month.

Baker Street

1. Handcuffed at the wrists and shackled on the ankles, we were led outside into the open air toward the van. I began to inhale deeply, over and over, to clear my lungs of a month worth of stale air. I felt dizzy and exasperated at the same time. The warm blast of fresh oxygen literally pumped life back into my belittled soul. *Up until now,* I had not even so much as seen outside, not even an overhead cloud . . . *not in over a month.*

2. I was loaded into the van and transported to another building a block away. We were led upstairs into the next altar of hell. I could not believe my eyes; porcelain toilets, hot water showers, water fountains, and windows. Windows to see out into the free world. Was I dreaming? We bunked up for the rest of the early morning, but I dared not sleep. I was too afraid it would all be gone when I woke. I remember lunging for the water fountain. This would be the first drink of that magical life preserving substance in a month. I had been living on juice cups and milk cartons for fluids.

3. My pod woke to a world of locker doors being smashed against their hinges. The noise echoed into my head ten times over, even after the banging was finished for wake up call. Role calls constantly interrupted the lazy days of sleep and the wakeful nights.

4. I signed up for a continued educational trade school class. What a joke or should I say, the egotistical SOB who taught the class was a complete clown. For a month, I sat in this guy's class and listened to his self-centered bragging of being a shoeshine boy. *How pathetic of a man to degrade inmates by threatening them in the company of guards.* If I met him on the street, surely he could only turn and run the other way in shame. For one month while sitting in that class for 6 hours a day, I did nothing but shine one pair of Deputy's boots. Sure, I gave them boots a good spit shine. Most of it ended *inside* the boots. *"Here's your boots motherfucker!"* It was more than any of us could stand; to listen to him brag of his worthless life for 6 hours a day. Meanwhile, other classes of cooking, woodshop, carpets, welding, and electronics, were moving ahead with progress. Most of us begged to be kicked out, but none of us wanted to be sent back to general population. I stopped going all together by keeping my name on the medical roster.

5. I diligently stuck to my routine of eating, sleeping, working out, and reading. *Reading* . . . now there's a renewed pleasure in my life. Since my incarceration, I have consumed thousands of pages by my mind's eye. Novels of suspense, scientific discoveries, dramas, adventures, religious, and so many other avenues of escape to occupy my time. We are constantly trading among ourselves.

6. This is the "Cadillac Bar" of jail units. An envied place away from the unsanitary conditions and uncontrolled environment across the street. This is a place where one "write up" could send you packing! Fighting in here among inmates is rare, except in the corners away from the camera's eye. However, this is jail and it's always unpredictable with inmates that just don't care enough to consider any of the consequences. They will revolve through this jail system all their lives. For me to knock knuckles with the scum of the earth only meant that fighting was more important to me than going home to my family. Occasionally, it becomes unavoidable. So once in a while, I have to become the "whipping boy", and open up a can of "whip ass". *Now . . . where's that can of spinach?* Here, one must prepare for the worst kind of fighting with no rules and no time limits. Nobody wants to stop it and everybody wants blood; biting, grabbing, stabbing, or whatever it takes to get the job done.

7. **And so it comes to pass, the days slowly melt into each other. Each passing moment is a struggle to maintain the hope of a better thought to carry me toward the next minute, or even the next second! This is the burden of my life to carry within my soul. I have become lost in an unforgiving system that hands out pain and punishment like samples in the aisles of a grocery store . . . only these don't taste so good.**

8. The summer heat warms my body through the tinted glass of the recreation door. It is the morning hours, which brings such contentment of solitude. The noise relief comes only *after* inmates leave for school in the mornings. The time spent soaking my bones in the sun's path is never long enough to fully enjoy. It would shine through a specific window for a short period of time, and then disappear behind a wall. I spent endless hours looking beyond the barbed wire fences toward the sky. The clouds eased on by lazily each passing day. They always became lost in the distance, as did everything else in my own life.

9. The uneasy shifting in my mind was obstructing my ability to function properly. The blocks of endless vacant spaces of time consumed my body from the inside. It ate at my physical strength. *My mental health deteriorated.* Depression plagued every decision I made. I stared blindly without focusing at things directly in front of me. My conscience had imprisoned me within these walls of confinement. I added up my days in. It had only been 59 days since coming to jail. How could this be possible? Already, I have toured four different prisons; two in Galveston and two here, in Houston. How could life stand so still for me as to only be in prison for two months? Had it not been four lifetimes already? Ever so deeply, I am experiencing many lifetimes of pain, and suffering great rivers of despairing regret!

10. **I have lost my home**. A beautiful warehouse apartment just newly renovated and decorated to the likings of all those who graced it's presence—including myself! Located conveniently on the corner of the most popular Historical District, I seldom was ever lost for excitement coming through the door. Entertainment was the current and it flowed freely from its plethora of "hot spots". Clubs, restaurants, pubs, dancing, pool halls, and drinking holes, all made up my own carnival of pleasure. A life to be envied. A life to be sickened by. A hidden treasure chest of contacts and vices. All of it lost now. A memory in the mind of my disbelief. I am unable to process its absence. *When does this nightmare end?* When did it start?

11. **I have lost by business**. A life of only moments a day. The ease of my good fortune attracts everyone who eats and all those willing to provide me with the lifestyle in which I have become accustomed.

12. **I have lost my vehicles**. My lifeline to the river of deep pockets.

13. **I have lost my child**; no . . . I have lost both my children. My first and oldest, taken away only days after coming back into my life. Gone to the clutches of abuse and neglect. An abusive stepfather and an ex-wife, unforgiving to the birth of this young child of mine. The anger raged on in my head as I played out endless scenarios of how to inflict my revenge upon their lives. How desperate I had become to escape this torture rattling my brain into the long hours of the night. My son's only remedy to fend off the attacks from constant degrading would be to rebel against them. How helpless he must be in the presence of such hatred. How abandoned he must feel with my absence. I prayed endlessly he would someday forgive me for leaving him this way. How do I explain my wrongdoings to him? *How will it be justified?*

14. And now, I am gathering up hints of abandonment from my present day, so-called loving and faithful wife. Well . . . that didn't take long, did it? **To lose your spouse,** I mean.

15. And for you . . . if you have so much as a shred of doubt of the stability and threads of unity that holds your family together, it will be the dagger that impales your heart to the wall. Unanswered letters, missing visitations, hard looks, and tears . . . that never come. All of this and more, to remind you that maybe your place in their lives are not as valued as you thought. As it evolves while in here, **your independence quickly turns to co-dependency**.

16. Check your family ties my friendly reader. How do you stand next to such scrutiny? Ask yourself here and now . . . if your life were to be turned upside down today, **would your family be there for you tomorrow?** Be mindful of the confidence with your answer. *Tomorrow can last a long time!*

Time to Serve

1. I did not want to go to jail that day back in June, and I am not prepared for judgment day today. I stood in the cell just behind the courtroom door and listened to inmates negotiate their time. How easy it seemed for them to sign away 1,5,10, and even 20 years of imprisonment for crimes committed without conscience. Each inmate told his story to an uncaring attorney more interested in the lunch menu, than the fate of his/her client's life. Each one of us attempted to sell his way out of the inevitable. We are going to jail today, and nobody, but nobody gives a damn for our pleas. This is a money game and the only winners are those who are putting you behind bars. I had (as all of us in here do) prepared several brilliant speeches for the judge, for my attorney, for myself, and for God. I went over them infinite times in my mind.

2. Slowly, the hours ticked away in the holding cell. The door to the courtroom kept opening and closing, giving me a glimpse of the free world. And then . . . it becomes my turn. It went fast. Too quickly to get a word in for any considerations on my behalf. An omission of guilt, and I was pushed back into the cell behind the beautiful wooden and leather surroundings of the courtroom. I was never allowed to speak of anything, other than "yes and no" answers. I longed to cry out. To even just speak my piece before the court. Won't someone listen to my suffering? Let me share my conscience of shame. Not to "sell it", but rather just to tell it. The way I want it to be heard. That chance would never come—*until now*. All of the considerations I wanted the judge to hear in my defense were banging around in my mind. I was not to be heard. Why won't the prosecutor talk to me? I can't even get a look in my direction.

3. Back to the cave, and the rest of the day is lost in utter shock I am walking in a daze. My head does not believe the news today. I am in jail today and I've just been told that I'm here for another four months. Another 120 days in the hole man! What happened to probations, or pardons, or forgiveness? What the fuck happened to "time served" already? Am I dreaming in hell that I would be kept here against my will for another four months? *And where the hell is my wife?* I do not see her in the courtroom this morning.

4.   And so it happens, I am looking around the courtroom for my wife. She is not here for the support I had so hoped for this morning. And now, all the years of love, energy, time, and patience spent nurturing this relationship are washed away. Endless conversations of faithful commitments to each other have become cluttered with broken promises. Is this the beginning of the end of infinite expressions of love gone by?

5.   I am angry now. And I am feeling the bite of betrayal. All the money she so took for granted. For six years, she never once laid a hand of labor in financial support of our livelihood. She never had to, nor was it ever expected . . . or required of her. But still, after six long years of unconditional love and support, I can't even get a letter of faithfulness from her. Unbeknown to me, she had already prepared to move on with her life . . . and somebody else's! She wears the sins of the flesh as if it were her evening gown. In the time that I have known her, I have replaced her youthful years of insecurities with praises of her beauty and character. But now, she has fallen to the shallow advances of nighttime crusaders; listening to what she has to say, and telling her what she wants to hear to feed an ego. It is the "simple-Simon" pick-up game of confidence pitching. If only she could have waited. I love her like no other before, and consistently showed my appreciation through unconditional love. I should've saw it coming. Years ago, she left her fiancé for me, and now she's leaving me for some other fun buck! I gave her six years. She couldn't give me six months. In fact, she didn't give me sixty days. Do you really want to go to jail today? *Can you mentally afford to leave all that will soon be forgotten?*

6.   Let me pray for the next fallen victim who is cast into the belly of this evil spell. "Don't look into ojos *del di diablo.* May the next guy find escape through the loving mercy of God? Don't let him be swept into her seductress empowerment of sex as a way of enslavement to her needs. Don't let him be a fool to give away the keys to his house, his cars, and his heart. For he too, will become the overlap of another relationship and a father to a bastard child. Save yourself from *el sangre del Diablo.*

7.   I have received a six-month sentence to serve as punishment for crimes uncommitted. Well, most of them anyway. It is August 17, 2004. I had, in fact, already served two months, so the arrangement is to spend another four months here in the county facility. That would not happen. I remember the judge asking how long I had already been incarcerated. I told her sixty days since June 18th. She never blinked an eye before jotting it down. I could've and should've said ninety days in already. To her, it wouldn't have made a difference anyway. It comes to this: there was no more fight left in my attorney. He had used up all the hours for the money we had provided. His time was up on this case . . . and so was mine! That's what happens when the money runs out. I suppose it's better than having a court appointed attorney who pressures you to do more time so the state gets paid. It's always obvious whose interests they have in mind when representation is state funded. Most inmates are threatened with more time through longer sentences if they do not comply with the

prosecutor's demands to sign a time sentence. Court appointed attorneys back up the prosecutors with their own subtle form of persuasion to put you behind bars. I was threatened with three years if I did not comply with the six-month sentence that was offered. It was just another finishing tactic to bail out from spending more time on the case. It worked . . . I signed and was quickly shuffled back to the bullpen.

8. I took one more brief glance around the courtroom as I was being led out. The décor of wood and carpet complimented all the nice furniture. My wife was not part of the backdrop.

9. It had been about a month since I had "money on the books" for commissary. Another broken promise from my unfaithful wife. How gallantly she would brag in the visitation room of sending me $50 here, or a $100 there. Never once did this transpire. I was, however, blessed with mom and dad's generosity. On the morning of August 19th, I received "necessities"; shampoo, toothpaste, lather soaps, sodas, candy bars, and the likes. This would be the first time in a month that I could enjoy "after dinner" chows. It's difficult to survive in here without food from 4pm to 5am everyday while in jail. The midnight hours drag on with hunger pains. I used half the tube of toothpaste when I got it. A week had passed since I had run out of toothpaste, so it was liberating to say the least. My gums bled with glee. I had not shampooed my head since the night of June 18th, when I was going out for my usual vices. It was also the night I had entered this system of hell on earth. Months of filth washed away down the drain. The sensation burned my scalp.

10. That evening after chow, my name was called up to the guard's cage. To my shock, horror, and disbelief, my routine becomes disrupted. ATW! How can that be? I had just been given four more months. I'm supposed to do my time here. What just happened? Where am I going? What happened to my attorney's promise of doing the remainder of my time here? When I questioned the guard's information, he laughed. "Pack your hit boy . . . you're going to state". TDC Baby! I had five minutes to pack. This is going to be one of the longest "hurry up and wait" periods of my pathetic life.

11. I had been saving my soda and soups for this evening "after hours" chow session. I never did get to feel that cool, crisp, taste of Coke hitting the back of my throat. Vulchers surrounded my bunk locker, as I hurriedly packed my books, sheets, towels, mattress, and whatever else I could take. I didn't even have time to trade soups for candy bars. It would be a long wait in the holding cell. The guards would eventually take all my books, papers, food, and hygiene from me as the early morning hours inched forward to my departure.

12. **And so it comes to pass . . . again, that I will give up every possession I have acquired in this pathetic, hellish nightmare. I have lost all my free world possessions by coming to jail, and now, I will give up every possession here too . . . except one!** Scrubs and barefoot sandals is all that remains with me right now.

A Simple Procedure

1. **Let's take a look at the simplest procedure gone wrong.** You're driving over the hill and are spotted by the police. You're clocked speeding. "Boss Boy" pulls you over. You roll down your window and hopefully; you can present a valid driver's license and insurance. You unkindly receive your unwanted ticket and drive away, steadily shifting your eyes in the rear view mirror to determine when it's safe to speed again. For those that submit to "guilty", and pay the fine, the court will allow about ten days to mail in your payment. And that's that! Mail your payment in and it's done . . . except for the fact that it will show up on your driving record.

2. Option two is to go to court and contest it. It is here, you will find yourself being delayed and distracted in a courtroom packed with disgruntled persons with the same idea; getting their tickets dismissed or pleaded out of court. You can wait there all day, just to have the plea of "not guilty" entered into the system. Now, it is up to the court to reset *another* court appearance for you to appear. Another day gone to the system. Another day wasted. For those of us working, the loss of pay and time is barely worth the price we pay to muster up the patience to deal with officials and the system. And so now, after the morning, and quite possibly the entire afternoon have passed, you're left with the anticipation of having to do it all over again. All of this with the hopes of having your ticket dismissed, dropped, or at least, lowered to a lesser charge. For the sake of this lesson, let's consider that a fine is imposed, and you're walking away feeling pinched. The court grants an extension of thirty days to pay. You will have this long to feel the pain of having to support your local corrupt police department.

3. **My mother is quick to remind me of all the retirement funds and/or equipment pieces I have purchased for law enforcement because of fines imposed on me. She says that I don't love money enough, because if I did, I wouldn't be spending it as fast as I got it. Instead, I should have been holding on to it with diligence and prudence for a rainy day. I tend to agree.**

4. It soon becomes thirty days later and you still haven't parted with that hard, cash money. It makes no difference if it was earned by, begged for, borrowed from, or stolen with . . . its still money you just can't part with. Not for the police anyway.

You know you've only got enough for the weekend and the "cop shop" isn't about to take your *"freaking for the geeking"* money that you've set aside for the up and coming shows. So, you decide to skip the payment. And now, the burden becomes policy. *Policy of truth that is*, because your name came up this morning for not showing up, not paying your fine, and not contacting the proper venue to extend your payment plan.

5. Now you have a warrant, and having a warrant means more fines and levies placed against you. It also means that an appearance before the judge is demanded of you. And finally, for those of us that like to gamble, it means from here on out, you take your chances in the car, at work, and in your home. The "chance" being that the law doesn't come looking for you. The law is betting they'll find you. You, on the other hand, are "banking" that when the unavoidable happens (and it will happen), you'll be a position of convenience. **You're hoping the dishes will be done with food in your belly, the bills are paid, the kids are asleep, there's money in your pocket, and the attorney's on call. BEEP . . . wrong anticipation! When its time to go to jail, there is never a convenient time to say you are ready to go . . . ever!** When that call comes knocking at your door to go, you are always going to wish that you were not going to jail. It is at this time, retracing your steps becomes most visible . . . and most wanted!

6. **This is the simplest of life's circumstances gone wrong.** You speed, you're fined, you don't pay, and you go to jail. *It's that simple.* And it's the same all around the country!

7. Alas, the time will come that you will go to jail if you don't pay your fines. Once you're there, you will quickly realize that jail time is slow time. And it will slow to a crawl. It makes no difference that your attorney is waiting in the lobby with a fist full of cash. There is a technical term for booking you into the system: it is called *processing*. Be prepared to shift your life down into *slow long play mode* if you're being processed into a large city or county jail. There is nothing here to please or satisfy your schedule. In case you have already forgotten the hardship of this task, just flip back to the beginning of this book to remind yourself. It should always be a sharp jolt to you as a reminder never to come here.

8. To spend any amount of time in jail is a loss of so much more than the fine imposed, or the time lost in your life. And if you do go to jail today, you will have plenty of thoughts and revelations of the other losses that it brings to your life. Let's consider your family for the moment. They are now expected to receive $15 dollar collect calls, in which they will end up paying for anyway. Then there's the imposition of raising enough money for bonds, fines, and/or lawyers. This is money they spent all day or night working for. This is the same money that you now want them to put out because you decided the diapers or formula was not as important as it was yesterday . . . or will be tomorrow. Gone is the new bicycle for your son's birthday, or the pretty dress for your daughter's first communion. Gone is the money that was to be used for groceries.

9.   Tonight, it was supposed to be steaks on the grill. Instead your family is eating dollar burgers outside the "cop shop" while being bombarded with the homeless bumming cigarette money off your kids. *Damn you for going to jail today!*

10. It is said; everybody reaches down to his or her own bottom. By going to jail today, you will be asking your family and friends to scrap bottom with you. *Are you sure this is the trip you want to take them on today?*

State Facility

1. About fifteen of us are being transported north to the state facility. It is about 5am. The bus is completely screened off over the windows preventing the public from looking into the cabin. Through the small creases in the mesh wiring, I can see out into the free world. Already the hustle and the bustle of the day were filling the highway with hard working citizens. I would give up both life and limb to be going to work as a free citizen right now. I'm sure everybody else could promise the same. Actually, I'm just thinking of giving up my life right now instead. The pain of this cage is too much to bear. The uncertainty of what my future holds has me in a trance with no escape. Escape . . . that's all I need. Just give me the chance. *Let me lead the way!*

2. The sun was rising behind the trees when we arrived. The silhouettes cast long shadows across the ground. The bus exited the highway. I peered through the screened windows of the bus. We begin to travel down a long and narrow road. Off to the left, I can see the baseball fields. They are empty. Now, I can see the soccer fields as we pass by them. They too, are empty. My eyes scanned ahead toward the front of the bus and as the soccer fields begin to fade behind us, I'm catching glimpses of more fences along the perimeter. Rows and rows of barbed wire fences surrounding the metal barrack style aluminum buildings in the distance. The bus came to a stop in front of the gate. On each side, guards stood holding shotguns. The bus was checked for contraband.

3. **In my mind, I know these are the gates of hell that we are about to pass through. It is a subterranean world. Enter, the fiery core in the center of the earth!** The bus rolled up to the barracks. We exited the bus in shackles and were led into the processing building. The sticky, humid, heat of the day had already started its decent on us. I looked over my shoulder before entering the door. Razor sharp, barbed wire, fences lined the complex. Beyond the fences were fields. Beyond the fields, were the forest; thick brush and tall Woodland trees. I can see that it is black inside. Beyond the trees, there is dense forestry to prevent escape to the other side.

4. Inside, we were stripped and placed in a single file against the wall. Holding cells lined the wall. They were full of inmates coming and going through the system.

Those of us that made it through with any possessions had them immediately confiscated. Inmates desperately tore up their expensive sport shoes so the trustees couldn't wear them. Whatever was salvaged from the County had now become the State's property available to burn, trade, sell, or donate away; clothes, books, papers, pens, and whatever else made it through were immediately taken. I wondered what the hell we were supposed to wear when we get released? What am I thinking . . . I'm not even able to focus into the next moment? Six hours from now, I will be led to believe that I will never make it out of here alive!

5. We all waited in holding cells for hours until being called out for grooming. Our heads were shaven bare to the skull. Every person of each race turned out looking like the next person. A freezing cold shower to numb the pain of exhaustion quickly awoke us to the realization that we were in jail. We were fitted with scrubs and slippers. My issued shoes were 3 sizes too big for my foot. I was told I could get them switched out later. I put in the request for months to have them switched out. I will wear them until the day I am released. I think my toes have extended themselves out another size. Blisters and calluses abound my toes from dragging my feet as I walked. Each of us was issued toilet paper, a two-inch toothbrush, a razor, and toothpowder. *That's toothpowder*—not toothpaste! Try brushing baking soda into your mouth for months. We would wet the little brush and then, rub it into a paper holder of the powder. It became a gagging struggle each and every time.

6. Bald, shaven, and showered, we are ordered to sit on the cold, metal, bench until further notice. Off in the distance, there are piles of mattresses. All of them are torn, tattered, and shredded of their filling. I scanned them carefully knowing I would eventually have to make a run for it, if I was going to get a padded mattress. What looks good on top is only met with disappointment after looking at all the tears and filth on the others side. The mattresses are a favorite nesting place for the dreaded brown recluse. Recluse bites are numerous among the inmates. The swelling is gigantic and the infections are unsightly. The resulting damage always leaves a scar. Other inmates from different County jails around the State joined us in the wait for our newly assigned pods. The mood in the arena becomes tense as different gang boys are thrown together. Most comply . . . others rebel. Just another hell house. One of the inmates who had just joined our original unit was visibly sick. He casually sat down beside us and began speaking about how happy he is to be back in general population. He had been in isolation at his last jail because he tested positive for HIV. He was now full blown with AIDS.

7. Once again, we are at the herding process. All sorts of "crimes" doing all sorts of "times" are placed together in the designated pods. It is a melting pot of criminals housed together under one roof. **Bunks lay inches apart from each other. Over fifty men residing in a room no bigger than a large apartment; eating sleeping, fighting, exercising, showering, shitting, and just passing time. It seems like we are here to live and die together! This is the place where anything goes.** It is the middle of August. I have not felt the pounding Texas, summer heat since July 2nd.

It is unbearable and unreal to me. The sweltering sun blazed down on us through the aluminum walls of the barracks. It harbored all the heat within making it hard to breathe the heavy air.

8. I entered and dragged my mattress across the floor to my assigned bunk. The heat remains still and heavy. The relays in the fans had been taken out to make tattoos. Zero circulation meant zero possibilities of receiving any relief from the suffocating circumstances of being in jail today. The red tape hanging on the A/C grill was not moving.

9. I am looking around at over 55 bunks of hot headed angry men, constantly engaged in heated arguments of nothing that should be important anyway. Fights broke out constantly. I was immediately approached for gang affiliation confirmation. I made it clear I was riding the rodeo solo. I set up my bunk and lay down on my mattress. The sweat poured off my body. There is no escape from the heat. There is no escape from this cellblock or jail. There is no escape from the realization that I am in jail today. I am suffering from heat exhaustion, intense constipation, massive headaches, and constant stress and worry from attacks by inmates and guards. Even the dudes in the county jail that had been transferred with me had stopped their bragging and boasting of previous tours through the system. I remain to be in a living nightmare.

10. Meals are served on geriatric time; breakfast at 4am, lunch at 10am, and dinner at 4pm. We are all herded outside down the center path to chow hall. Thousands of us are being released from our pods, and filed up for eating. Here, I discover the most efficient feeding process of all time. Thousands of inmates being fed systematically. We are rallied through two cafeterias each containing five rows of tables. On "paper", it says we've got twenty minutes to eat. I know personally that I was never once allowed to sit for that long . . . not once. Nobody ever was while I was here; 7-10 minutes is the norm. You sit, choke it all down . . . and learn to taste it later! My mouth was always full as I took my tray to the counter for cleaning. We would stuff ourselves with this slop just to fill the void.

11. The guards yelled continuously throughout the cafeteria for people to get up, move over, fall in line, get out of line, and to "shut the fuck up". Even when there is no one to yell at, they are still yelling. And then it's back to the pod. Those of us that risk a 2nd tour of mealtime and get caught are stripped naked in the center of the walkway and ordered to stand in place . . . sometimes for hours. Whatever significant privileges are given . . . is easily taken away at the discretion of guards who have absolutely no positive influence on your life. They are there to intimidate by numbers. That's all. Most, if not all, are despising and so very out of shape. And so it goes on, day after day; rest, fight, argue, workout, eat . . . rinse and repeat! Arriving inmates are not allowed to purchase commissary for the first two weeks and we are not allowed to have visitors for a month. I am truly feeling lost and deserted in despair at the same time. I am feeling a lot of things right now. All my thoughts are out of control. Where is my family? Where is my wife? Where is my

life? Surely, this is not the way it has to end for me. *"Please God . . . don't let it end for me in this nightmare"*.

12. Letters did eventually arrive. The postmarks were sometimes two weeks old because of the transfers and delays. Sometimes, those letters gave hope. Other times, they reminded me of all my wrongdoings, to others and myself. Either way and whatever the content, they always broke me down. I struggled to keep my fears and my tears hidden, but the "shaken in the sheets" was always a giveaway. There is no room for sentimental considerations here. You can love and miss your family, but nobody cares. Most everybody else does too, and those that don't will be the first to tell you not to inflict any of that crying bullshit on them. You can take your choice of riding this rodeo solo, or teaming up with your own kind for support and good company, so to speak. Just be prepared to defend yourself from all sides.

13. Immediately upon entering, I was sized up and approached. There's a burning question to be asked within moments of entering a multinational dorm of inmates; "whom are you running with?" Pick a color and place your bets on the winning team. There's a price to pay for that protection, especially if you turn the wrong glance at someone with the wrong kind of attitude. The fires of unsteadiness brew continuously. It's also the price of freedom in here; freedom from picking a table to sit at, and what shows you get to see. It is the freedom to know you don't have to always look over your back. It is also the freedom to know someone's always "got your back". I took my chances and told the runner "I'll ride solo . . . my ride here is a short one this time." *This time . . . like as if there's going to be another eh? No way!* He said, "That's cool, we understand." I later became friends with the dude.

14. I watch guys get in arguments as an excuse to show off their "ass whipping" talent. Some fight out in the open, while others prefer to "catch a corner". It's about finding a place where the cameras are not viewing. The fights are continuous here. The enemies of color fighting during the day are the same brothers praying together in the evening and then, become bitter enemies later that night. *Hypocrisy,* this world is full of liars, snakes, and fakes. *Trust no one.*

15. The day has turned to night. I am sitting and observing the daily routines of inmates. I just waited and watched, not really wanting to talk to anyone. *It is enlightening to see who are the predators, and who will be the prey.* All this time, I have been silently fellowshipping with God to show me He is glad I have come back to his love. At this point, I will be the first to say it is out of necessity. What else do I have? I am a "have not". But secretly, I have been wishing for death, just in case I don't survive the wave of attacks. A heat stroked, heart attack would be a good start right about now. It is humid. My eyes are burning through the sweat. Even at night, the temperatures remain in the upper 90's. It never lets up.

16. How can I keep up my health and strength in such conditions? The water system here is filthy and too unsanitary. We are forced to drink water from a stream on top of the commode. We rinse our bodies several times a day to wash away the sweat

and grime that comes from these dirt filled floors and walls. I remain on constant guard for recluses coming my way.

17. In the county before arriving here, I saw dudes pushing the numbers; stomach crunches, sit-ups, and push-ups, reaching 300-400 a night. Here, the "rough and tough" punched out numbers up to 1200 a night. Imagine the discipline, the time, the strength, endurance, and the dedication. It is a show of force and attitude within the numbers game. *"How can I compete?"* One wrong move with one of these dudes and its lights out baby! I don't know anyone here from the outside to be able to fall back on. I suddenly felt weak. I knew I had to find an edge . . . somehow. Enter the badest dude on the block. *"Country . . . Big Country"* that is. He's not the tallest fellow, but he is the most avoided and toughest. For whatever reason, I don't even care. What does matter is his immediate interest in the book that I'm presently reading. Fortunately for me, he had no glasses, so I began reading my *daily lessons of life* to him. Soon, others joined in to listen in while I read stories of success and courage.

18. In return, *Country* showed me how to workout on strength resistance training with a broom handle. I dedicated myself to a daily ritual of muscle and cardio workouts. I owe him this: the realization of being able to reverse the effects of age and ill health through a serious commitment of improving the quality of my life . . . no matter what the surroundings! *Thanks Big Country!*

19. So here it is, in the middle of hard-core state facility inmates, within the aluminum walls of hell's sauna, I befriend a White Supremist who instills a life long "addiction" to properly up-keeping my health. And in exchange, I read perfect English, inspiring stories of hope and courage from pain and suffering. We did not discriminate. *Country* helped me with the workouts until I became proficient. So now, the broom handle joins the long list of everyday, household items used to strengthen my arms, stomach, and back. I guess it's better than getting that broom handle shoved up my ass. That never happened. We became adapted to the horrid conditions of the summer heat and grimy filth. We had no choice.

20. And so it goes, the routine of being an inmate sets deep into my soul. The days are melting into the nights leaving me more exhausted with each passing moment. A typical day brings with it so much stress and too little rest. Within each 24-hour period, I am taking 2-4 naps rather than the usual 8 hour sleep. It's terrible to awake to the same day each time I open my eyes. To wake up from these short cycles bring forth the suffering of time standing still. It is still the same day . . . over and over. ***This is the nightmare of being incarcerated . . . time. This is time traveling in space. A space with infinitely small intervals. My life has becomes the State's to do with as they wish. I am forced to do whatever it they want. I do it, or suffer the consequences. This is the punishment within the confinement of my sentence.***

21. Attempting any classes offered was like attending adult ADD "kitty corner" classes on speed. It was impossible to control with any and all directions unknown. IQ testing was a futile effort on behalf of the authorities. Most inmates just filled in

the blanks to go through the motions until finished. I did find out something of myself during these days of testing: I should've been a doctor.

22. Days later, my life is being uprooted again. This has to be the worst of all stress factors for me. It requires one to leave a place of familiarity and routine, to experience the discovery pattern all over again, and again, and again. Just when you become familiar with the routine and sociable with a few good men, it's time to be moved into the unknown. And the next place is usually worst than the last one. Just when you become compatible within the routine . . . and just when you know who to watch out for and who you can get along with . . . just at a time you can let the towel slip from around your neck while you sleep . . . and just when it's safe to sit at a table among others to write letters and read books . . . just when it all comes to a level of toleration, you are pulled into a world of unknown surroundings again. I thought it could get no worse, but this is jail, and I have to be here today. Sure . . . tomorrow will eventually come, but only if I can get through today.

23. Upon entering, I could immediately see this was going to be the worst that I will experience. As I walked into the pod, there were two different fights going on at the same time. The guards ignored them. Gang colors and tattoos decorated the pod. Territories were clearly marked. Here, the biggest, badest, dudes inhabited the cellblock. I quickly jumped on the workout schedule. I was luckily uprooted the very next day. This time, it was in the middle of the night.

24. I soon found myself with most of the original inmates that had come over from the county with me weeks before. We were being transferred to a new facility. But where? It was two days before my parents and wife were scheduled to see me, but now I am leaving. There are three possibilities: Austin, Houston, or Beaumont. So far away. It was always so close, but now it becomes so far away . . . again. I have become so distraught and lonely. Not knowing. It's the worst of all anxieties. Fearful human instinct. When will it end? Where am I going? How soon will it be before I know? Why doesn't someone tell me something? The fear of not knowing transcends our mind toward a world of insecurity that brings with it, a stress factor that extends beyond the Richter scales. My body tenses with the thought of adjusting to the friction of change. You can try to mask over it, but it always peeks through. You can laugh about it, but it ends with the sound of a crackle. You can worry about it, but it never goes away before it's time. This is jail, and you will remain on a "don't need to know anyway" basis.

25. We checked out our possessions and it was off to the holding cells for preparation to leave. About ten of us sat in the empty cafeteria waiting for further instructions. Knowing that I could be transferred hundreds of miles away was gnawing away at my brain. Finally after so many hours, we were led down corridors to another holding tank. But this isn't just any holding tank that we were about to endure. *This is K block.*

26. **In all my life, the question of whether or not I want to go to jail today will stem from the memories of these next hours. It is the motivation of my life to be kind**

and considerate to others, while I seek a higher ground. It is easy to submit to finding a life of God, health, and emotional stability, after experiencing what comes next. To live life to it's fullest in satisfaction and gratitude ... every minute of it! To believe in this, so that today, tomorrow, and all the next days of your life, you will never have to experience a single day in jail ... *Not ever.*

27.   . But before I take you into the belly of the beast block, let's talk about why you personally don't want to come to jail today. Never mind the filthy conditions, violence, loss of identity and property. Forget about your family's sorrow and anger for a moment, and start thinking about yourself having to endure being a caged animal with really abusive circus trainers. Trainers so terrible, that it's only right that things could go so wrong. I'm talking about the guards. What I'm telling you now is real. **It is factual witness testimony by me. It is not hearsay. It is reality ... from my eyesight to yours.**

The Guards

1. I've sat in enough holding cells at the beginning of the processing to see many officers come in from the outside door with prisoners of all types. I've watched them check in their gun at the door lockers . . . and their oath to serve and protect. Be warned. Once those metal doors close in on you, your human rights and civil liberties are at the mercy and discretion of those in charge.

2. The first things you notice are guards cursing at guards. The vulgarness spewing from the gutters of their mouths is intolerable to listen to. The cursing is not so much at each other, as it is within their conversation. You are bound in cuffs, pushed into a cell, and left to sit indefinitely. The cop finishes his report of the arrest and prepares to leave back out onto the street. Their faces of consideration are slipped back on and they are back out the door. Outward appearances are so deceiving and deceptive.

3. It is a fact. You can't herd sheep with a chicken or a rooster. But you can herd them with a guard dog. And this is how they do it: train human beings to be guard dogs. Not much depth of thought is involved here. But the brash, growling, barking, and gnawing of the teeth is a prerequisite. I'm curious, does it take a certain breed of human to be a guard dog, or can all walks of life be trained to be so evil minded and thoughtless of any human dignity.

4. It is not my intention to crucify all persons that I came in contact with during this time of incarceration. However, in the 222 days of hell in jail, I can only recollect a handful of descent people. They are in the administrative and school testing departments. On the other hand, within these same departments, I witnessed others, as well as myself, being subjected to cruel remarks, screaming, and beatings for any possible reason. Even when there was no reason to engage an inmate, the guards found a way to instigate agitation.

5. Guards, in general, are always angry and are not shy or hesitant to show it through brute force. Violence and brutality are alive and living dangerously in overly packed cells across the nation. *If only we, as a people, could slow the movement of persons through the penal system*, most of these animals would be without a job, on the street, or in jail themselves. "Under educated" and "no breeding" within their upbringing

55

is the picture that comes to my mind when being cursed at and threatened by the scum of the earth guards who feel it is necessary to push someone down in order to get a rise.

6. Patience, self-respect, and confidence in your own life are major requirements of dealing with, and protecting yourself from the guards. Most of the time, you'll wish you had never even looked at them. It's either that, or you check your sense of respect and understanding at the door. And most have chosen to do just that! A guard's only response to whatever it is that ails you is *"not to come to jail anymore"*. But realistically, each one of them is happy you're here today, for they are not bred for anything other than "guard dogging". Guards are predictable. Their anger management is satisfied directly through you or the other guards. The only therapy they are practicing is in your face "fuck you, and the horse you rode in on baby". You are to be punished, and that's exactly what they intend to enforce. It is the punishment of cruelty within your sentence. Or didn't they tell you to expect that?

7. Now, I want to tell you this: In the free world, we are all required to wear different hats throughout the day whether it is as a parent, worker, teacher, student, husband, wife, etc. We display public characteristics to manage these responsible roles in our lives. I believe consistency is the key to success here. I'm doubtful that when confronted with mind altering and challenging circumstances, a guard is able to leave their work at the door. They come to work half-baked on bars, coke, and pot. They finish ready to leave the rest of the world behind. Patience of any kind is not required and is definitely not expected of guards. *There is no conscience for the living here!* Simple requests for the most basic needs are usually slammed back in your face.

8. Within the confinements of a cell containing fifty grown men, there is an unspoken sense of order. We maintain our own order and progress. Leave it up to the guards to disrupt any such place. So . . . with the growing number of inmates passing through the revolving door of freedom and incarceration, it's no surprise these guards should live in fear. They spend their days glancing over their shoulder. They share the same Wal-Marts and Quik Stops as the rest of us. It would do them no good to run, for most would never be able to escape the wrath of a disgruntled ex-inmate.

9. Almost all guards I have encountered in the state facility are severely out of shape. They are, however, trained to be beat you into whatever shape they want. And they do this by the numbers. Guards attack with piranha-like aggressiveness; they do this all together at the same time. It is done by the force and strength of numbers. But meet one of them on the street, and most would turn and run the other way if they saw you coming. I often notice that guards make it a point to have you believe that you are an interruption to their day. Ironically, they are there because your incarceration is their livelihood. Many sleep while in the safety of their "chicken pens" and couldn't be bothered to give interest unless it was required. Most, if not all, are confused about the significance of their lives. They actually believe that their

lives are more important than ours just because we happen to be incarcerated. Stay here long enough and they will have you convinced of this lie about the importance of your own life. It's up to you, as an inmate, to remain distant and unnerved by their torment and intimidation. Remember, prison is always to be thought of as a temporary shelter . . . even if it is for the rest of your life. It's still a temporary confinement for something so much bigger than anyone here.

10. **If you go to jail today, make up your mind now, that no one or nothing will allow your sense of inner wellness (if you possess any at all) to be dissipated. Keep your quality of life close to your heart always. Act upon it whenever possible. Remember, this is a temporary situation, no matter how long the stay. There is a beginning and an end. How you face the days gone by will be your proving ground. You can tolerate . . . or annihilate: To tolerate will be to self-preserve, and to annihilate, will be to self-destruct.**

11. *Toleration* requires that you separate yourself from what the guards can give in the form of cruelty. Preserve your safety and your sanity. Slip to the back away from the line of fire. I tended to . . . no actually, I made it a point to avoid any such eye contact or communication with guards in general. They are rude, and feel it's not necessary to consider any of your worthiness within any type of interaction. *Fuck em! I didn't feel the need to kiss the ass of the same animal that would later strike out to wound.* I chose to speak to them only when absolutely necessary.

12. For those that choose to *annihilate*, it becomes torturous. Your pain becomes self-inflicted. Most confrontations with the guards, if not all, end up in a wreck. **Guards, given their unlawful right, take every opportunity to verbally and physically degrade whoever is visible to their grasp. It is their way of life and their train of thought. We, as inmates, go to sleep with it, wake up with it, and endure it throughout every waking moment of every day and night.** Most of us are sound enough in our lives not to become the "crash test dummy", and the select few of us choose not to even get in the car. This is the best and most sensible choice an inmate can make; steer clear of the guards. Not because you're afraid of them or they deserve the respect of being bullies. But more so, ignore them because you personally don't have the time or the space to endure the emotional turmoil of one more person in an already unforgiving place. Those of us here that make the regrettable mistake of initiating the skid, usually end up in the notorious K block.

K Block

1. Upon leaving the F block unit, I was rejoined with some of the original inmates that I had come here with from the county jail just weeks ago. It seemed way too long ago since I had seen them, for each day was an eternity in hell. All of us were taken to the cafeteria for out-take processing and inventory. We were then led back through the corridors to the place where we had first been processed. And beyond that, we are led down another corridor to the center guard cell. It is elevated and round with windows all around it for complete circumference viewing. A walkway surrounded the guard station like a mote circling a castle. Each cellblock extending from the mote was in the shape of a slice of pie.

2. We entered and immediately the cages rattled with noise pollution reaching deafening proportions. **We were bombarded with questions of the free world. Some of these questions were from events so far back in the time. How long had they been here? How long will they stay? It turns out, some have been here in the same cage without once leaving for up to six months at a time.** I quickly summed up all the sludge that I had been dragged through for the past two and a half months and realized that it had all been "Kiddie Corner" *up until now!*

3. **K Block is angry and rebellious. It is dark, isolated, filthy, and unforgiving. It is all that can be unpredictable.** Between the walkway and the day room there are 6 cells stacked 3 on 3 in a quarter circle. Although they are beside each other, the curve in the design allows for inmates to have the slightest view of each other as they press their face up against the cell bars. I'm looking across the walkway into the cells. I can see only a few white guys. Most of them are black and Hispanic. Each of the 6 cells contains 6 to 10 inmates.

4. The conversations between the K block inmates and us quickly turned to slang, shouting, and threats. Threats of pain became promises, and promises of violence were being reinforced with shows of force. Gang signs hung outside the bars. They had us backed into the corners as they flung freezing water at us from higher ground. These barracks were already below 60 degrees. We had been subjected to the sweltering heat of the Houston sun for weeks, and now it is the A/C we cursed. Everybody was shivering through to the bone. And getting sprayed with cold water

is not helping. It was cold. I assume this is to deter the growth of bacteria and viruses that thrive in the warmer temperatures. And so the agony continues. The clear spray water soon turns yellowish green, and the stench quickly turns sour. Urine littered the floors. We pressed further back against the wall in the corner. Inmates filled squeeze bottles and shot their infected waste across the floors. The guards stood by watching. They appear to be amused.

5. One of our posse boys is clearly AB. He soon became the object of all that is to come. He begged the guards to let him go up to fight the fuckers throwing all this waste at us. The savage scum's began jerking off and attempted to throw their semen down on top of us. Soon to follow was the make shift "exploders" made of food and vomit. The mess was everywhere we stood. There would be no place to sit down or rest between reloads. The guards continued to ignore our pleas to allow us to go up and satisfy our quest for retribution. However the guards did nothing to stop the filth of these punks from being thrown down at us. There was no way to get up to where they were being kept. Complacency is the norm for the guards. It has been everywhere I've gone so far.

6. At about 2:30 am, we were moved to another slice of the pie; different unit, but same kind of inmates. Any type of rest tonight will be completely out of the question. We endured continuous riot-like antics. These 6 to 10 man cells were being destroyed however possible. Breakfast was served at 4am. The sugar content of syrup on the pancakes immediately surged through the veins of the undead. Trays full of syrup and slop were thrown back and forth between cells and along the breezeways. It wasn't long before it was our turn to eat. Most of us took advantage of the food, while others joined in the free for all. But this is no ordinary food fight like in the school cafeteria. No . . . the objectives are much different here.

7. **Fights are breaking out within each of the cells. Inmates attacking each other with bits of broken trays trying to cut their fingers off while holding onto the cell bars. So many inmates got left without a tray and of course, the guards assumed they were lying. *They weren't*. Like savages competing for the kill, most meals were sacrificed just for the fight to prove who should eat . . . and who won't be eating at all. The floors were littered with food, urine, and feces. The water compounded the problem as the nauseating mix flowed everywhere.**

8. I am remembering this one particular fight breaking out between two young men in one of the cells upstairs. They are small fellows but their strength of force was intense. At least five inmates stood by watching while these two warriors went at it . . . hardcore! Punches over punches, and kicks into the face and body from both these guys had blood spilling freely in no time. As the fight continued, all but one of the guards stood carelessly about. These inmates were fighting like I haven't seen before . . . and I've seen some great ones. Casually, one of the guards strolled upstairs. The two fighters ignored him until he stood against the bars and shouted something for them to stop. He quickly left without ever turning back around. The moment he had turned his back on the fighting inmates, they continued their

bloodbath onto each other. Finally, the two animals separated due to complete exhaustion. They sat near their bunk on the floor actually licking the wounds on their hands and body. I guess the warmth felt comforting. Once they had gotten their breath back, they went at it again. Who, or what, had started the fight at this point is irrelevant. They fought to kill each other. Each unsuccessful. But each gets my vote for an "A" for effort. Pound for pound, it is *the most gruesome fight I have ever seen between two people.* They both fought until they could fight no more. Even as each one of them literally crawled to his bunk, I could sense it was not over yet. *God save them from their torment.*

9. The cleaner came in to sweep and mop the walkways of all that littered the floors. The cells remained as they were though; stinking, soaking, and smelling, of food, urine, shit, and puke. In a matter of minutes, the inmate sweepers were covered in the same mixture they attempted to clean. They retaliated with buckets of filthy mop water. These buckets of freezing, poisonous, wastewater were poured onto the floors through the bars and into the cells. The inmate cleaners then hurled buckets of the same up onto the bunks from the walkway. The bunks, sheets, towels, clothes, mattresses, and all other possessions were saturated. I'm told this is the norm between them most every night. It will remain unattended to for days until linen day arrives.

10. This K block has transfer inmates pass through here all the time. It's hard to imagine this is the way of life each night and early morning. Many times, the meals are missed or delayed for hours. There is no way of telling what time it is for there are no windows. This block is result of catching serious cases toward other inmates in general population, or for instances of violence against the guards. I look back and consider how many times I came so close to striking back or lashing out at guards for the verbal and physical abuse I had to see . . . and what I had to endure myself. All of us suffered the same tyranny during some point in time. Much of it consistently worsened as time rolled deeper into a never-ending nightmare. But I knew I had to hold onto homeward thoughts. To strike back would have meant my conflict here with the guards or other inmates was more important than getting home to my wife, children, and family.

11. Let it be known here and now to the reader. *Nothing . . . and I mean nothing, is more of a priority and mission to me than getting back home to them, and into the arms of love and compassion. I will save this family and will not allow someone else to take my role as provider, lover, and daddy. Everything I do, and consider doing, in this God forsaken place is to allow me to function better, sleep easier, and wake hopeful knowing that I will still be a significant part of my family's lives. As I'm being told through sporadic letters, I am being encouraged to get my time done and get back home. This is the motivating lifeline I will cling to.*

12. Little did I know, at the same time that I was receiving hopeful and loving letters from my dear wife, she is also sharing a daily dose of both from someone else. Hope is supposed to be the answer when death and despair are knocking at your

door. For me, it is the hope of being loved again and considered a significant asset in someone's life. Looking ahead, I can say I'm glad I didn't know the true facts and the extent that someone else was sharing my bed, for if I did, the life force of passion would have killed me. It is said that when a man is tired of pleasure and passion, he must be tired of life and the continuing quest to exist becomes null and void. She was my best friend and lover. My extension of character and person of pleasure. Unbeknown to me, she has betrayed me many times. Much because of feeling rejected and insecure. I just could not believe the news nor can I comprehend that my wife could do this while I am in jail and being left for dead in an unforgiving system. She is being seduced by the good ole doctor boy routine. So very typical of someone attempting to latch onto that label. Money will never buy her the good breeding she longs for.

13. The early morning hours are dragging on. So is the marathon of unexpected surprises and tragedies. We keep hearing screams from the bottom cell. The lights are out, but we can see movements within the cage. None of us wanted to approach the fence separating the walkways and cells for the thought of getting soaked with urine and feces had no appeal to any of us.

14. We can see an inmate jumping from the top bunk to the floor and back up again. He is screaming "stay on your bunk, stay on your bunk". I can see the rope. It is made from garbage bags braided into a lengthy tight coil. It had enough strength to support whatever is going to be hung from it. It was tied onto the bars leading up to the top bunk. "Tie yourself up, tie yourself up" echoed through the cellblock. The young man screamed as the predator continuously pounded the helpless inmate. He spoke in a fake Asian accent to mimic playing out the role of some Vietnamese or Japanese war torture character. This man is actually American black and is tragically disillusioned into being the capture of a POW. He was truly caught up in a sadistic world of kidnapping and torture. Soon, the young inmate was forcibly tied and the aggressor flung himself back and forth off the top bunk. He continued to beat the helpless victim.

15. **How is it that an inmate can go this length of time beating a tied up victim without being noticed by the guards? Or . . . is it the situation is just being ignored by complacent and apathetic guards? Yea . . . that must be it! Guards who don't get paid enough to give a rat's ass about some two-bit hustler criminal in jail tonight. *Is this where you want to be tonight?***

16. The young man wept silently in his bunk. I can hear the whimpering. He's in trouble now. The plastic rope is now bound tightly around his legs, body, and neck. The animal inmate begun to instruct the victim how to choke himself. This, of course, is not very effective with his own voluntary movements, so the predator inmate began pulling on the rope to tighten it further around his neck. He went into a frenzy as the young man began to grasp for air. He actually got off on watching this prisoner suck back deeply while struggling to get air. This bastard now begins to jump off the back of the top bunk, forcibly dragging the choked man down with

him. I could see that if the victim didn't follow him down off the side of the bed, his neck would snap from the force. Every cell in my body was a raging inferno. I knew any plea for him to stop would simply aggravate him further. We turned away for a while only to steal glances back in his direction. He was enjoying the spectator's attention already, so we didn't want to encourage him to continue with his sadistic ritual any more. The other inmates in the cell with him just watched and laughed throughout the entire ordeal. The young ones snickered out of fear. I could see it in their eyes. Each one is wondering if he is next.

17.   I had my face down in my hands quietly praying "oh dear God, when will this end?" just as the steel doors of the cell opened up for us to be moved. Right now . . . I'm giving thanks for still yet another prayer being answered. We are being moved to the large open room where we had originally come in just two weeks ago. It seemed a 1000 life times ago that I was here being stripped of all my possessions, identity, dignity, and even my hair. It was here; I had been forced to give up what little left I had tried in vain to hang on to. I had been literally stripped to the bone . . . and to the core! As we were led to the exiting holding cell, one inmate was stopped and returned back into the corridors leading back to hell's kitchen. I am pleading that doesn't happen to me, and that my terror trip here is over.

18.   It was over! I am leaving on a bus to *"I don't know where"* and *"I don't care"*. As long as it's far away from here, it should be better. There are possibilities of three different places. Two of the locations will send me further away from home and the other will put me closer to my family. We all had that nagging feeling we would be sent further away from our families and homes. That concern was now put to rest as the bus rolled up to the launch pad. A small victory for the group of us. For me, it will be just another terrible beginning to a tragic ending that will not go away.

19.   **I have survived this menacing place. It has been, and will always be the worst memories of my life. I will remember every second of every terrible waking hour I have spent here. Images of the heat, fights, food, guards, inmates, filth, diseases, exhaustion, torture, and the feeling of abandonment flash before my eyes . . . even to this day.** A small glimmer of hope has been given to me with the news that I will be transported back down closer to her.

Bus Ride

1. The sun had not yet risen as we boarded the prison bus. It's darker inside due to the steel fence and wire mesh over all the windows. We can still peak between the spacing in the bars to see outside. Upon leaving, the guards take their loaded shotguns and lock themselves in the back of the bus. There is a separate compartment for them to sit and watch inmates during transportation.

2. We drove on the road along side of the prison facility. I can see where the rows of barbed wire fences end and become endless acres of green soccer fields. It soon becomes baseball fields and then finally, the highway and other buildings come into view. *I can see civilization*! The feeling of euphoria is overcoming me in waves. I can never forget this moment in time. I can now see the sun rising in the distant. I am looking all around, taking in everything; people, cars, billboards, buildings, . . . all of it! I am looking at all the busy bodies getting to work. It's amazing to see just how many people are up and already on their way to work or school this early in the morning. Whether it was school or work, I never had the hours that required such early rising. I've always scheduled around it . . . or should I say "after it". Afternoons and evening have always been my forte for functioning. Maybe if I had done the early thing instead, I would not have existed as a creature of the night for all of my adult life. I surely never had to deal with traffic like this in the mornings. Only in the evenings. But right now, I'm missing civilization terribly for all that it entails and what it means to me.

3. This short look and small taste of the world outside this prison bus had me thinking about how different it had to be now. It wouldn't, shouldn't, and couldn't be the same as it ever was this time around.

4. I peaked through the thin slits of metal plates and looked at the fancy trucks, cars, and other vehicles passing on the road beside the bus. I looked below at the car driving beside us: pretty blouse, short, sexy skirt, one gorgeous leg propped up against the door and the other on the gas. Her legs are parted amply enough for me to imaginarily fondle my way into her sense of pleasure. My hormones exploded! It had been too long since seeing such opportunity. The touch was out of reach, but the sight is embedded in my mind. I quickly relieved myself in the dark as her car

moved back and forth along side the bus. She will never know the appreciation of gratitude I have for this treasured pleasure that she unknowingly afforded to me. My handcuffs rattled all the while. I had no conscience to who was listening . . . or watching. I knew it would be too long before I would get to see such beauty again. Surely, it would never come from the guards.

5. Before you decide that you want to go to jail today, ask yourself just how damn great your sex life is, and are you really willing to give it up. Do you thrive on lust and sexual pleasures of intimacy and comfort with your loved one? Is it the "one thing" or a combination of many things that keep you coming back for more over and over again? Do you want it to die and become a faded memory? I say, "do you" because if you do go to jail today, the sex doesn't have to fade away for your spouse and lover . . . but it does for you! Think about that before you go off and do the deed that puts you in jail today.

6. **I am confident that I am the absolutely most exotic, intimate, and physically satisfying lover to my wife. We both know this. Yet, I was replaced in less than a month with someone far less capable of giving any kind of passion and attention that I would constantly give to her. But this makes no difference. It is the intimacy they seek after you're gone to jail. And they settle for anything to get it. You had better check your love life before you leave the house today. Examine the strength of your bond. Find out whether you're an asset or a burden. Don't hurry though. You'll never get the results you want overnight. It takes time . . . lots of time.**

7. While the letters I received were encouraging and comforting, subtle hints of communication painted a different picture than what she was describing. False truths became the looking glass of clarity. It was promises undone and words unbecoming that tore through my heart like jagged teeth tearing flesh away from the bone. All I could do was keep writing letters of my progress, my hopes, and my renewed strength of faith. I avoided false promises and empty threats. Instead, my encouragement came from my own self-awareness that I had been the "walking dead" in overdrive. It was simply a matter of too much money, too much time, and way too much idleness that put me here. That, and unbeknown to me, a lying, cheating, and thieving wife

8. The bus continued to roll down the highway south to the city. The sun has broken through the morning clouds now. I took notice. I am thinking about these last fourteen days. Still hidden in the dark confinements of the bus, I broke down and cried. I held my breath quietly as I have learned to do all the times in the past. But my body continues to shudder with the pain of unbearable realizations.

9. As the bus turned down Baker Street, I immediately knew where I was to come again. I sensed the familiarity of my surroundings, as I had been escorted down this road many times for trade school while in the county jail. However, I'm not going to the County jail. This is the downtown State facility across the street. I had continuously prayed for my transfer to this location many times. As it's been told

throughout the system, this is the place to do your time; cleaner rooms, football lockers, air conditioning, regular commissary days, and daily outside recreation. The appeal of these services was to deter inmates from exacting their wrath on the guards and the other inmates. Damn, I'm just looking forward to communicating with decent human beings. Up until now, I have felt deprived of any intelligent and/or stimulating conversations. It doesn't have to be book smart or professionally degreed shit to talk about. But rather, just some good old fashioned barroom talk. Anything but all the jailhouse bullshit I've been listening to. I've been living in my head and it is reaping its torture upon my soul. Yes, this is what I've come to look forward to and this time, I've got great expectations. I would be able to enjoy contact visits with my wife and children. Finally, after two and a half months, I will be able to feel the soft touch of loved ones. It will be better than knocking knuckles with scum of the earth.

10. The bus rolled into the garage. The door slid down behind us. We filed out in chains. Instantly, the familiar sound of vulgarity echoed the unloading area. This is nothing more than the same verbal and physical threats we have come to endure as inmates. *"Be careful what you wish for"* was my first thought upon entering the garage door. I had been praying and wishing with God for me to come here. After enduring and adapting to such horrid, sub-human, and sadistic conditions of human suffering for the last 75 days, *I was told my future residence here would be a breath of fresh air. Why then, after breathing in the cool, fresh, morning air, was there a really bad taste in my mouth?* Right now, I'm wishing I had gotten off at the wrong stop and I was getting back on the bus. Already after moments of seeing and hearing the spiteful filth coming from these nasty guards, I am missing the hot, crowded, conditions of where I had just come from. The open space, abusive guards, unconscionable neighbors, and the endless 24/7 noise pollution that littered my ears, has instantly become a wanted hall pass back into time. I longed to be me again. But that's not possible, for at this moment, I am being herded into the prison dayroom for processing as a "nobody" along with a bus full of others. I am nothing more than a head of cattle going in for the slaughter. It is the morning of September 2nd, 2004.

Keagan State Facility

1. The Labor Day weekend is upon us, however, the parties are so far away. It's not going to be that fun filled, party weekend in the sun I've become so accustomed to. *There is no booze, babes, or buddies here that I want to be hanging around with at this time.*

2. We are being prodded through like cattle, and herded up to our new housing units. The design is the same as the county facility across the street, but definitely not as sanitary. At least it is air-conditioned. Adjustments are always easier in the cool air. Looking back from where I had just come, anything beats the 110-degree heat index of the north facility. I have almost made it to the half way mark of my sentence. I'm at this table counting days to go and I do not believe what is to come. It has only been 75 days since first being incarcerated. I'm adding my days gone by, but I cannot engage my brain to function any longer. How can this lifetime of suffering be within such a small frame of time? It already seems to have been years gone by. How could time have traveled in such small intervals? Has the world slowed down to this just so I can do time. How can this be? Having only 75 days in meant that I still had at least another 90 days to go for the cause. **It *is* true then! The world *does* pass you by when you're in jail. I have become overly burdened with grief. I have experienced suicidal tendencies several times while being incarcerated. It is now my prevailing wish to end this already. I am tired and tremendously exhausted from thinking my way through this ordeal.**

3. I suddenly felt the aging process kick into high gear. There is no telling what I look like. I hadn't looked in a mirror for months. It's more of a metal plate scarred with dents and scratches. There is just enough reflection to see my structure and shape. Shaving is difficult. I have learned to do it in the shower without having to look at myself. The blades are terrible; the cheapest single edge blades that last one shave. We keep them for a week and must shave everyday if we want recreation time. I guess even in the worst of conditions, even the smallest conveniences that we take for granted become a wish list of better commodities and conditions to come.

4. I feel like I have been abandoned. I have not received any letters from my wife in over three weeks. She is, for the most part, moving on with her new friends, career,

and motherhood. My letters have not been sufficient enough to keep her heart full of love and contentment. The lust and sins of the flesh marinate within her. No longer does she have the daily compliments of beauty and brains from me, so she has gone searching elsewhere. During the nights out on the town, it is easy to find attention from anyone willing to listen and it's even easier for everyone to talk his or her own game. Her being taken by another was only a matter of time . . . and time had just moved into fast forward. **I wonder if the wives of hostages captured in other countries were out socially gathering up their flock of night calls from any men willing to lend their time. Probably not, but this is not a hostage situation and I'll never be a hero for coming to jail.**

5.   Desperately, I fight to control the rage from burning my flesh. I am trying to keep busy with daily activities of reading, writing, recreation, and sleep, but no line was being written or any thought completed without my inferno re-kindling into overdrive. It would only get worse for me. I continued to write. She continues to lie. The excuses became useless; too busy with school, work, and mothering to write me. But even when the letters did arrive, she always left out the dating, and the constant character attacks she made to my own social circle. She has infiltrated my circle of friends to spread her disease of lies. It's what a cheater does to remain on the winning side; turn your own friends against each other. It's a simple military tactic. She says anything to justify her actions of deceit. She's had plenty of time for lunches and dancing with new companions.

6.   And so it comes to this after six years of complete bliss (but not without strife). After a half a million dollars in vacations, vehicles, city tours, dinners, clothes, and a child, she couldn't wait six months for my release. It turns out she didn't even wait a month! I have been used and abused right out of the playbook. All the love, energy, dedication, and struggles. All the good times, walks, talks, and laughs. All the reconciliation, and the sentimental considerations. It became all about her now, without any regard to what I've given to her. How quickly the pleasures of life afforded to her are forgotten. And now with school about to finish and a career in the works, I will no longer be the branch she swings from. She has already reached out toward another and I'm sure, has a handle on it. She will soon be letting go completely. I am devastated, lonely, and in great despair from being lied to, rejected, and replaced.

7.   **And so it comes to pass, my life as a man in society reflects everything that is broken. I am without a single penny to my name. I have no dwelling of my own to go home to at the end of any given day. I do not own a single thread of clothing within my reach. I have a wife unfaithful and a child not knowing the truth. I come from a family of parents and siblings that is now torn from the patience of a hard, cold, truth; never knowing if I made it through to the next sunrise.**

8.   *My life, however insignificant to you, has ceased to exist. I feel that I've reached my date of expiration. I am no longer able to function in my mind. Regret and remorse*

exist far beyond my endless flow of tears. It stabs into my soul, stinging with every breath. I cannot see inches in front of me or consider even brief moments in time ahead of the present. I have arrived at the point of no return. And now . . . with every physical possession gone, there can only be one thing left . . . freedom. It is the freedom of nothingness. It will be the freedom of knowing that nothing vital is at stake except . . . ?

9. It has taken much pain and suffering to get to this point. Days and nights of reflection, mediation, repentance, and begging for forgiveness. It has been creeping into my skin and winding through my veins. After wishes for death, cries for desperation, and struggles for safety, I have finally come to a new place in my pathetic life. A place that knows no threats. A force to be reckoned with, an inspiration to my life, and an affirmation to my soul; a replacement is in the works. I am under construction and definitely under new management. But this time, it is not going to be of this world. **This time, it's going to be so much more glorifying and powerful. No insecurities of anything worldly shall ever again be put first before my belief and imagination of a most powerful and infinite love and trust. This is the love of God and it is more than good. This is the trust I am to put before him. A low down, dirty, sorrowful, and pitiful end . . . to a pure, uplifting, bright, and worthy beginning. This is to be the cleansing of my soul from all of its impurities.**

10. The visit from my wife was too predictable. I'm reading her like an elementary book. She bombarded me with questions and complaints. I was left to scratch the surface of nothingness as she shared past disbeliefs and burning questions of nothing that mattered at this time. She dazzled herself with what will become more broken promises. She says these things in front of others just to enjoy the sound of her own voice and to hopefully gain some admiration from people she will most likely never see again in her life. She grants these promises to me in public in hope of others speaking highly of her in her own absence. I am hitting the hammer on the nail when I tell you these things about her.

11. I have become the sponge of scrutiny to her friends as she shares her own feelings of me to them. Of course, these are her friends and they have already set her up with whoever else needs to get laid today. She is convincing herself I will never get out even though it's only a few more months until I'm released. Just another example of living like there's no tomorrow. Her friends have seduced her into believing she will have a better future without me. This taste of the single life will eventually leave her child a bastard. He will not have me as a father. I don't plan on sharing this one with other men coming and going into her life. I struggled to say the right things to her. I prayed God's love would guide me. I spoke sincere and without promises, but what I was saying became beyond a struggle to keep. I tried to renew our love through a transformation of right way thinking. What I offered was as pure as Holy water, but she's been marinating in the *sangre del Diablo*. I prayed for her salvation but it is easy to see (and hear) her soul had been sold to the highest bidder of worldly promises.

12. Anyway, beyond that . . . I'm out of chips. Every time she spoke, she tried to squeeze the last crystals of hope from me. She would then begin her ramble of nothingness. I think of locusts when she comes to mind; scavenging the land and leaving nothing in the wake. Nothing of substance . . . and nothing of conscience. Before she left here this afternoon, she threw this dog one more bone about sending me a $100 a week to my inmate trust fund. She boasted of all the money she had saved for us. She tells me our apartment would be ready when I came home. She must have been referring to someone else. She stopped writing for a while after she left that day. Could it be because I wrote and condemned her for her infidelity and pathetic attempts to buy me into continuing my struggle to remain faithful to our lives? She keeps telling me to hang on to *us*. She had me on the hook. It's hard to let go of what little correspondence you receive while in prison.

13. Hopefully, a strong faith in God and His power to heal will give guidance to my life. I'm hoping He has better plans for me. Now, I just had to figure them out. I knew I would have to build a stronger foundation of my life . . . from the ground up. One so solid, that nothing or no one will ever deviate me from the path of well being again. *Oh Lord, how will I ever find the strength to do what I intend to do, when I have no earthly idea what I'm trying to accomplish in this life?* And then it hit me! There has to be some type of spiritual intersession here. That, and some very creative and savvy earthly ideas of prosperity. I keep telling myself that it's good . . . and it's only going to get better. This is going to be the necessary train of thought I need in order to prepare myself for the worst yet to come during the long arduous road ahead. Or . . . maybe I'm just kidding myself.

14. This is a very difficult time for me. One week while visiting me, she had mentioned something about a new male friend. I became immobile with shock. I was shattered. I hammered and condemned her about it in my next two letters. While I remained to be trapped in a hole, she was finding it rightly so to hang our relationship out to dry for all the public to see. Even after all the reassurances from her about keeping our lives private. She always did have "diarrhea of the mouth". **The week gone by has become endless. Each and every moment of every second of my waking hours, minutes, and seconds, have become unbearable. I longed to see my mother. I desperately wanted to see my family again.**

15. I wept uncontrollably under my sheets while listening to prayers meetings from a distance. I eventually began to attend. Each one of us added a little prayer for each other . . . and ourselves. I began to give motivational talk sessions to some of the inmates; glimpses of wisdom. We gave thanks for our health and God. We came to terms (and at odds) with the realization of the sufferings of our families for what we were putting them through. It was a big concern for us. The gatherings grew larger and larger and within a short period of time, the numbers had grown to at least 20 inmates. It is an overwhelming comfort within the confinements of such a dark place. One evening, some of the inmates approached me while I was reading on my bunk. They mentioned to me how the attendance for the prayer meetings

had dramatically increased because of my involvement. I felt a rush of satisfaction surge over me. *What will I discuss tomorrow?*

16.   The next Saturday has finally come. *"45 bunk! You got a visitor"*. Is it my mother finally coming to see me? Is she with Jack, or my brother . . . who? I am ordered downstairs through the stairwell and on to the garage door where we are to be strip-searched. We are required to bend and cough before entering the visitation area to see loved ones. I signed the sheet and turned to see the faces of all types sitting in the picnic area. I am scanning the tops of everyone's head for familiarity. I'm seeing my mother stand and rise in the distant. Tears immediately swell in my eyes. It is difficult to hold back. I cannot see properly because of the "emotional drip". My heart thumped out of my chest when my son stood up on the table next to my wife. This is a rush to see them all. Immediately, I'm thinking this is the time to say, "I'm sorry" to all of them. This will be a chance for clarification and a time for unconditional love to be shared between us. I held on to my mother for so long. Then I wrapped my arms around my son for a great big hug. He is smiling from ear to ear with beautiful, bright, teeth. I am alive with elation. I then, leaned over to kiss my wife.

17.   What a mistake I had made sending her those letters of malice content. I wanted to make it so right no matter how much wrong I believe she had done to our relationship in the past. It couldn't be any worse than I had already done. She herself never could send that letter of faithfulness as I had requested so many times. I guess it wasn't that important to her after all. In any case, she's here with me now, and I'm convincing myself that it is out of pure love for this family and me. I'm telling myself over and over, that she's here to make things right. I have sensed she has given up on us several times since my incarceration. I will not dwell on it. Rather, I will concentrate on serving her instead of trying to change or control her. I realize the wrong moves will only drive her further away. It is time to put the shallow state of mentality aside . . . for good!

18.   **God has removed everything from my life. He must have done this because everything in my pathetic life was in disarray; my lifestyles, my routines, my destruction, my existence. Now, all that remains is an empty shell full of hope. I have to take this time to become a better man. It is time I become responsible for what I do, and have, instead of what I wish I had.** Please keep in mind, these revelations did not occur overnight. They have come from many hours, days, nights, weeks, and months of suffering, remorse, and regret. And through much reflection, mediation, research, and prayer, answers have begun to appear and become clearer. I no longer will seek out that letter of faithfulness from her. It would be pointless to even consider any truth within its foulness of lies.

19.   And so it comes to pass, after the longest days of my life. Longer than any lazy, summer days in the history of time, longer than the most freezing winter nights stuck in your car. *Longer than my* . . . . well, maybe not that long . . . but anyway, I have come to acknowledge that quite possibly, the worst days of my life are

over. So to me, the belief knowing that wherever I am, whatever I'm doing, and however I feel, I should always be graced with the presence of appreciation of my freedom; my freedom to do, and my freedom to choose. Now, this is not to say that before my life ends here on earth, I won't be subjected or spared from additional horrors or thrillers that go "bump in the night". It may very well be that the worst of conditions are yet to come, and I have not yet begun to feel what it means to suffer at the hands of God. I do know that up until now, I have been scarred for life with what my eyes have seen and for the emotional turmoil in my heart. Finally, **the scars of pain that I have caused toward my cherished loved ones remain to be the burden of responsibility. It should have been easy to see it coming . . . and so much easier to avoid it.**

20. The following days came and went. I have 91/2 weeks to go. But in considerations of that number, there is no seductive intimacy here. Instead, it is a time of rape and pillage of my self worth and dignity. Most conflict comes from the guards. Actual rapes are not happening here like in the other places. I was fortunate enough to have defended myself well enough to survive the onslaught of predators.

21. The weekend passed uneventful, but during the up-n-coming days that followed, I slipped back into a winding depression. Looking back the last few months, I have come to realize that all of my emotional struggles are stemming from the lies and deceitful circumstances surrounding my relationship with my wife; broken promises, undone chores, unanswered obligations, lack of interest, and outright, unwarranted blame. How many times will I have to be kicked while trying to get up? It was so many things.

22. Monday night becomes our worst "shake down" yet. The guards remain on a never-ending power trip to control us with dreadful remarks and obnoxious noises. Endless patience is required. I am finding that the justice system has found a new source of labor for immigrants coming in from Africa. Most have little or no education or other job skills to speak of. It appears these African nations are lining their people up to be correctional officers in our state facilities. They are "FOB", or "fresh off the boat", and speak with such severe accents, it is difficult to ponder upon what any of them are even attempting to say while trying to convey to their message. They have memorized the all too familiar phrases of "shut up" and "get on your bunk".

23. The lights never went out last night, so we gave the guards hell to beyond and back. And in return, they hit us with a "shakedown" just as we were all getting quiet for breakfast lineup. These "busts" are worse than any adult "kiddie corner" exercise that you can imagine. And it's done all for the sake of demonstrating human crowd control. The CO's, sergeants, and Lt.'s, bombarded our dorm with all the force they could muster up. At the time, we were ordered to strip to our boxers and go downstairs to the freezing cold dayroom. We sit there for hours. Upstairs, lockers are slamming, trash is being thrown about, beds are being stripped, ripped, and shredded, to the inner linings. All of our possessions are being piled up in the middle of the room to be

sorted out later. Lockers rattled until all of our contents became part of the common heap. Garbage bags are filled with what is considered contraband. This is nothing more than 3-day-old newspapers, magazines, kool-aid packs, and "sweet things". Few weapons are found here in this facility. These simple things of possession are enough to cause alarm for the guards who write us up. Here, in this facility, the results of write-ups mean that you can expect a trip down into the N dorm. The most trivial of infractions are the very ones that will put you in that hole for up to 30 days.

24. **We arrive back upstairs several hours after the shakedown to see the obvious; two hours of clean up. We search for our clothes and possessions that have been thrown into a common pile. Fight are breaking out everywhere by people looking to get back their commissary and other belongings. Even those that had nothing, fight for what they want as their own.**

25. I am not waking up for outside rec this morning. I am too tired and way too depressed. It will be my first significant loss of productivity in my quest for health. Thoughts of betrayal and the menace of depression are eating away at my desire to succeed, even if it is just working out.

26. I slept until lunch (10am), got up, ate, and went right back to sleep until dinner (4pm). After dinner, I eagerly crawled back between the sheets until nightfall. I opened my eyes to another full moon. It is more beautiful than I ever remember. I am trying to read, but the effort is futile. I am not able to finish a simple short paragraph without drifting toward some intangible worries without a solution. I convinced myself to read 20 pages, but quit after fully realizing I still haven't paid attention to a damn thing I've read. Gone are the early days of incarceration when books of 500 or more pages were completed in 3 days and nights. These are the worst of times for me. I needed help. I am overwhelmed and desperately looking for answers. I am watching the fullness of the moon slide beyond the view of my caged window. My mind slipped into the darkness of the field past the railroad tracks below. I fell asleep soon after.

27. I am awaking with the encouragement of this day, Wednesday. Will it bring with it, a bittersweet beginning of a very long 9 weeks to go. Who am I kidding? The justice system of incarceration does not operate that way. Here, it's all slow long play. I am dreaming of death to end this day.

28. Her face is nasty looking. Her hair has got that burnt smell to it. It is gelled and rolled into Shirley Temple curls hanging loosely down in her face. She appears unkept and is obviously a drug and alcohol abuser. *She is a guard.* She has the reputation of sucking her superior's dicks for extra concessions and privileges as a guard. Her language is vulgar and crude. This is the norm for her type. I know my "paid bunk" will not be mine today. She is checking ID's closely and she knows my trading partner; the guy I bought the bunk by the window from. I retreated back to the front isles in the center of the dorm. This is the original bunk that I had been assigned. The A/C continuously blew freezing air directly on the bed. I hated it here, but knew it was only temporary until the end of her shift.

29. And now it is here in this very next hour, I am watching this bitch guard in full frontal view abuse her right as a CO. She is sexually harassing and abusing one of the "funny boy" inmates. For the most part, we all just leave the funny boy alone and most want nothing to do with him. However, I've seen a few inmates take him into the showers at night to get their cocks sucked, but he stays out of everyone else's way. A few maggots befriend him for his deep commissary pockets. He is never without food and hygiene products. He is protected for those reasons. *Who isn't going to protect someone in prison while they're offering blowjobs, food, and drink?*

30. I am watching this guard attack him without conscience. She is calling him all the usual names of bitch, whore, lezzy, slut, hooker, babe, etc. He is ordered to strip, bend, and cough. But this is not the usual strip search. He's not going anywhere for it to be warranted. This guard is satisfying her own demented agenda. She states that she wants to know that the funny boy is actually a man. The "State" already knows that he is a man. He has been in the system for two months already. So the guards have this she-man standing out front and center. She is humiliating him to the point of despair. He is ordered to stand and not move as she continues her escapades. Everyone is at their boiling point with her. *Each one of us is praying someone will "take one for the team" and beat her like the mangy dog she really is.* I am struggling with my own conscience not to attack this filthy animal. I made a nasty comment to her and was immediately ordered to the sergeant's office. She said she could make me disappear. I should have knocked her teeth into the back of her skull on the way out the door.

31. I stood in the hallway and made a comment to another inmate about how I was so tired of all the idol threats made by the guards. As I said that, a Lt. exploded into the hallway and although he didn't see who said it, he threatened to shut everyone's recreation down for a week if someone didn't speak up. For me, it was either a weeks worth of ass whipping from my fellow inmates or take the isolation punishment from the system. What do you think? I spoke immediately. In his office, I am breaking down. Not for the punishment that never came from this incident, but for all my days in jail thus far. It is a compilation of stirred emotions from the recent past. For the first time since coming to prison, I have found someone listening: *all of the hatred and cruelty; all the verbal and physical abuse; and all of the pain and suffering from being incarcerated has taken its toll upon me.*

32. The Lt. knows this breakdown did not stem from this past incident at hand, but rather, from the compilation of stirred up emotions from the recent past. His first concern here is my suicidal tendencies. Mine is from the betrayal I felt in my heart. This burning sensation in my heart and in my head should have only felt like a match burn to my skin, but instead, it has escalated into a scolding fire of jealousy and hatred eating away at my flesh and soul. I tried to ignore the Lt.'s concern any longer and attempted to retreat back to my bunk, but the attending nurse had other ideas for me. Whether it was for his own job safety or not, he maintained a hopeful ear and then referred me over to the chaplain.

33. The man of God sat and waited for me to divulge my regrets, remorse's, fears, and sins, but then became immediately sterile to what I had to say. I knew there was nothing anyone could do to help. I knew that nothing, and no one, other than my estranged wife's voice of dedication and commitment to our family would help. It is all I needed to hear to make it through to the next moment. I longed to be free and healed of these dreadful feelings of abandonment. The chaplain attempted to read scriptures to me in order to fit in and relate where he could, but it felt all too stale and rehearsed. He can sell it to the next person because I wasn't buying. I've established enough confidence with the Lord in my own fellowship and with other inmates. He handed me a used bible and another book, a book of armor. I, within my own faith, am praying for God's strength in realizing that nothing else is vital other than His love in my life. But I cannot avoid the reality that my head is filled with despair and my heart still burns with the devil's breath every time I open my mouth.

34. I sat for hours in the nurse's station while being monitored. I was then released back to my dorm for lunch. I am being told I will be heading north tomorrow for counseling. I will be seeing the same guy that interviewed me a month ago. I remember this "psych" visit. It consisted of *"Hello, how are you? Ok, that's it . . . you seem fine. Good to see you. Bye!"* . . . *"Next please"* I'm thinking to myself that I will go north to see him just so I can get a chance to see civilization from the bus during the drive. Even if I have to squint through the thin slits from the bus windows. Hopefully, I won't be visiting K block again. Little did I know, it would be closer than I thought?

35. I long to be intimately touched. To feel the slight of her hand across my back. The press of her body against my now muscular physique. To feel her arms draw me in to kiss her lips. I wanted to experience the needful, passionate experience of love. As the poet Robert Frost once said *"I have the irresistible desire to be irresistibly desired"*. **But this is a tragedy, and there will be no passion of love in jail today or any of the days to follow; not the hormone drenched lust of newly-weds, or the compassionate holding of hands between two grandparents. No, there is no family love here today. I am lonely . . . and I feel very alone.**

36. Who has been here for me during these worst of times? Surely not my wife! She never did know how to love me the way I truly desire to be loved. Will I have to start my search again? Will I be able to muster up the patience to go slow and get to know someone again? Can I be consistent in my desires for companionship? Who will accept such a man now? Where will I start? Should I not even begin this journey again? Is it that this is not the time to think about relationships? Is this my cue to refrain from the envy of couples? Shall I seek the domain of solitaire? Should I build myself a foundation of life, happiness, and spirituality based on my relationship with the Light, rather than the flesh? Am I answering my own questions here?

37. I'm tired of these concerns about her infidelity. I'd never know now anyway. How can I ever make love to this woman knowing she could always run back to his

arms in the morning? As great of a lover as I am, the fear of inadequacy strains my confidence. This is the pain being handed down to me by her. This is the feeling of doubt keeping me wondering. This will always be her form of control over me. I can only predict that it would always disable our progress of trust and growth. The shoes must become untied! We can no longer be soul mates. It is no longer for the good of two people. This is my own personal therapy. **This has to be my strength. My life has to change its course. I will not let worldly worthiness or intentional ungodly sins perverse me into temporary lustful moments with her, only to be followed by confusion, regret, and anger, of a time already gone by.**

38. *My desire to be loved and accepted has been the primary source of my emotional pain.* And I realize the longer I wait to free myself from this one sided love, the harder it will become to untie these shoelaces between two lost souls. *This co-dependency of the need to be loved and accepted, weighs heavy around my neck.* I can no longer endure the thoughts of her own sins. Does Satan bribe her soul with a vow of secrecy? Does she keep him a secret? Does she hide him from shame from her neighbors? Will she shut him up in the attic of her heart out of sight? Will she only let him out for those wild embraces of lustful acts in secret hiding?

39. **It is difficult to think about even brief moments ahead in time. I long to break free from this co-dependency and create a new history for myself. A history that does not worry about the future because of past mistakes. One that allows for positive growth to stem from making the right decisions. I need a future to look forward to . . . not one that I will keep dreading. This should be a future that does not leave me feeling criticized and scrutinized. It should be a future that grows with the promise of the present process of personal gain, rather than self-destruction. And finally, a future that exists without lying for personal gains or suspicions by reading too much too little. One that leaves it in God's hands. At this point, I have nothing else to rely on. It's all I can do to continue onward.** Of course, this is so much easier said than done. We'll give it a try!

A New Perspective

1. I'm sitting on my bunk meditating about what one of the inmates had spoken during a nightly prayer call. Of all the people that I've come across so far, this guy is the least expected person to bring such comfort to my restless soul. For the most part, he is continuously and constantly brash and untamed in every manner of his character. Vulgar and loud, his class-clown antics always sounded off to the tune of cut-ups and defamation of other inmates. For the life of me, I couldn't figure out why nobody hasn't killed this fellow yet? I'll get to his interpretation in just a moment, but first let me express myself to let you know where I was at upon entering.

2. It is our first and foremost belief that we'd rather be on the outside functioning as a free man, rather than spending a stressful extended "vacation" here at the dreaded State facility. Whether it be during our rebellious outbursts on the guards, and the system in general or, while marinating within the solitude of our own regret, most of us would like to believe that we would be better off in the free world, rather than within the confinements and control of the demanded rigors of any jail routine.

3. **Tonight however, I will be shown a different point of view. It will be a new perspective on "the never-ending search for . . . Why?" This fresh outlook will spark my battered faith into a thankful and appreciated smile of why I am here in jail today.**

4. *My life was dead*! I was a walking shell of lust and drug infested cravings. Still socially acceptable as a fully functional addict (along with all the other young professionals), I continued to role through the days playing worker, parent, husband, and in general, everybody's "good time Charlie". Now, while these vices were not the deciding factors that sent me to prison, I knew that at the time of my departure, I was the walking dead, full of booze, and enjoying grand sexual addictions. *My only concern was for how long I could keep it going and what would I do if it all went away?* It was a plethora of liquor, laughter, and lust. But I knew if it was taken away somehow, I'd really be bored to death. Or so at least I thought. I mean, I'm thinking how could I live without all of these wonderfully, terrible, foreign substances in my body? Well, it turns out that my life wasn't ever going to reach a point of all

these vices just going away. *They had to be taken away.* And it certainly was not of my own choice either. Rather, it was something within these turn of events that demanded it be taken away when I got arrested for other events in my life. At the very instance of being arrested that fateful night, my life became publicly announced for all to see. *I became the wake up call for many life stories that night.*

5. **And so the demand forces me to give up all the empty joys of nothingness to be here in the cavity filled cells of the walking dead. And for this, I am being told that I should be giving thanks and praise! These are the lessons of being spared from the continuous torture of my endless journey down into the dark. The drop off had become endless; a bottomless pit of intolerable wantingness and needingness. A pain . . . self-chosen and enveloped in agonizing needs.**

6. *And now comes this fellow's interpretation of why we are so lucky to be here.* He expresses to us that many others are not, and will not be as lucky as us to be in prison. They are the ones lying in the streets; doping, boozing, beating, stealing, deceiving, . . . and being murdered. And they are dying in those streets . . . by the numbers. Most won't make it. But maybe . . . just maybe, the lucky will make it here, *to the sanctuary of jail.*

7. **Jail is a place of complete and utter relinquishment of rights and civil liberties; a nightmare turned reality, a reality turned sanctuary, and a sanctuary turned self-actualization. A revelation of realizations. A safety net . . . so to speak. Safety from the harsh realities of the free world. The very free world in which inmates are not capable of functioning in, while remaining to be within the boundaries of the law. And so now we are here in jail. Spared, even though it has been unbeknown to us . . . until now, from further slowly killing ourselves.**

8. Now, the responsibilities are minimum and if we refuse to accept what little responsibilities are handed to us, we can be punished further into having nothing of anything anyway. Right up until there is nothing left to lose of anything. And so now we have to ask ourselves: is the suffering worse out there in the free world where everything we have, we stand to lose? Or, is it in here during the continuous suffering of our incarcerated lives?

9. Some are just destined to remain here and will enjoy the ill effects of not having to ever fend for themselves. Here, we are fed and eventually medically attended to. We have "three hots and a cot". Conditions are surely not the best, and many times, are the worst that you *can't* even imagine. But here, inmates are spared the burden of what we were recklessly trying to let go of anyway; responsibility to others . . . *and ourselves*! To some of us, maybe this will become the safety net of salvation beneath the drop off. However, life's unfortunate, circumstances dictate that for others, it will become the agony of permanent defeat.

10. **This is a place, which fuels the fires of disease, divorce, destruction, despair, and eventually death. There are so many choices, and so much time to think about them. For those of us that choose the salvation of life, it will become all that is good, acceptable, and perfect. Many will choose the unconditional,**

gift of God. **It will be given through the Book of Christ. It will be within these pages of the Good Book; you will realize that salvation truly lies within.**

11. I think I'm started to sound like a preacher. What else is there to believe in when everything you know to be true has vanished? *I hope I never forget it!*

The Day Trip

1. The morning of Thursday September 30th, 2004 is bringing with it, the anxiety of knowing that I will be riding *the chain* back up north for a psychiatric evaluation. I have become unable to cope with the guard's abuse. What I don't know yet, is that I will be leaving there in good shape within one aspect of my life, and far worse in another. Four others and myself are being shuffled into a holding pen just after 4am breakfast. The cell is no larger than six by seven feet. Two of us are sitting on the familiar cold metal bench while the other three lay out across the worn and stained, filthy, floor. A nasty toilet showcases as our centerpiece ornament. Several hours will pass before we depart. The wait is uncomfortable and I continue to shift due to my severe constipation. Finally, we rode the familiar ride to our destination. This is why I came too: to see civilization along the way. It looks ever so good.

2. The bus arrives and it quickly comes to mind what happened here just over a month ago. It's most likely still happening here every day and night. It's hard to believe that it's only been 28 days and nights since leaving here. It has been an eternal ride into hell and back. It seems so much longer than that because of so many short-term sleep periods. With the little sleep we get at night, there is a constant need for short day naps. I've calculated that I've actually awaken at least a 100 times within the last 28 days.

3. The short intervals of time are having its way with me. And from what I'm seeing right now, it *has* taken its toll upon me. I am looking at the dented steel mirror of the bathroom waiting area near the medical facilities. My face has aged many years in such a short period of time. However, my body has become more physically fit than it has been in over 20 years. I am encouraging myself that this day will breeze by without a hitch. *But this is jail, and it will not be mine to control any such outcome.*

4. We will sit for 4 hours before ever being seen. The four others have dental appointments and the dentist is not in any kind of hurry until the 5 o'clock bell sounds to go home. There are no predictable outcomes here.

5. My appointment with the psychiatrist went well. I came away from his office feeling better and less burdened with the lack of faith within my relationship. I feel better

than I have in a very long time. However, nothing can be done to find reason within my inability to continue coping with the guard's constant verbal and bullying abuse. I have become numb to any fear of being pushed around by any of them anyway. It would be a pleasure . . . and once I started, nothing could stop me!

6.   Confidently, I know none of the inmates of my cellblock are plotting against me. I think I've earned enough respect here to know that nobody will be putting me down without some serious conflict. My strength shows and my body ripples. My endurance from running and boxing enables me to workout hard and intense for well over an hour without feeling fatigued. My body weight routine is frequently copied but no one has ever shown the same discipline and consistency as I achieve on a daily basis. Every fiber in my body says, *"thanks for the change"* Every thankful function except for one . . . my bowel movements.

7.   Constipation has plagued me. Suppositories and fiber are doing nothing to loosen the blockage that prevents me from passing waste. The stinging sensation that tears away at my insides is unbearable. It will become so much worse in the up-and-coming days and weeks. Every moment of this time here today is spent adjusting myself into a position that will aid me in finding some type of temporary relief. The efforts are futile and the stinging in my ass refuses to subside. There is no escape from the rotating pain. It has me squirming in my seat and rolling in my bunk. Sitting is an incredible task of shifting, pushing, and tucking. The constant moving is preventing me from achieving anything *but relaxation.*

8.   As the other inmates take turns getting their teeth filled and pulled, I am shifting and squirming in my seat. I am not allowed to stand in the corner to relieve the torment of sitting. At about 1pm, during the guard shift change, I attempted to achieve some understanding from the incoming guards. The "bitch dog" guard quickly cursed me out without any considerations to my visible pain. Now, understand that I am in a locked cage already, but am not allowed to stand up in the corner. I am beckoning with this she-man guard to consider my situation. It is documented back down south at my cellblock. S/he will not verify.

9.   Just as I am giving up on any reasoning with her about my discomfort, a sergeant walks in and is informed of my dilemma. I called out to him. He never stopped once while vaguely interpreting the info being told to him. He blurted across the room to me that *"if I didn't like it, then don't come to jail"*. This is the catchall phrase they are all trained to say. It's all they know to justify any complaints or nagging requests coming from inmates. When he walked out of the room, the CO went ballistic on me for "pulling rank" on her: a term used for going above the hierarchy of levels in command. She pulled my ID to start a case against me. The sergeant came back through, but paid no attention to the case being drawn up against me.

10.   Over the next few hours, I continued to be denied any medical attention or medicine to relieve the severe pain from this constipation. It is demanded that I *do not* get up off the metal bench for any reason. Threats of K block continue to ring through my ears. I am in critical pain. Finally, it is dinner (4pm). A large grossly overweight, bastard of

a man enters and stands before me as I explain the fact that it is impossible for me to stay seated, and it would help to stand in the corner to relieve the unbearable stinging in my backside. The simple remedy of standing in the corner to shift my weight will temporarily ease any conflict here. The fellow responded to me by letting me know that if he heard another word out of me, he will be re-locating me to K block and the *"stinging in my ass"* will be the least of my worries.

11. On that note, I've decided to give up trying all together. I know I wouldn't survive the rest of my term in that hellhole. I did attempt to quietly relay my dilemma to the medical staff, but was received with *"that's not my job"*. I had to go through the guards to get medical attention. Once again, I am being ordered to shut up or be sent to K block. I can tell you that *I will find a way to hang myself before setting one foot in that notoriously satanic hole of hell.*

12. **I have lost my faith here today, and I am cursing any belief in something good within this vicious world of hatred and denial. I have discontinued my prayers. I have failed to keep my faith when it's supposed to matter the most.** I am hiding my face in my hands as I quietly weep uncontrollably from the pain. I will remain in silence for hours as the tears run down my face in waves. Once, during those hours, a woman's feet came into view. "Are you ok?" she asked while walking past my seat. She never did wait for a response, and I never gave one.

13. New scars have been cut deep into my flesh with this unwanted abuse of power and lack of compassion for the human soul. I came here today for therapy to deal with the blatant disregard for human dignity that is eating away at the fibers of my sanity. What I'm getting are reminders of the gross negligence for any considerations of human compassion or respect. What I've received today are $10 an hour human guard dogs posed in a position to deny even the most basic of civil liberties. And it's happening right here in the good ole' USA.

14. **My faith is lost in a whirlpool of complete and utter disgust. I realize at this particular moment, no amount of fellowshipping or praying will stop the human race from killing each other. It is too late. The willful and malicious episodes of hatred and violence will always thrive in places of such desolation. I wonder how much longer it will be before I too, become a predator within this corrupted system.**

15. It is after 7pm. We are being called out to the van for departure back to the downtown facility. It has only been 13 hours since arriving. I have been sitting on that steel bench this entire time, except for the two 15 minute intervals of chow. Other than that, I was not allowed to stand once except when leaving. Try that with intense constipation and internal hemorrhoids burning your ass! It seemed like days since I had left my cellblock down south. I am longing for my bunk to lie down. I am wishing desperately for home. I am pleading for a life . . . not of this world.

16. Once again, we are passing through the gates to leave. The guards are loading their pistols and shotguns in full frontal view as a reminding consequence of any considerations of escape.

17. The amazing sun is setting in the distance beyond the trees ahead. Its fiery glow is pulsating in the atmosphere. I am being reminded of those lazy summer days I missed so terribly much. Beyond the gates are the soccer fields. And beyond that, the baseball diamonds. Civilization is just up ahead. The fields are packed with families. I see the moms and dads playing out their childhood memories with their kids. The evening air is warm. I can feel the breeze through the vents. Screams of laughter and cheers are ringing through my ears. Its just another missed opportunity of cherished times that should have been spent with my family. Will I live to see them, *and us,* together again?

18. **Before you decide to go to jail today, consider the absence of your place within the branches of your family tree and what it would mean to loved ones if you were not there: To have a missing branch. A gap in the symmetry of order.** *In my opinion, and I'm sure the likes of millions,* **the family circle is the most critical and necessary unit that holds together the threads of society. These are the ties that bind our world. It is the fabrics of brothers, sisters, mothers, fathers, sons, daughters, and grandparents that are woven and entwined together to bond our securities of love and protection. How could I have left the comfort and security of my family to be here, in the belly of danger and harms way? How did it come to this?**

Nature Calls

1. My *Owl of Minerva* is tired of its flight path. My wings long to rest upon a branch without the threat of being knocked off. The struggles to remain safe while in prison are taking its toll on me. I am tired. *So sick and tired of being sick and tired.* Not even the comfort of longing for peace and tranquility at home can suffice. There is more conflict back in the free world beyond my actual knowing. I am hoping for the best, but know that I should expect the worst.

2. I'm still watching dads practice baseball with their sons in the baseball fields as we pass. The genuine role of parenting; the mentor and the protector. Hunting and forging for food and shelter (all in a day's work) is finished for them and they are all enjoying playtime together. I longed to be the head of the household again; to be the silverback ape.

3. It is observed in nature when two baboon groups come together in the wild, the resulting outcome is to fight or join . . . or enviably both. During any part of this conflict and ritual, the female baboon will find the dominant male from the other group and mate. It is considered to be for the good of the colony . . . *and its species!* *This is nature's natural selection process*; to pass on a more preferred and able offspring. Has my wife acted out these animal instincts in familiar circumstances? Her purpose, of course, being to pick what she believes is a more suitable mate for her ongoing quest for security and to bear more children.

4. I knew in my heart, it would be difficult to receive her in complete forgiveness. I could understand her abandonment during a life sentence . . . *but this was only 6 months!* After six years, she could not wait for six months. It turns out, she didn't even wait sixty days for the next sixty years. I guess if those of us who are continuously fed and taken care of, were to be cut off from a constant supply, we too, would eventually grasp for the discarded scraps upon the trash can lid. And when our bodies are starving of food and sex, we would naturally seek out satisfaction, until full again. For her, I know any amount of money in her life could never buy the breeding she so desires. For me, staying in love, means being a beggar of emotional support. *I continue to tolerate being scrutinized, criticized, and lied to, just to feel the temporary lust of a lying love.* I know she will never be so loved by another in

her lifetime. It is a love that extends far beyond the pain she brings forth toward my aching heart. She will never reach into something so completely beloved as my unconditional love for her. It is a love that says *"I love you in all circumstances and no matter what the conditions."*

5.   The bus finally passed the baseball diamonds. I felt that time had stopped all together for these brief moments of reflection. We entered the street to civilization. The sun is disappearing into the horizon bringing dusk to the city ahead. As the bus continues down the highway, *I am clutching my heart to seal the open wounds of a lost love from pouring out onto my body.* Thoughts of despair are swelling around in my head. It is hard to interpret what is real, and what is not. Who is right and who is wrong doesn't matter to me anymore. I am lost in the confusion of events surrounding this ever-so-complicated life gone badly.

6.   The van is pulling into the prison garage just about 15 hours after leaving earlier this morning. An 80-hour workweek would have been easier. I am glad to be in the familiarity of my dorm. I am looking forward to falling back into my routine; eat, sleep, read, write, workout, *rinse and repeat.*

Dad's Visit

1. This Friday is bringing forth another day in the life of . . . I missed commissary yesterday, due to my *day trip*, which basically means that I will have no nightly food supply for the rest of the week. The little chow that is rationed to us is supposed to equal 2000 calories a day, but most of that count is in the "sweet things", or other pastries.

2. The evening is a breath of fresh air. We are outside in the rec area listening to a Christian faith ensemble of singers, players, and testimonials, of hope and prayer. It's nice to be sitting outside in the cool evening air listening to all the people speak of hope from the outside world. Many inmates have come outside . . . just to be outside. It is easy to see who is moved by such generosity from the ensemble. We are grateful to these folks for coming here to be with us. Still, I have not returned to prayer call at night. I have begun to notice strange things going on in that corner as I watch and listen from the distance.

3. It is Saturday morning and I have awoken to an amazing sight upon the clouds. I am looking out my caged window from my bunk. The sun has not yet risen above the horizon in the distance. And although I cannot yet see the sun, its rays are stretching its glorious warmth up toward the sky. It has set afire, blazing leaflets of golden clouds. As I continued to watch, the clouds became ablaze from the sun's reflections. Then, they scattered in the morning breeze. You would just have to see it to believe it. Some of you already know what I'm talking about if you have witnessed this phenomenal sight before. It is short lived as the clouds form together thickly, in the morning air. The day will eventually become black and white; mostly overcast and gray. However, the caged outline of my breathtaking view will remain with me forever.

4. It is 12 pm. I am hearing my bunk being called for visitation. I wonder why she was coming so late in the day. Everyone knows it's best to come in the mornings. She must have stayed out late and was just getting around to driving up. I got dressed and brushed my teeth (with my two inch toothbrush) and headed down to visitation. I'm doing the usual strip search before being allowed outside. When I got outside into the garage area, I looked around but saw no one. I'm scanning the tops of heads

and glancing at all the civilians with their inmates. I see no one I know. Where is she? My heart is sinking to my stomach. Has it been a mistake? I don't want to go back upstairs without being seen. I do not want to miss this opportunity to sit outside in the fresh air. *I don't want to go back in period*! I proceeded to turn back into the strip search area just as I saw why I had come down here. He is definitely a sight for sore eyes. How well he is dressed. Just as I've always known him to do. My father is passing through the gate. Fear and disgrace is quickly marinating with sighs of relief and comfort. He rapidly hugs me, just the way a father should hug his son. I am happy . . . so very happy. It is bittersweet.

5. We found a table to sit and talk. I am telling him of my regrets, remorse, and pain. He s talking to me of a better tomorrow. I am holding on to it without actually being able to touch it. It still remains to be just out of reach. I could not quite grasp it yet. I remain to be in despair. *It pains me not to be able to get a fix on it and immediately change the future from this very moment.* I want it to play itself out already. I know this will take lots of work and up until now, I still have no idea of where to start. I know I had better start by letting go and leaving her . . . not behind, but in her place. I am challenging myself to break free from the co-dependency of love and lust. I am looking to find myself a place in this life that does not include working to please her . . . or any other woman for that matter!

6. She has completed neglected any, and all requests to piece together unwanted questions remaining from my business. She leaves it totally unattended, even as my family struggles to put forth all the resources of info and money to support the finality of tying up any loose ends. All she had to do in order to satisfy my family's requests was to forward already printed information of my customer lists. My father enlightens me of all the unanswered promises, half-truths, and lies spewing from the gutters of her mouth. Truly, now I know that I have been betrayed. I will continue to let her believe that she was still in the drivers seat. Her deceitfulness is so deep, she refuses to realize her lies are in the open and everyone knows already. My family continues to build a firewall between her . . . and us. She would like to believe she's still in control and in the drivers seat, but unbeknown to her, she's headed for a wreck. She's forgotten to let off the gas and pull over.

7. And so now it comes to pass that my "Owl of Minerva" has taken on a new course. At the critical time, when my back is against the wall and my feet are to the fire, a consciousness of critical thought and a renewed sense of spirit and courage to stand-alone takes on a new priority. No longer can I be content in having the lust of a woman as my motivating factor. Never again, will I be insecure about money *I don't spend*. No longer will I need to spend on women to impress them *or myself*. She has become a termite in my life, eating away at the very fabric of my soul. I used to think that being a great lover was enough to keep a woman, but that's a fantasy. It means nothing unless money is in the bank to back it up. And now mine's all gone, *and so is she*. For me, it's been a fortune spent and bent on the "next best thing". It has been a temporary remedy in an attempt to maintain an "endless love".

8. I am sitting on these thoughts in reflection: *Passion . . . man's greatest incentive.* Our greatest motivation. How foolish of me! How reckless of us! Men, willing to throw it all away, and willing to break all the rules all the way to the top. To sacrifice a life's work for three minutes (or three hours) of pleasure with an outsider. **Infidelity can kill a man's desire to be all that he has dreamed of and worked for all of his life. He is willing to give up and sacrifice his children's well being, all of his possessions, his piece with God, and the woman he so loves. Lust of another (while being married) is able to disrupt any future guarantee of a peaceful and tranquil retirement. And it is within this passion of lust, man's greatest incentive becomes his greatest adversary; his greatest killer. Lust of another (while being married) is like an iceberg unseen until it slides up underneath your belly and rips your insides out. It's a shark attack ferociously slamming up against your body, picking you up, spinning you around, and throwing you right back down on your ass . . . *Whoosh*, and then you disappear beneath the surface!** I think I'll stop this confession right here. I swore myself to secrecy . . . and to them.

9. The rest of my visitation with dad went well. We talked and laughed. He looks well and actually appears to be content. It's nice to see him in good spirits. Even to this day, he never says *I love you*, back to me when I tell it to him. He just says *I too*. And that's ok. I know he does. He reminds me that it is my responsibility to make the right decisions. I'm feeling inside that my family is willing to help; I know I will have to make it through this ordeal first. I will have to earn my keep. I knew that upon my release, I would have to hit the ground running, pound the pavement, and turn myself into a money making machine! My skills are expertly refined, but I've got to get organized to channel my success. I've been the best of the best in this industry that I work. And I've been the best in the country for the last 5 years. Six months in prison is not enough to take that title away from me. I am known across the country in circles from Seattle to Orlando and all points in between. I'm talked about in bars till wee hours of the morning. (Too bad it wasn't the church instead). They went to bed thinking about how I do it, and they wake up in the morning wishing I could hand them a "day in the life of . . . me". *Very convinced . . . but not conceited.*

10. Sixty days will not come soon enough to begin again. I am busting at the seams to start right now. This time, it will have to be different. I am consciously thinking about this. Maybe this is why I have to wait just a little bit longer. This is a continuing reminder of why it has to be different. This time, I will have to concentrate on stock piling my money instead of pilfering it away as in the past. This time, a standard of living must be maintained; a standard way below my means. It will be the only way to succeed. To save a lot more than I was spending. *I figured that the ways of the past are surely no way to the future.*

11. *Future* . . . mmm, now there's a word I had almost forgotten. Maybe that's because I've always been guiding someone else's future instead of my own. I want a new

beginning. *And what a trip this will be!* Preparations of a new government in my life have already begun. But I am not yet ready to depart. It must be nurtured longer into strength unmatched by all those who will aim to destroy it. *God, Health, Family, and Work*: These are the ingredients of my government. The four corners of my mind. The make-up of my life.

12. Dad talked about all of his "mini-vacations" and seemed to be happy talking about them. We were both happy to be able to spend this time together. We said good-bye and he went on his way. I heard him say to the guard on his way out of the caged door, "Listen guard, take good care of that one for me, would you?" The guard shrugged him off, but I still felt genuinely loved with thoughts of dad for the rest of the day. *"Thanks Dad, for your company, and for your love. It means everything!"*

Sixty Days

1. *How can I occupy time?* I need to keep influencing myself with positive re-enforcements. Everyone seems to be happy on the outside. They are maintaining themselves by managing their lives. I found it difficult to do so.
2. Here, I am always in the fore and aft of my life. It has become the scope of my horizon. I find it impossible to just stop and relax . . . not even for a moment. Not even to enjoy the freak shows. It will be difficult to endure 60 more days. I will spend it living in my head.
3. I have spent this Sunday mostly just writing. In all, it's been an okay day. My hair is coming back and I can actually lay it flat with the help of lotion. I have shaved and am looking good. Now all I need is my satin shirt and micro-fiber pants to match these black slippers. *Then I'd really be cruising eh*!
4. I've written my old partner in Ohio looking for work during the Christmas holidays and hopefully, thereafter. It would be nice to have the blessings of work when I get out. Money to provide for my children. Maybe even enough to pay for the debts that have accrued since arriving in prison. I have my health and I have the faith of God in my life. I do not have my family or any work lined up yet. Both are in ruins at this time.
5. It has been almost a month since receiving a letter from her. I guess every other week was too much time away from "whoever" to drop me a line more often. I expect she has just given up on us, and any ideas of reconciliation. It is impossible to defend myself against the constant chipping away of trying to make sense of it all. She is not leading the life of a married minded woman, as she would like me to believe. She has become too inconsistent and absent in her support of me. I knew it would take much consistency, patience, and gentleness to win her back, but the expectations of this new past between us has strained my forgiving heart. The secrecy of whose heart she now possesses, stirs in my mind. The agony of knowing she is sharing the bed with another has me whipped into cream. I have become a useless, pathetic, mass of heartache.
6. I have 8 weeks to freedom. *But freedom to what?* I have to reach her. She is the heart and soul of my family. Without her, I will starve to death as a caged animal.

My soul will never ease into contentment without her. **I continue to exist living in my head . . . day after day. I am finding it difficult to communicate with others, even on the most trivial of matters.** I've become shallow in my will to live any kind of life without her.

7.   The next couple of days have been uneventful. **It is unbearable to endure this nothingness. The seconds within every minute drag on. Each second has it's own story of despair. Each moment is being stacked upon each lost thought, leading back to nowhere . . . *but here!***

8.   It is Tuesday afternoon. I have just received a stack of books from my mother. A couple of novels, a journal, and some work books about events and activities in my life. They have inspired thoughts of a life gone by. A chance to record turning points and family influences of my chaotic life. Topics, which stir memories of childhood ways and romantic interludes. The pages surfaced memories of softball days and lazy summer ways. Vacations and geographical monuments share the spotlight of family outings. A flood of emotions has swelled in my eyes. It is difficult to see. I am overcome. **Please God; turn back the hands of time! Just long enough to make it right and then, to come back to a better day. It is a single thought. A brief moment in time is all it would take to tie the knots of strength back into my family history.** It happened thirty years ago, but it is so clear in my mind. *Vividly clear* . . . like I'm watching those few minutes unfold before my eyes at this very moment. That significant factor . . . that decision on that fateful day, forever, altered the course of my life. That day is not here though and I have no business talking about it now. I have to let it go. I kept on reading my new books. But even as I read, I constantly want to record endless thoughts of what I should be writing. I can never get it written onto the pages quick enough though.

Living in my Head

1. *Do ya know when you just know?* Well . . . I just knew. And the suspected truth is gut wrenching. I can feel the impact of knowing she is gone. Out of my life into the world of the single-minded woman; having fun, shopping, sleeping around, one-night stands, and all of those loquacious conversations of how better off she is without me. I wonder if she tells them about how she took and/or used up everything I had. I know now, she is not interested in my progress. She has never responded to my questions of concerns in my business matters or about our relationship. And when I push it, she threatens never to come back. That's a hard thing to let happen when you are in prison. *You will want to keep all lines of communication open with whoever will bear the time and considerations.* Frankly, I'd accept visits from anyone willing to take the time. It is vital to stay connected to the free world. She never showed happiness during the last two visits. It's like she's creating these mood swings to find excuses of her easy abandonment. What I am seeing, besides the addition of new wrinkles, is the cold, angry, slant, shifting in her eyes. Betrayal has become the dominant factor of her anger.

2. It would have been easy to destroy any regret of a lost love while living in the free world. "Go-betweens" could have filled my lonely nights. And right now, I could really stand to enjoy a new taste test of women to keep my palate stimulated and from going dry. **I craved to interact with people of my own liking; people to talk to, laugh with, and lust for. I need a displacement factor. Something real and tangible to buffer the pain of loneliness**.

3. Why has she turned against me? Isn't it enough to just finish our relationship quietly between only us? Why is she finding it necessary to fight at the gates of hell to put "us" out there, and band together all those that would choose to hear her contemptuous desire to marvel in her new found, but still just as stale, glory. She is screaming to all that can hear. But I don't think anybody is caring anymore. One day, when I'm out of here, I'll say it while everybody's actually listening. *I'll only have to say it just once.* All of these hidden agendas that she feels is necessary for her own self-image comes down to one thing; Her own lack of breeding within her family circle. She has never been a truthful and faithful companion in her life . . .

not to anyone. Not even to her family. She has lived her life as a trollop. I know all these things are truth about her. But I did not create her, so I refuse to judge her. *Isn't that what love is?* Knowing the worst things about someone and still believing in him or her as a person and that something good still exists within them. Actually believing that something can change from the past to break from the destructive cycle. But I am wrong. It turns out that "we" are no different. She will cheat on whomever she remains to be with. This is her history. This lack of character will follow her for all of her days.

4. I have begun to masturbate to a different tune. The thrill has gone out of any lustful thoughts of my wife. I try *not* to imagine laying on her, caressing her, and participating in love. No longer, would "anger fucks' suppress my need to punish her. I'm sure though, I'll get that chance soon enough. It's always been easy with her. But right now, that milestone feels like a country mile away. *And that's a long way when you're counting time by every second!*

5. I am thinking about the women to come and the beauties gone by. How fortunate my life has been to attract such an exotic species. I know I've been blessed (and cursed) with such encounters. But I'm thinking about a different approach to all this now. One that would mean never again giving all of "me" to the women I meet. To *"put it all out there"* left vulnerability in my life that I will never be willing to sacrifice again. I have to ease up on that romantic and sensual bullshit that keeps them coming back for more. It would only complicate a life, already full of uncertainty. In here, that uncertainty remains constant without end . . . every moment of the day and night.

6. There is a burden of truth stirring inside of me as I begin my 8-week march to freedom. There has to be a completely new and original way to manage my life. I am feeling the anxiety of new responsibilities. And I say "new" because while it may be ordinary for the mass of populations, it was novelty to me. I'm talking about taking responsibilities in other areas of my life that I have so long taken for granted.

7. I wonder how I will be accepted back into my family of parents, brothers, and sisters. And my Son, Nicholas? I sensed my son's compassion for me that day so long ago as he watched me through the glass. Will he listen to my story? Will he believe my honesty as I explain my failures away? Will he end up following my footsteps into the wastelands of being a menace to himself, as so many young children do watching their own fathers? It takes a long time to wither the body away; sometimes years, and many times, even decades. Will my story be the chaos that threatens my son's own existence? *Or will I be the lesson that saves his life?* Will he, as I've pleaded with him many times, turn and run the other way with the slightest scent of dope, or the uneasy thrill of a crime at hand among his so-called "friends"?

8. What about her? Will she admit to her wrongdoings and abandonment in this time of desperate needs? Can I ever face her as a friend again? I am considering not ever returning upon my release. That would be the easiest solution. *And the simplest!*

It could very well be the most cowardly act of all too: to abandon all contact and responsibilities to her and her son. But this is her doing and she has chosen to let another man father this child. One that she feels will be better able to support her growing needs of greed. *Fuck her . . . let him if he wants to!* How feeble and weak of her to fall into anyone willing to give her a few moments of her time. She needs anything and anyone willing to help her with that belittled self-confidence. She continues to gather compliments wherever and however she can. Everything remains divided in my mind.

9. On to better things. I do not want to "shell-shock" myself into a different time zone with the same old chaotic routine of too much time with too little to do. I know the day will come soon, to start retuning my day into a recognizable and productive schedule. It's hard though. I am lost inside myself. I want these memoirs to be over with already. That would mean I was out. I want it to be over with already. My final chapter to be written into eternity. Maybe it will create a movement amidst the simple burning question you must ask yourself time and time again as a reminder of what you *don't* want . . . *Do you want to go to jail?* It is a question that should rise to the occasion when you bully someone, get in the car to go somewhere, or even just before you tell someone to *fuck off.* Yes, I wish I could end this book today, but I can't. The rodeo isn't finished yet. The first time is always the longest time to ride . . . no matter how short your stay.

10. **I'm thinking about the simplicities of being arrested. How the resulting factors can bring so many complexities to our lives, and how everything becomes so unavoidable and irretraceable thereafter.** To be in the public domain; as a pedestrian, as a driver being pulled over, or waking up to see them hovering over you. *To be arrested,* will be the burden of truth; a threatening reality that has not yet occurred. *A constant concern.* Being arrested brings up so many regretful pasts . . . *oh so very fast!* But then it's *always too late.* By then, only *time* can be the remedy. Will I become just another inmate among the missing within the penal code? This is the horrific terror that has become my nightmarish reality.

11. How did I let this happen? Why did I choose to leave the free world to come to jail? Was that slug right? Had I been saved from the shadows of the valley of death by coming here? Am I being spared from any more temptations from the free world by being in here? Will I remain trapped in here for defending my own life against predators? Will I live out my days within the proximity of hell and smothered in sin? Will I spend the rest of my life . . . preparing for death!

12. **I am struggling to make out some sort of organized and predictable answers to life, but it's not working. I just can't see clearly. I'm being swallowed up in a black hole. All of a sudden, it has become a burden to be alive. My despairing life has left such deep scars on those dearest to me. If only I could release them from all the anger, worry, and fear of me being here in jail today.**

Thursday Oct. 7ᵗʰ, 2004

1. The days are getting cooler in the yard. I can hear the trees rustling in the wind. I can hear them, but I cannot see them. There are no trees in the prison rec yard, but when the wind blows, the leaves blow over from the other side. I can close my eyes and listen to it. I watch the birds fly over from the other side to the razor sharp fences. It may seem trivial to say it, but if you are in jail, the sight of a bird's freedom and flight means so much. How tender footed they are to be able to jump all over the sharp wire fences. To be able to come and go as they please. If only . . . it would be so easy to get to the trees on the other side.

2. I remember the year spent in Utah. My work crews and I would work all day and night, Monday thru Saturdays. Sometimes for months without end. Most Sundays, however, were spent in the hill country with our horses. We saddled up early and rode our stampede of horses all day, venturing up into the mountains. We would dress up in our ponchos, cowboy hats, and riding boots. We rode up through the creeks. The water creeks cut paths through the woods, so we could follow its trail deep up into the mountainside. During the fall season, the trees turn amazing colors of purple and teal, red and orange, and green and yellow, revealing long stretches of patterns for as far as the eye could see. Sometimes, this brilliance extended itself all the way to the edge of the *horizon*; where the skies meet the earth. It is a place where time and space become separated and together at the same time: *A place where everything is part of something.*

3. If you've ever ridden a horse, you are familiar with the awesome strength it can have; to feel its hind quarters move under you. Especially as it climbs up embankments. We would climb high into the clouds through paths and creeks. Deer played "hide and seek" with us as they darted across clearings in the grass back into the woods. The sky carried the cool Northern breezes, pushing the trees into a swaying dance of colorful glances that constantly changed in motion with the wind. I can remember this memory in an instance. I enjoyed several months of quality living while living in this part of the country; a most productive time of my life. Anyway, it's the trees I'm missing right now. I'll never forget the trees. I haven't thought about it for a while. But now, I'm outside in the yard . . . in the prison yard. Here . . . all I've got

is *up*, and the gray sky looking back down on me. *Here . . . it is all about the walls and barbed wire fences to keep you in and remind you that you are jail today.*

4.   I hurried to start my workout. It's the best way to keep warm now while outside. I have a routine of strengthening my arms, legs, and stomach. I have managed to turn a semi-soft pot roast belly into a rock hard washboard, fully equipped with side arms full of bi-ceps, tri-ceps, and forearms. I've even got the legs and ass to carry up the rear. I am standing proud with the way I physically look. And I have only one person in mind as my audience. I have this burning desire to show it off. I have done this for her. Every moment of pushing harder has been motivated by what her response would be when I got out. Hours and hours, of days, weeks, and months, have been spent pushing and pulling myself, up, over, and across in every type of resistance training we could imagine. It has been my plan from the tenth day in prison to never waste another day of my life without some form of exercise.

5.   Inside the prison, we have to work out in secrecy. If we get caught, the guards write cases against us. We constantly look out for each other and watch the doors for peeking guards. For those of us that do get caught, it means isolation or suspension of commissary and visitations. And in here, you don't want to be without either. *Inmates live for loved ones to visit, and paid food to eat.*

6.   So, if you plan on plan going to jail today, be sure to tell your kin to come visit. And hopefully, if you do come to jail today, you'll have some money in your pockets for the little extra things . . . that will mean so much! If you don't have these precious things in your life, you'll become a lonely beggar in an already despairing place.

7.   I remember when I started this fitness crusade: I told myself how good I needed to look. I told myself that when I walked out of those gates, she would take one look at me . . . and another . . . and another . . . and then, blink in disbelief of how great it is to be looking at me. I want to see her draw in her breath. I want to see her look away, and glance back again in sheer delight. I want her to quickly open the door and wish me away all for herself, knowing full well, *it was worth the wait!* However, as it appears right now, I am to be the benefactor of my own work. She has not shown interest in my studies of parenting, self-awareness, or spiritual growth classes. She seems oblivious to my progress of a new found, healthy minded diet of mental and physical exercise. *It is impossible to impress her.* I can't even get her interested anymore.

8.   How can I get her involved in my courageous journey from getting where I was, to where I am going? She has not responded to my letters in over a month. And what's worse, I feel that I have to refuse her visitation this week (if she even comes), so that my dad will not be turned away after driving over 200 miles to see me: This prison only allows one visitation a week unless special circumstances are arranged. Surely, if she gets turned away, it would ruin any chances of her belief in my commitment to her. At the same time, I'm having to bear the burden of knowing that the last time she had wrote or visited has already passed.

9. Why should I continue to put her first in my life? Am I not supposed to be worshipping something so much bigger and better? Why should I concern myself with whether or not she shows? It would be better to spend time with the love and support of true family members, than a lying, cheating, sorry excuse, of a wife. What's the point of seeing and listening to the very person who continues to lie and deceive me? She still actually believes my family doesn't know about all the filth spewing from that gutter in the center of her face. These continuous lies that she blindly hangs on to, buffer her own guilt of wrong doings.

10. Will she come to visit or write? Will she re-evaluate her sense of commitment? Can she not see the changes of circumstance? Should I continue to believe I could win her over? I am being tortured by my own imagination . . . a slow, agonizing, torturous, death of hope. *It is killing me!* Each time it hits, I am praying for death with my last breath gone by. And then some spark of senseless and fantastic imagination that she will change and clear my interpretations, releases me from this despairing grip. Very soon after though, my torment follows back down into a new chamber of grueling, brain crushing, pressure. It is useless to go on. I'm never getting the answers that I so long for. My thoughts are wondering continuously. Even while I'm reading and trying not to think about it, I'm thinking about it. My thoughts keep coming back to the future of us. The unknown continues to pre-occupy my every moment. An enormous force is willing it. The pressure is like a boa squeezing the life out of me. Will I leave here a bachelor out on my own, or will I be received as the loving, passionate, father and husband I am being groomed and encouraged to be? This love is too much to swallow. I am choking in it.

11. I am now standing at the far end of the rec yard, shivering in the morning air. *I can't remember how long I've been standing here silently screaming my life away in useless worry.* I'm looking around to see everyone working their routine. Some have already worked up a sweat in the cool, morning air, so I know I've been standing here for a while. I'm missing out on my self-inflicted pain. I'm looking at my hands. The palms of both hands have blisters on each extension of my fingers . . . each and every one of them. I am tired of the pain. I loudly curse to myself as the boil of blood runs through my veins. I am struggling for one set of pull-ups and dips.

12. I'm standing here motionless, with my head leaned back toward the sky. My eyes venture beyond the wall, through three sets of wired fences, and into the heavens above. I am focusing directly above me. Straining, I am gazing far into the distance toward the clouds as far as I can. I am not letting my peripheral vision catch sight of the memory of imprisonment. I am looking beyond the walls and the wires. I have extended my arms to the side. I am raising them slowly and outwardly, keeping my elbows behind me, never bending either one of them. I am inhaling a long, deliberate, intake of cool air. My outreached arms continue to move upward as I shift my voice into *gear*, release the clutch, and begin to let it out. A slow, deep, drawl begins to voice up from my throat. My lungs are filled to capacity. I know this one will be good. I will push out all that is hurting in my life. This will be a

cleansing of the soul. Today, here and now, I will shed my skin. The entire yard is echoing with my upheaval. It is an outcry of four months of suppression. I am shifting into *second gear*. This is a response to all the times I haven't reacted to countless inflictions: The "snap" I didn't take in fighting back all the filth that was thrown my way. Of course, most being from the guards. *This is the yell to end all screams!* The walls are responding with clarity as the vibrations bounce from my voice to the buildings and back again. I know it is carrying through the windows and inside the dorms. I know it is reaching the distant streets and beyond. The roar of my voice is gaining momentum now, as I shift hard into *third gear*. My arms have reached the sky and are lost somewhere in the clouds. My skin tightens now, as my fingers grasp to reach higher into the heavens. I could shed my skin right now. It is lasting way beyond my expectations. I realize the strength of my lungs have become enormously powerful. I'm pounding into *forth gear*. I am feeling taller, thicker, and to say the least . . . I feel better. It is never-ending. I can hear the decibels reach its maximum peak. *I'm off the scale baby*!

13. And now, it is time to release my grip on this intensity and slip back down into third, second . . . and finally neutral. I've coasted to a stop. A deafening silence has fallen on the rec yard and I'm looking around to see everyone staring. They are just staring, but the look is in agreement. They know. You know when you know . . . you just know. However short-lived, it carries with it, a most satisfying memory of how long the fuse can burn. I continued on with my workout.

Friday Oct. 8ᵗʰ, 2004

1. It Friday morning just before "chow rolling". She has awakened me from my sleep. She frequently wakes me from my dreams. It always leaves me hurting in some way or another. At first, I thought the soaked sheet role was from sleeping drool, but it's not. I can feel the stickiness near my eyes so I knew it was from crying . . . even in my sleep! Having a pillow would be nice right now so I could bury my face in it for a few more minutes. Actually, having my bed, pillows, comforters, *and* my beautiful wife hiding just below the warm sheets would be even better. I love it when she shows me only her eyes as she stares at me. The rest of her remains hidden beneath the sheets. That's an endless fantasy, but always quickly lost in despair.

2. **My rented bunk, however, does give me the luxury (and the torment) of a view to the free world; highways, cars, buildings, and people in general. It is nothing more than a view of life passing me by. Much of the time spent looking through the caged window leaves me in absolute depression. Many of the inmates refused to look. Some make it a point not to come near the caged window at all. Others strain their eyes to see something that remains the same anyway; a burdensome wish. For me though, it is sacred no matter how I positioned myself mentally. I can never be without it. I need it during all different times of the day. Whether it leaves me hurting inside or smiling contagiously, I need it. I use it as my sanctuary of escape.**

3. In the mornings, the sun's rays become visible before its outline actually appears. The air currents sketch splashed colors of fire and ice under the clouds, revealing streaks of purple, orange, red, and silver. By 8am, the sun shines into the window, casting shadows of the cage directly on my bed, extending from my head to my toes. It's always cool enough inside this dorm to be able to enjoy the warmth and brightness without reaching boiling point temperatures like some of the last places I have recently been.

4. For me, it's easy to believe this is God's sacred light still shining down on me. The same light that I found long ago in the dark that night I re-discovered my faith. Here, that faint light in the blackness of hell shines bright for me, each and every morning. **For me, the faith of God has become a necessary means of survival.**

If being so close to hell's navel has, in fact, brought me closer to Heaven's belt, then please God, help me respond to a better tomorrow!

5. Even on mornings like this with overcast, I know it's always better than not seeing anything at all. **I am able to experience God's newly painted canvass on the horizon each and every day.** *Priceless!* **Each day brings forth a new print. The arrival of each day brings with it, another day gained toward freedom. Each day that passes is another day lost within the penal system. Watching the window has become my never-ending silent moving picture.**

6. The bunks we sleep on have no width. To lay in a fetal position, means that my knees are pushing through the rail and my ass is hanging off the other side. It is not possible to roll over on your side while lying in your bunk. It is, instead, a matter of rising, turning, and landing back down in another position. My scrubs are rolled up as a ball and fitted into a sheet to make a hard pillow for neck support.

7. I am tired of waking up and going downstairs for my breakfast to be handed to me in a paper bag. I'm tired of waiting to exchange my laundry every morning at 5am. I'm tired of listening to the nasty, bitch guards yell and scream for the respect they'll never get. They live for engaging in the disruptions of our routine. *It is an endurance of moments in time.* For them to add unnecessary intervals of redundancy by interrupting any chance of a calm, cool, collective environment, is the norm. They look to disrupt any harmony among us. It's always a question of how long can you go in tolerating the cowardly authority of the guards. They all have their different strategies of trying to get inmates to comply. But the usual orders of the day are *"to get in your bunk"* and *"stop talking"*. Most attempts are useless. There is no way, any guard is going to stop 50 grown men from talking, especially when the bunks are only 8 inches apart. It's all we can do while bunked up . . . sometimes for hours. So, the resulting responses from inmates are usually *"fuck you"* and *"go home"*. Each shift brings with it a new guard trying to throw their own form of discipline at us: *It's really just like coming home to an abusive bitch every night. They deflate our spirits every chance they get.*

8. I am finding it difficult to talk to anyone unless required. Besides, any conversations in here are made up of lies. So many lies poison the air. It's unbearable to listen to all the made up stories. Most sentences contradict the next and so on. **Most stories told in here are actually events and circumstances created from other people's stories overheard in the past. People naturally do this to make their lives seem a little more important than it actually is, in order to enhance their own self-image. Every person wants to seem and appear better than he is for a greater recollection of himself.** Whether it's to be smarter or tougher, we each have our bullshit game play for better stage presence: *the entire world's a stage and we are merely players.* One guy that comes to mind is memorizing several words a day from the dictionary just so he can use them in sentences. Nothing he spits out makes sense. I'll be the first to tell you, it's great to learn new words in order to

become more efficient in your efforts to become a great communicator, but what I'm hearing from this guy is mass confusion.

9.   **I'm listening to so many untrue stories. There are 20 year olds who are telling us they've done everything. Whatever topic is being discussed, it seems they've done it! They are telling us of all the jobs in any industry. Whether it is with a small private company or some huge public project, they've done it! They've driven or owned every vehicle on the planet . . . including prototypes. They have ventured to any place on the globe mentioned in any conversations. Whether it is some large city or a far off, remote region of the world, they have trampled on it with an entourage of partygoers. Even when they can't pronounce the name or have no idea what continent it is a part of, it has been visited somehow and sometime in their short pathetic life.** *It is obvious*: **most of the distant lands said to be visited, are being traveled to via photo magazines and literature.**

10. I am tired of listening to shallow philosophies and crimes, but it is impossible to ignore or avoid. The walls are echoing and the sounds carry throughout my head . . . pounding my temples with every heartbeat.

11. I realize that most of us in here (and out there) enter into exaggerated conversations everyday. They are easy to discuss and brushed aside without worry because they happen and end quickly . . . *unless you are being called on to answer to those short lies.* People in general, will talk about money (they don't have), and possessions (they wish they had), for hours on end without taking a breath. However, it seems that when it comes time to talk about their raising their family, the conversation becomes nothing more than a few gestures. Here, there are definitely not any inmates willing to talk about how unfulfilling their marriage and home life is while sitting around the chow hall.

12. Looking around, it is easy to conclude I have been afforded a much higher paying career job, but this is not the place or the time to talk about such unimportant jargon. What fulfillment could it possibly bring to my depressing life anyway? Besides, I have nothing now. Mainly, because I've spent it all trying to keep her comfortable.

13. **Damn, I can't wait to do my thing out there again. I was the best at what I did in the industry (and across the country) before I went to jail that day. But that best will only be mediocre to the standards I possess today. There is a fire in my throat and I am prepared to quench my thirst for the successes, which I desire. Eventually, my time here will come to pass and I will be released to the endeavor of scratching, clawing, and dragging my way back up to the top of the food chain.**

Saturday Oct. 9ᵗʰ, 2004

1. I'm standing in the yard feeling lazy this morning. I worked out twice yesterday; first in the morning with pull-ups and push-ups, and then I ran for two hours in the evening. I do this barefoot on the concrete floor, knees high on the spot. My calves and legs feel no pain due to intense muscle conditioning. My lungs have no limits to the endurance of time. Earlier this morning, I slept through chow hall and linen change. I felt no need to get up. My scrubs are clean and there's food in my locker. It's a treat to not have to face the bitchy guards so early in the morning.

2. Right now, I'm just laying back on the cement block bench in the cool, frigid, air. I'm looking up toward the sky. **I'm laying here pondering the very essence of the existence of my life. Everything that *hadn't* mattered to me, has now become pivotal points of influence and priority; my faith, my wife, my life. I'm thinking of my duties to protect them and myself. I'm thinking of my integrity and name to carry on for my children. There are so many things to think about. It never stops. It's beating away at my head. It's eating away at my life.**

3. **So much of my life has been swallowed up beneath the wreckage. I am pondering the goals in my life . . . *and* the ones that have slipped into distant memories. The ones never ventured since so long ago. All that was left behind has slipped away into the midst of an unwanted history. All that I've ever wanted is flashing through my senses. I can see and hear my history sliding into a black hole of forgotten failure. I can smell the agony of defeat. The aroma is making me sick to my stomach. Being here now isn't about surviving the others *or the conditions*! It's about reviving myself from the torment of guilt. It is about bearing the torturous burden of sinking into a life chosen especially for me.**

4. I was half-ass awake, and daydreaming when the clouds broke above revealing blue skies. My head is spinning. What I'm seeing is amazing! My daydream must have left me gazing at something close, because my eyes are having to adjust to the distant sky above: The clouds passing by opened up a hole in the heavens, revealing the beautiful blue sky. It was small at first, but soon the entire sky came into view. I am looking at layers and layers of thinly sliced clouds moving at different speeds on different levels of altitude. Some clouds are passing by slowly on one level, while

others, on another level, move much quicker. There are several different layers of clouds moving in the same direction, but all are moving at different speeds past my viewing area. Beyond that, slow, puffy, explosive shaped, cotton ball clouds are becoming visible at different time intervals each time all the levels of clouds break a hole into the distant blue sky. I can actually play "froggy" in my mind while trying to get to the top level by jumping onto the entire passing ascending clouds. What I'm seeing next, I know my eyes have never noticed before. In all my years of sky gazing, I have not witnessed this "something" which probably happens everywhere, everyday. I have to get a landmark to make sure that it is not an illusion from looking up into the clouds. I thought I would get that motion feeling you get when you look up at buildings from below. The moving clouds above are giving me that tipping over sensation. But this is not a mirage in the sky. One of the levels of clouds is actually moving in the opposite direction from the rest. *I can't believe it*! This defiant breeze channel has these clouds going the other way in between three different levels of clouds. I am quickly re-formatting the "frogger" game in my imagination and am venturing up through the clouds, *far into the sky*. Wait . . . what am I seeing here? I cannot quite focus on whether it is my eyes or the sky. Thousands of miniature lightening bolts flashing and spinning before me. What is this? I am afraid to blink. I do not want this other world in my eyes to go away. What's really going on here? Definitely . . . *too much time on my hands*.

5. Saturday mornings are for visitations from loved ones. I haven't heard from her via letters so I'm sure she won't be showing up anyway. At least she won't be disrupting my visitation from dad this morning if he decides to show up. It turns out, neither one of them showed today anyway. I'm looking at her last letter. It has been over a month. I've been swept aside and placed in the attic. Replaced and forgotten. I've waited all day. They call the daily mail call a "suicide watch", but that only last for 5 minutes. Try waiting 10 hours for a visit that never comes. Time is being measured in half-second splits. I've been crying under my covers for most of the day. Waiting . . . wondering . . . wishing. I watch the sky from my caged window way up on the third floor. It is actually six stories high because each floor has two levels within it. Once again, I'm seeing the clouds move in opposite direction. This time, I was able to catch the view from a side angle since I am looking across the sky toward an uninterrupted horizon from my window. *The laws of diminishing return have come into play, and the wonderment of it all doesn't taste as good during this second helping.*

6. I am becoming very bored with myself in here. I want nothing more than to write my days away. It seems my only struggle while writing, is getting my ideas, thoughts, and memories down on paper quick enough . . . before they flash by and disappear forever. Sometimes, there is just simply nothing to write. Other times, I can't put the pen down until the ink runs out. "Lights out" usually comes first. Whoever said, "*You cannot, not think*"? Hell, I'm always forgetting what I want to remember because of all the distractions. It is time consuming in a place that refuses to hurry up.

DO YOU WANT TO GO TO JAIL TODAY?

7. As I continue to write these memoirs, I realize that my experiences are being expressed most vividly during the times of "bone-crushing" setbacks. My depression has generated much creativity to write during the very times that I find my spirit being deflated. **I have been robbed of my anticipated future, and now I have been left in the belly of the devil, close to the proximity of hell, hiding in the shadows of the valley of death. I have become the recipient of all that it entails. I have received all that it offers. And right now, because of all of the events unfolding, I am lying in a septic tank full of hatred. I am a lifeless, mass of flesh, cooked to the bone, and rotten to core!** But still, that isn't enough. I've had to reach down just a little bit further down to find my bottom . . . *and I have!* And I've had to do it all by myself in order to get any type of resolution to whatever it is that eats away at me. I have ventured all the way down into nothingness and back again several times. After being bombarded by all the sludge within this cruel system as well as from the free world outside, I am courageously surviving a lonely struggle to build a solid foundation for future survival. I have already developed myself in so many ways that will bring forth great health and wealth. I know that my own personal government still needs much work, but I confidently know it will succeed. And I'm not about to give into a coup. Now . . . if I could just receive that letter from Ohio promising me a job.

8. **I want to experience fresh, new happy occurrences. I long to wake and smile for the whole day. I want to be happy about where I am, whom I'm with, and what I'm doing. Most of all, I want to be happy about *why* I'm doing it. I long to be at the peak of my game.**

9. I want to express to you my love for writing. I've always loved it, but never took the time to properly record and document my revelations. In the past, throughout my life, I have recorded many "evolutions of thought" in personal journals, random pieces of paper, and even on receipts. I would keep them long enough to become just another lost sheet of life's script. Moving, carelessness, and lack of motivation have created a puzzling paper trail of missing pieces. Most of my history recorded has been lost over time.

10. I wonder if this will be what *finding myself again* is all about? Is this the creation of a new history of personal growth, godly worship, family values, healthy minded living, and superior work ethics? *I hope so!*

11. I am considering three more books to write. One of war, one of the mind's eye, and one of the sensual kind in nature. I will wait till I get out for the last topic to be written. It is foremost on my mind though, as I'm sure, it is on everyone else's mind too.

12. It is Saturday night in the State facility; TV junkies, artists, readers, exercisers, and me . . . *the wanna-be writer*. Writing gets harder to do on the weekends. The days and nights last so much longer than the weekdays. The lights stay on till 2 am, but even then, everyone just keeps on till 4 am chow. Waking up on the weekends is worse. I've got inmates crawling all over my rented bunk to search for family

members below in the waiting area. Even worse, I have to listen to inmates returning from their visits downstairs. I had to listen to their renewed sense of spirit and hope from spouses and family that are sticking it out till that inmate gets released.

13. **I feel cut off from the rest of the world. I guess that's the whole point of being here eh? Alienated! My imagination runs rampant. It fuels my hatred, my despair, and my regrets. My body responds by twitching, tensing up, and getting ready to snap! It is hard to breathe sometimes. Not just because of the shitters, but also because of my inability to cope. I have become brittle to the point of breaking. I am chomping at the bit with anger. My life has become disassembled from the inside out. There is no one to talk to, and more importantly, there is no one to listen. Nobody wants to listen to anyone's struggle to get out while in here. It is a barren world . . . full of barbarians! I have become separated from myself. It is as if I am existing in a completely different time zone, sliding from one world into the next and back again. My identity has been erased. I have become out of sight and out of mind from life, as I know it. I talk to myself constantly and many times, have embarrassed myself, knowing others had heard me already before I get a chance to stop.** *So fucking what*!

14. I am constantly thinking about what to say to her. What do I reveal? What remains quiet? There are so many unanswered questions. Where do I start? How do I defend myself against the flurry of questions? **My imaginary jury is crucifying me. The consequences of my incarceration will last forever. I am the product of a multitude of bad decisions.**

15. I so badly want her to write me. I need to read words of love. I am fantasizing of our coming together, but it keeps getting interrupted with thoughts of abandonment. I keep dreaming about running down a tarmac after the plane. I can see her looking down at me. Her son is a youthful man now. They are leaving on a jet plane far way from me. *Please . . . come back*!

Sunday Oct.10th, 2004

1. I have opened my eyes to see my "cellie" standing only inches away from me. *Hey what's up?* I say. *Good morning* he responds. *Are we going for the French toast slam this morning? Yes we are,* I say. *Good, let's get the racing form, and after breakfast, we'll go down to the stables and watch the morning workouts. Hey buddy, be sure to bring a change of clothes so we can go eat lunch and make the 1 pm post time.* It was going to be a big day so we knew all the ladies would be wearing their finest hats and the men would be sporting their best jackets. If only . . .

2. What a glorious day that could be if we were really out there in the free world. It's a game my cellie and I often play. Anything to escape the realities of being in jail today. Wow! How nice it would be to hold this ticket in my hand; to be the favorite; *to win the race, to win the day, to win my life back.* Or should I say . . . my next life! The one where I actually start living for myself first before I ever consider dedicating myself to anyone else. **I'm thinking about the life where I become successful in so many ways, so I can continue a better, more normal, healthier, and enriching existence.**

3. Considering the circumstances, I'm feeling pretty fortunate to be in the G dorm. Except for the occasional "fuck you" between the same antagonist mouthpieces, there have been no serious contacts in this dorm *up until now.* That would soon change for the worse though. I remain to be a spectator too much of the horseplay and pranks. I find myself laughing aloud to much of the practical jokers. The excellent sounds of voices singing, sends inmates into a cool, soulful, rhythm and blues beat for hours at a time. It is a relaxing break from the echoes of bullshit conversations that constantly surround the brick walls and steel bunks.

4. **A lot of these guys are considerably patient with their given sentences of time. They can relax and enjoy the moment and do not seem to be stuck in the free world. They are strong-minded individuals who know the importance of living in the present. Unlike myself . . . I am forever caught in the deceit of my past and the robbery of my future.**

5. There is a slight connection among us while we endure the same anguish brought forth from this place by the guards. **It's not so much as a likeness to each other**

as it is an agreement to pass the time with each other . . . rather than against each other. I long to engage in conversation of my own liking. It doesn't have to be smart talk, but it sure would be nice to have a truthful conversation with an honest person. I am tired of all the babble. I would like to be able to sit, drinking coffee, and have a relaxing conversation with someone that does not depend on passing out samples of bullshit to get you by. **The truths of my own consequences have been pushed up against my mouth and as I lick my lips, it leaves a bad taste in my mouth.**

6.   In the evening, as the moon rises diagonally across my window, it initiates the never-ending search to seek out new stars becoming visible in the dark. When the moon passes out of sight, I say my prayers and lay down to sleep.

Monday Oct. 11ᵗʰ, 2004

1. I finally went to "store" today. It's the jailhouse food/supply commissary. It feels good to have food in my locker. The money came from my mother and father. It did not come that neglectful, lying, cheating, tramp, and slut wife of mine. She made excuses to me about not sending money because a female inmate at the hospital told her it would be used to buy drugs in here. It was such a lame and pathetic excuse not to send me money to eat. I get so hungry after my workouts. *The weights are finally fixed.* Today, I am outside pumping iron and "getting paid baby"! The weather is nice, but I know it won't last for too much longer. I can feel the fall breeze. It's time for "sweater weather".

2. I wonder if I'm making a fool of myself by sending her an "I miss you" card and a poem. *"What the fuck does she care"?* I'm thinking to myself. And if she does (which she doesn't), where is she? Everything she is doing has become so contradictory. I want to tear up the card . . . *but I won't.* I still have 6 hours before Tuesday's mail call at 4 am. I feel like I'm reaching to a place where my arms aren't high enough. I long for so many needful things and love is the foremost desire on my mind. I could starve to death in the next 20 days if I knew she could be here with me, holding me, love me, kissing me, and sharing my final days until my death. I am secretly blind to any kind of worthwhile future. *I think I'll get a Seeing Eye dog.*

3. Deep inside my despairing mind, I know she has become tainted goods. She is dirty and soiled in anger lust from lashing out her own frustrations. She has the luxury of answering those calls impulsively: satisfied in a moments notice . . . whenever, wherever, and with whomever she wanted. If only I had noticed it, I could have prevented it and more importantly, guarded myself from it. Looking back, I cannot overlook all the silent and hidden abuse I have endured over the years; the possessiveness, threats, and public outcries of false accusations every time she felt insecure. Still, as much as she has hurt me, I continue to find myself coming back to her . . . to serve her. All of her gain has been at my expense; my finances, emotional stability, criminal record, and mental well-being. *Is this the trap of co-dependency?* Is this what it means to be trapped in a world of domestic violence? Is this what men and women around the world are being punished and killed for: trying to right

107

someone else's wrong while enduring a continuous proving ground to satisfy the relentless cruelty of control? I've been had. And I didn't even know it.

4. The status of our relationship has been based on my success. I've been labeled only as good as my last performance. The sex, possessions, dinners, parties, admirers, status, travel, and all the attention have been directly proportional to my success. I am a victim of *the performance trap*! It was a lie . . . a terrible lie. So much wasted time, energy, love, and passion, was spent trying to get her to hang on to my own life. I did everything to keep the closeness and look where it got me.

5. **How's your relationship these days? Will it survive the time sent away? Will you both survive the time together while separated by bars? Will the distance of sight blind you into believing you'll never see each other again? Can you both survive the onslaught of needed change within your lives? Do you dare make the commitment of a revelation in your life? Are you prepared to answer to that change publicly? Can you live up to your words to those that count?**

Tuesday Oct. 12ᵗʰ, 2004

1. I'm mailing this letter this morning at 4 am. It is a romantic "I miss you" letter. I'm also sending a separate letter with a poem in it. It will probably be passed off and given to friends to ridicule. I think it is a waiting game for her to see how long it would be before I give in and end up writing a sobering letter. This *should* be my last attempt at any reconciliation.

2. As I write this, I'm making a vow to myself right now, to discontinue all intimate expectations if she does not respond to my outpour of love, commitment, and promise. I immediately regretted placing the letter in the mailbox. But I also knew that if I didn't, I'd never know any different. By mailing it, I could at least give myself closure within a couple of weeks if I didn't hear from her. I tried to make it easy for her by accepting her decision to be with another in her time of struggle. But realistically, I am raging inside to punish her. I'm scoffing at myself for compromising my acceptance of her galloping to the beat of a trollop. This will be much easier to deal with when I'm released. I just hope I can walk away without screaming my pain down her throat. I truly will find no peace until she feels what I have been enduring all these months: containment, abandonment, and judgment.

3. I wish my mother would write. She is on the other side of the globe for three more weeks. Maybe, my friend will write, longing for me to get out. Better yet, it would be great if my product supplier wrote telling me of all the work available up north and how my plane ticket will be waiting when I am released. Now, that would be the solution to many obstacles in my life for so many unpaid obligations. **When a man works, he is able to fend for himself. Without productive work, it seems that nothing else falls into place.** I am formulating new strategies and adding more strength to the successful plan of my business. This new beginning is hinged on one promising letter. *When will it come?*

4. **I miss my work**, and I especially miss being out on the open road, driving on the highways through canyons, valleys, and long stretches of curving roads. Whether surrounded by the woodlands or seeing miles of grazing, sloped pastures, it is the discovery of newly found geography around every corner that I find very satisfying to my sense of curiosity. Soon enough, I will see the snow peaked mountains of

109

the west and the north. I long to feel the rain or snow falling upon my face. I will linger in it without caring, even if it keeps me in bed the next day.

5. **I miss being in all those wonderful cities**; the suburbs, strip centers, malls, restaurants, clubs, and downtown. And oh . . . about downtown. How I just love being downtown; all the people, stores, shops, social gatherings, and party establishments. My thoughts are venturing into the clubs and pubs. To sit back on the couch, watching cool bands, and listening to beautiful music. I want to feel the vibrations of the walls and thumping of the bass against my chest. I feel my body rocking to the beat of the drums just from thinking about it.

6. **I miss** the Island that I have come to love so much. I remember hating it before I actually moved into **my own place.** For 5 years, I had to endure her parent's home during visits. Always stale and rigid. Everything so set in useless ways. What was thought to be secure was actually just plain and boring. At every chance, I shed money for a hotel so I could avoid the stuffy and hot house. I enjoy my own schedule. I knew the Island would be my home the very day I moved into a beautiful warehouse style apartment. Words cannot describe the feelings of elation in my life to be surrounded by such historical, downtown, buildings. To hear the clip clop of horse and buggy outside my open bay windows, or to listen to the whistle of the train trolley as it passes by the front doors. The Island is always packed with tourists sightseeing. It felt good to be a local. To be a part of it all. I used to sit right outside the doors early in the morning and watch the tugboats turn the huge cruise ships around to dock right in front of me. What a sight to see up close. No sounds except for the low humming of the tugboats. Everything else is quiet. The ships were always packed with colorfully dressed tourists standing against the rails on all levels. It's all still there . . . but I'm not! It will forever be etched in my mind though. I think I'll take a cruise with my son when I get out. *I wish I were getting out today.* The weather is so beautiful in the rec yard this morning during my workout.

7. Truly, **I do not want to be in jail today**. Nobody ever should, but we continue to fill the prisons beyond capacity. I feel wasted with disgust as I look around. **Everything, but everything is here to remind me I am in jail today** . . . *and I will be tomorrow.* **The constant reminder is constantly reminding me** . . . that I will *not* be hearing the horse's hooves against the brick road. Nor will I be hearing the whistle blow as the trolley glides down the tracks. And finally, I will not hear long, bellowing horns of the great cruise ships. Yep . . . all of this and the great people of the Island that I've come to love so much are out of reach, *and out of sight!* I cannot see or hear the fun and laughter of the sights and sounds of that cozy place I long to call home again. I want to be there, even if it means living alone without her.

8. **I am tired of taupe colors, hard chairs, loud guards**, and so much more. Or should I say . . . so much less. Simple things like shaving have become gnawing, painstaking, events of disgust. I must stand with my legs spread over "the pisser"

struggling not to slip on the wet spots left by the bad aimers, while straining to see the reflection of my face up close in the beat-up metal plate. Of all the makeshift mirrors up here, the one over the pisser is the only one with a half-ass reflection to see myself. I have resorted to pulling off the top of the coffee pot for a better glance.

9. The threat of dropping soap on the floor is not from the "backsliders" as much as it is from letting the soap hit the filthy floor. Actually, there really is no threat of any sexual predators in this dorm. The only activity of that nature here are the bitches sucking dick in the shower stalls. But they are harmless. What matters is that your soap stays off the scum floors of the shower stalls. Unless you're using a body scrubber and liquid soap, count how many times your bar of soap hits the floor while bathing. I can't tell you how many times I've thrown away brand new bars of soap just because I couldn't hang on to them while taking a shower. I've just resorted to showering with shampoo and a rag instead.

10. *Fuck this place, man!* **I'm tired of showering only when I'm told** and between certain hours. I'm tired of eating what I'm given, and eating only when I'm told. To talk only when I'm given permission, and told to shut up whenever they feel the need for silence. To have to sneak in extra workouts at the risk of "being cased" and eventually sent to restricted dorms. To be herded like cattle through the halls and corralled like a stallion on your bunks. I will forever hear the words "shut up and get on your bunk" from freshly imported African guards. The scum of the earth guards who take pride in getting in your face. These are the ones who get off threatening 50 grown men at a time, knowing full well that most inmates will not retaliate because of the law sentencing us to more time for violence. **No matter what the activity or whatever it is that you are doing, thinking, saying, hearing, or feeling, there is always something within proximity to remind you that you're in jail today.**

11. **We walk around in scarcely washed scrubs** given to us by the nastiest bitch of all whores. She is constantly angry with us and even at the inmates she puts to work. It's deafening to hear her voice yelling and screaming threats during the entire changing process. She could never get laid. She's too ugly . . . *inside and out*! We are given holy socks (with holes) and overly baggie boxers.

12. **We wear slippers that never fit** and get haircuts that are never right unless it's bald. We drink water from a dirty water cooler, and eat food from a plastic tray filled with thick calcium spots. Food stains are visible from the last meal *and the meal before that.*

13. **We live among open trashcans**, stained floors and use dirty rags to clean, but all it ever does is spread germs and filth from one location to another until it's time to spread it back the other way.

14. **We live among those who constantly fight** and argue their way through life. We contend with constant interruptions of shakedowns just so the guards can stay alert and earn their measly paycheck. They too, fight the boredom of being in jail today.

And they take that frustration out on the one thing that can trigger responses of violence . . . us! Inmates never win in here, but it is gratifying to occasionally see a guard get their face completely smashed in by an overly zealous inmate. But those days come few and far between. There's too many of them, and they keep coming. Just like the days forever rolling into the night . . . they just keep coming.

15. **Want some more reasons to stay out of jail today?** Good . . . because I've got 'em and the list is endless. I hope by now I have your attention and you're actually reading into this book, and not just merely "glazing" through it. I'm trying to get you to feel what I'm feeling without actually having to experience it. **That's why you're reading this: to fix things.** Or . . . to undo what has already been done. **There is still time.** You must ensure that your rights and privileges of being a citizen *remain to be your right!* At least be grateful that you are actually able to think about what you're reading. Try doing this in a cement room filled with metal bunks and nothing else to buffer the echoes, grunts, and bullshitting of 50 grown men wallowing in the stench of noise pollution. Yes, the noise will have you up to your ears in it for the entire duration. The silence you are hearing right now in the comforts of your own home or at school must be deafening. *Where is the luxury of opening my eyes from my own restful night? When will I lay upon my own bed, with my eyes open in solitude and silence, reflecting peacefully on the day ahead?* That day will not come soon enough: 51 days will not arrive in time for my sanity to remain. And with all the short naps in between, it means I will awake at least a 100 more times to the reminder that I'm still in jail today.

16. **Now, you can sit there in comfort and pretend to agree with me on various subjects, but unless you've been in jail, you truly have no idea of what I'm talking about in terms of the physical and mental deterioration of the human spirit.** My wife screamed at me once trying to express to me that I didn't know what she was talking about because I wasn't her. All she was doing was cramming for a test she had put off. The usual norm. She said I didn't understand what she was going through. Damn . . . lest she dare spend a day in my oversized ragged jailhouse slippers. The fact of the matter is that we'd both be in jail if the authorities knew the truth. "Authorities", now there's a word that spreads a blister across my heart. For me, the word itself conotates all that is evil. Sure, I can be agreeable with most laws and I am willing to abide. I just disagree with the makeshift authorities that guard it and enforce it. Especially in here.

17. **It is said "don't bring your work home with you". In the prison system, the guards bring the horrors of their own home here to work. They punish us for the instabilities of their own lives. They mumble and grumble to themselves while balancing their checkbooks. They argue with spouses and punish their children over the phone. They sleep in the cage where they are protected and read to pass the time away. They are overly paid babysitters for a room full of grown men.**

18. I've just looked up from my paper to stare outside. There's not a cloud in the sky. I'm watching this bird on an electric pole feed itself. It's glancing around nervously

while picking at its food. He reminds me of how I have to guard my own food, but he looks much more paranoid. I'm going back upstairs to my own perch by the window to stare out in the free world and the horizon beyond. *I want to go home.*

19. I'm seeing so much abuse of power from the guards. I have been witness to so much more than I've taken or received in terms of punishment. Even so, I will always hold the scars inside from the verbal and physical attacks on me. I don't want the guards to be nice to me whenever they feel like it. I want to stay angry with them for all their cruelty. *Why should I respond kindly to their good moments, only to be again harassed by them on their bad days . . . which is everyday anyway.* It is harboring a lingering mean streak inside of me. None of these guards are actually very strong or tough. They are just able to command authority and throw around because none of us want any more prison time.

20. **I am looking around the dorm at the other inmates. Most of us sleep in the lazy afternoons between lunch and dinner. Some are awake though. They stare blindly, as I know I usually do too. I can see it in their faces; the pain, the loss, and the would'ves, could'ves, and the should'ves of their history. It's not any one thing, but rather, a long list of small things that changed their lives in very big ways. It is a multitude of bad decisions.** For me, I am attempting to undo 28 years of all those bad habits exposed to any one person. I had spread those habits among my family, women, friends, and co-workers, so that no one person would be subjected to my overdrive of wasted days and partying nights. It has been 28 years ago to the month, since I turned 11 years old and began slowly killing myself with some type of dependency.

21. Today though, and for the last 4 months, I store no foreign substances within. I am no longer caught up in a race to continuously chase the high which picked me up, spun me around, and pounded me right back down, flat on my ass. **This was my time of calling to quit: To break free from the cycle and reverse the deteriorations of a reckless life. It is closure to the never-ending quest of involuntary attempted suicide.**

22. And now comes one more dependency that has brought slavery into my world; *the lost love of my life.* This is a dependency that leaves me exhausted from constantly seeking approval from her. I have endured years of emotional trials and metal anguish. I have been a self-inflicted sacrifice; a slave to her approval. And now that I have sent her through school, my services are no longer needed. My services have been discontinued. I have been replaced and I have become obsolete in her future plans. I realize now, that the proximity of our relationship had been based on my degree of success. No longer could she ever face me, for I know the guilt of her wrongdoings must be so great.

23. Is she being forced to discontinue all contact with me? Was it her boyfriend, family, friends? I wonder how she truly feels. Is she torn? I want the truth, but I'm not even sure I'd know what to do with it when I got it. And how could I possibly know how far from the truth it would really be if I did get it! *What the fuck is really going on?*

24.   These concerns are not suspicions of extreme paranoia. My worries are real and warranted, as are her inconsistencies of actions vs. words. I wrote her again asking her to help me get through the rest of my days. To reach out to me . . . as a friend. Even if there is someone else in her life, maybe she could still find enough compassion to answer my cries. Something . . . . anything of contact to preserve my sanity. After all, wasn't I supposedly the father of her child? *Am I not her husband and true soul mate? If I am as she says, why do I feel like sole of her shoe standing in shit?* I must snap out of this crutch. **I figure, if my imagination can be the killer of my spirit, then why not make it my savior too.** I have poured out my heart to her, sometimes expressing the most important of feelings. She often mistakes my sadness and pain for anger and many times the anger surfaces within the pleading. I have shed my skin completely. I want forgiveness between us. Why can't she see the better part of what has come to pass through all this turmoil? *I've tried to salvage her faith in this relationship from prison, but it is like trying to fight the good fight and win from the sidelines.* I find myself paying attention to thoughts normally never considered before. I'm thinking about having to die without her. I wonder what the last thing I will see before I pass. I want it to be her. Damn it! I'm becoming completely unraveled again. I have to stop writing. **I need to workout to burnout this smoldering fire before it ignites**.

Sunday Oct. 17ᵗʰ, 2004

1.   Depression has set deep within my soul. I have gotten sick from something in the air. I have been bed ridden for the last two days. My sore throat stings when I swallow food. It worsens every time I breathe in the foul air. I have covered my face. My body aches from fever.

2.   I am again, giving up any hope that she will show for the short, but oh so significantly important two-hour visit. I have tempted the lure of death several times this past week. Each time with more intensity. I pray for it to come and end my suffering quickly. *I want it so bad I can taste it.* But it isn't the cold taste of steel in my mouth that could remedy my quest to rid myself of this rejection. *It is only her that can cure this mental illness of feeling rejected and abandoned.* Where is she? If she has become a nurse, where is the compassion that comes with it? As a child growing up, and even now as an adult, I have always been aware of a nurse's ability to provide the spirit of healing through touch, talk, and affection. Tender, loving care can bring forth medical miracles when used in the right doses. It brings back the will to live on. It instills the passion of life within to survive and succeed. So where is my nurse? This bewilderment consumes my every breath. *It is a cancer eating away at my passion for surviving.* I am losing this fight to remain. Her absence is shrouded deep in secrecy. Only facts are of any concern now. The suspicions have become real to me. Everything that I could imagine must be true! Is this her time of glory now? Is this the revenge set upon me only because of her own suspicions? Because of what she thinks she knows to be true? She holds no fraction of an idea of what really happened out there. *And she never will!*

3.   I will write her tonight asking her to save my life. I once read on a cup in a bathroom *"when a man is tired of pleasure, he is tired of life"*. She had been my pleasure, but now she is gone. And now, I am tired of being her painful struggle to remain. I am tired of being her pain. This is her ultimate win. There will be no rematch. She will be the lying, deceitful, and abandoning champ until the next title fight. *God help the next contender.* I'm thinking if I could just hang on for 43 more days, I could top it off like icing on the cake by letting her watch me slit my throat. She could

115

watch from a distance, or come really close and knock me out so I don't have to die choking in my own blood.

4. Is this what it has come to? The wonder and worry of not knowing about her change of heart? Not knowing how she is? Missing her? Thinking about her days or what she does when she gets up in the morning? How, and with whom, she spends her evenings? Is her new partner so great that I have quickly been forgotten? *I can't do this anymore!* I can't go on with my own life while always wondering about her. I thought the powers of faith could have healed some old ways, but she couldn't even wait, and I can't maintain something I can't see, touch, or talk to, in some way.

5. It is said, *"hope is an unseen thing"*. If this is true, then I have become a blind man. We had everything together. I thought she could have waited for that "something more" to come from nothing. I thought she had the ability to forgive and heal. Her letters, when they rarely came, gave so much hope and expectations of a better life together. Is this all a lie? Why is she doing this? Why am I being covered in lies? Wasn't the money enough to take from me? Is this her way of hanging on to me to get still . . . the very last drop of whatever else she can take? Why doesn't she have the strength to just let go, so I can move on to the next phase of my life? I am caught in her trap of not knowing what to expect when I am released. It is clouding my decision process. Must she be so cowardly? It's just one of the characteristics of a liar. If only she had the courage to step forward and enlighten me of whether our lives will be together or apart. I wish it would be soon. Then, I won't have to feel the sting of the blade in my neck.

6. I live in a vacuum surrounded by 50 men and a revolving door of unnecessary shouting and abusive guards. I speak to no one unless I have to. Tension comes at me from all sides. Everyone is always trying to show their "colors" through intimidation. It would easy to start something of disrespect with someone, only to be killed or maimed for life. But I can't bear to suffer anymore. I have had enough already. Enough for infinite lifetimes. *I'll decide my own death . . . not some young, fucked-up punk trying to gain clout within his circle.*

7. I am considered low risk, but it means nothing when it comes time for someone stepping up and kicking your ass. There is no protection from anyone's anti-social agenda. I am tired and so very lost inside my head while I remain in this hellish nightmare. The revolving door brings the anxiety of knowing new conflicts will arise. Many familiar faces have left to other dorms or have been released. New inmates have arrived. Many with vendettas about their lives. They walk around with a chip on their shoulders. Some hold boulders upon their back. They are always looking to strong arm. I find them to be weak and pathetic in character, no matter how rough n tough they are in brute force. I myself am now very in tune with my own physical well-being. I have never seen myself like this and I haven't even looked in a full-length mirror. But I know it's good from the way that I feel. However, with that aside, I *still* feel worthless as a man.

8.　I don't want to start all over again without her. I am so strong now, but yet, I am too weak. I don't like these feelings in my life anymore. Total rejection is the best way to describe what is being inflicted upon me. It is complete and utter denial of anything she wants or needs in her life. I feel worthless to the core. I am toast . . . *burnt fucking toast!*

9.　She has won the day, she has won my life, and she has taken it all from me so she can give it to someone else. She must be reveling in her silent celebration so that she does not create too much attention for all that I have given her. Is this what it means to be alone? I don't want it anymore. The pain of it hurts too much. I cannot bear the burden any longer. I can no longer hide it away under my sheets in the dark. *Please God . . . save me from this suffering.* Just to hold her hand could be my remedy, even just for a moment. *Just give me the chance!*

10.　I've just looked at the calendar and I am in disbelief. I have just crossed over the halfway point since coming to this facility. I came here on Sept. 2nd, and now it's only Oct. 17th. This is unbelievable. It has only been 45 days since arriving in this dorm. No, no, no . . . this can't be right. I'll never make it. Doesn't time ever leave this confinement? *Will time ever end here for me?* I have become a victim of my own demise. My prayers have ended in vain causing me only more pain to my already broken heart. I gave up on praying for her faithfulness a long time ago. It will be nice to seduce her one more time though. Easily said . . . and much easier to do. To feel her under me. I can see her hair flowing across the pillow like micro-fibers; so fine and well groomed. I want to kiss her neck and caress her breasts. I want to inhale the scent of her body while she is spread out across our bed. I can smell her here with me now. My desires are overwhelming me. My blood is overflowing with lust. I want to be pushed far down into her abdomen regions. My lips never leaving her skin. My arms lifting her torso off the soft bed exposing her finely trimmed fleece of love. It is here, down there, where I love to be. Never wanting to leave. Always wanting more. To taste her anticipating scent of me . . . inside of her. Yes, she would want me. Being inside her is too much to think about while being incarcerated. Sex was always the best, always encouraging, and always so very intimately physical for us. Whether it was a blissful quickie or a full evening affair, we always wanted more. I've never been disappointed. Neither has she—*ever!* But now it is gone . . . *and I want to be too.*

Monday Oct. 18th, 2004

1. I'm waking up this morning feeling better. It is a Monday and I've decided to have a new outlook on things to come, no matter how short-lived it would be. I hate the weekends here. It starts with the long nights of Friday. The lights never go out until wee hours of the morning, and even then, they are only out for a short period of time; abut two hours. The noise never stops from the loud TV's, arguments, and of course the worst pollution of all . . . the guards. Saturdays and Sundays are torturous with inmates crawling all over my bunk to see if they will get a visit. My rented bunk is the best view in the house. But with it, comes the constant interruptions. Most are just looking for hot chicks to gawk at. However, some are actually looking for their loved ones. Attitudes and demeanors immediately change when they spot a visitor coming to see them. Inmates have a way of spreading good cheer within the dorm knowing they are about to communicate with someone from the outside. But three out of five times, they come back disappointed because of some conflict within the family circle.

2. So having everyone jump all over my bed is the price I have to pay for having a rental by the window. The price is worth ten times what I paid for it. Three months by the window for $20 worth of commissary. That's all I had to buy for him. Joey ended up becoming a great friend in this place. What's funny about it is that the guards would come by and check ID's and the faces to match the picture at least six to eight times a day. Not one of those idiotic, blind, hateful, pigs noticed that *it wasn't me they were staring at* on the offender card.

3. The bunk is the best investment I could have made while being here. I couldn't begin to imagine being in the center of the room having that freezing a/c hitting me in the face 24/7. *No way.* It is the center of traffic and three feet from the showers and the shitters. My rented bunk, however, is in the corner at the back of the room and against the window. *Each morning, the sun rakes through the bars across my body, warming my skin into a submission of a relaxed state of mind.* My morning views of the rising sun and the evening glow of the reflected moon grant me an added escape from the confines of my punishment.

4. I have missed my workout today because of the fire alarm downstairs but it doesn't even matter. I've enjoyed the silence of sleeping in this morning. I can hear soft-

spoken conversation from the early morning risers in the background. It must be "old schoolers" or else the noise levels would have awoken all of us in moments. The "old schoolers" have a way of containing themselves, unlike the "rascals" who continuously jump around and get in each other's faces all the time.

5. I'm laying here on my bunk thinking of better times to come my way. I'm daydreaming about the holidays approaching. Family gatherings: I wonder how, and in what manner, family and friends will accept me? I want to start over . . . clean. **I wonder if I can create a new history for myself? One of calmness, coolness, and collectiveness. A new, uneventful, and peaceful history. I will not ponder or burden myself with all the events and people that could let me down. I do believe I can make something more of my life from this nothingness.** I'm wondering when that day will come and if, if fact, it ever will? What if I never leave here because of new charges against me because of conflicts with another inmate or guard? I try to avoid what is sometimes, just unavoidable. What about the old lingering charges that may surface before my release. I should really have someone check these possible charges out *before* that time arrives. It could count as *time served*. I just couldn't imagine my release date being delayed until the New Year because of some unpaid traffic ticket. I do know that my child support payments for my son are backing up while in here.

6. I am 39 years old and have become completely dependant again. I have no money, job, prospects, or home. I am the victim of an abandoning wife and child. How's that for a bleak future! All because of a lying, cheating, back stabbing, wife. And still, I love her. I will always love her. My thoughts are reflecting back to her beauty and our past life together. No matter what she has done, or is willfully and maliciously doing now to disrupt my life. I will always love her. And . . . I know I will always want to be near her.

7. This turmoil of coming to jail could have been a "walk in the park" with her dedicated support. It was supposed to have united us. The pain was to give us strength: *to bond us the way everything else did in our lives.* So many trying times sowed our strength into a woven blanket of security to each other. It was easy and natural to count on each other. It was a given. Instead, *this separation has given way to any such predictability or accountability in our lives.*

8. There has been no connection or consistency on her part right from the start of "*you're under arrest*". And now, she plays a violin, and loudly sings the "blame game" for everyone to hear. She spend her social hours finger pointing at those who have to listen to this crying she so easily bellows out of that gutter in the center of her face.

9. We continue chisel to away at each other's character. *Me;* because I'm hurt from the deception. *Her;* because she needs an easy way to justify her way out. It has fumigated our ability to breathe a deep sigh of relief toward reconciliation. There is no comfort anymore when considering each other's feelings. Damn it! We had been so close, so comfortable, so exciting, and so adventurous to each other. We were

never embarrassed or uncomfortable with each other. It was easy to laugh together. We were unconditionally appreciative of our passionate skills, pleasantries, and comedy routines of each other. I miss it. There were so many silent celebrations of our lives together. But now, those memories are becoming over-shadowed by the screaming outcries of trial and error.

Tuesday Oct. 19th, 2004

1. My bunk was just called for mail. My heart skipped a beat and then, thundered it's way up to my throat. Actually, for the past week or so, I've been experiencing another kind of heart concerns: a surge in the frequencies of heart murmurs. It is an inequality of heartbeats. Sometimes, it is flustering and fibrillating, beating very rapidly like a vibration. Other times, the beats are thundering, yet slow and hard, pounding against my chest. *This isn't right!* I'm supposed to be in the best shape of my life. But now, I have to contend with this threat. I don't want to die. Not here. Not like this. *Please God . . . not alone among strangers and uncaring chaperones. Don't let me die without knowing the fate of my wife and children.*

2. The letter comes from my father. He has written an entire page to me. It is the first time I can ever remember ever receiving a letter from my father since I moved away at 17 years old. That was 22 years ago. Usually in the past, I would just receive a blank page or maybe a quick line with a check inside the envelope. I am instantly ashamed as I reflect back at all the money wasted on the never-ending quest to end my life. But today, I have received his letter and it feels damn good. I will read it several times.

3. My "cellie" hands me another envelope and I immediately draw in a deep breath. Euphoria quickly overcomes me. I am stumbling back as I look down at what he is handing me. We always made it a point to pick up each other's mail since we had switched bunks. He's been holding this one for the last half hour while I hung on to my dad's letter. I hadn't even heard my other bunk being called after I had dad's letter in my hand. All this time, I had been drowning myself in his encouraging words of love and affection.

4. The next letter is from my wife. A glaze is quickly swelling up in my eyes as I leap for the privacy of the hidden corner behind my bunk. It is here; I will open that fateful letter. I am trembling and expecting the worst, but hoping for the best. I open the letter and glare over the two page typed letter desperately searching for the words of *love* and *miss* and *want*. Frantically, I'm looking across and down the pages to find any substance of a "wife in waiting". Fearfully, I am dreading the unwanted signs of a relationship gone badly and a fading memory of the past.

Regrettably, what I'm getting is so much more. What I'm getting is a trip down the long and winding spiral of betrayal. I am being reminded of terrible deeds and irresponsible acts. Some not even remembered . . . and even a few that are being made up from the demented imagination of a sick mind.

5.   The letter is simple enough to read. She needs these absurd creations, in order to buffer her justification of all her lies and deceit to me while I am here in prison. Meanwhile, she is out there fucking everything and anything with a pulse.

6.   Her pain is exploding from the pages in clear vivid illustrations that are burning impressions into my skin. She is turning over explanations of what I did to remind me of my negligence and self-abuse. Whether it is opinionated or not, doesn't matter at this point. I'm feeling the daggers piercing my skin. I finally stopped skipping around the lines and have submitted myself to reading this death sentence from top to bottom.

7.   The first few lines are accepting me into the light of complete wonderment. She has received my card and poem. And it is good. She said it brought tears to her eyes. Instantly, I needed her. A flicker of light is shining brightly in my eyes. I have to continuously wipe away the tears as I read on. I am clinging to every word as she reminds me of the good times, and our passionate times. She is also telling me about a few of the terrible and tragic times never to be forgotten . . . or ever to be relived again. I know she is sitting on the fence with this, and it has got me standing in the field next to her. I am imagining her feet dangling over on my side. I want to reach for her and gently pull her towards me. I'm praying that she will not fall backwards on the other side.

8.   I will write her immediately with words of love, respect, and of course, some funnies. Laughter has always been a good pathway to her heart. I want to become the light at the end of her tunnel. *Can she wait?* I know I want to believe that. If not for herself, then at least for me! The rest of the day will be easy. My sleep will be content. This has been a day in my favor. *It is also another day lost to the system.*

Wednesday Oct. 20th, 2004

1. I was awakened by the abruptness of my bunk being rammed by a 200 lb man landing on my rails to get a closer look at a passerby. *I know it's not the weekend yet*, so why is *"fat boy"* thinking he can crawl all over my bunk, especially while I'm sleeping! Of course, it is most likely a woman of sorts he's trying to catch a memory of for tonight's sleep. I tell you, *one slip of my foot, and he'll be breaking off body parts on the way down to the cement floor.* I will refrain from knocking his teeth out this morning and instead, I will join him for the look outside. I'm quite sure it is someone that I could not find any interest in, nor will I appreciate the efforts of getting up out of my bunk. But I am wrong . . . way wrong!

2. Before me, down below and across the street, between the County and State facilities, two women are pacing back and forth along the sidewalk. I know that the prison system allows for special visitations from visitors at least 300 miles away or more. Was the young lady here to see her man? I'm wondering if the elderly woman is the young lady's mother, but quickly evaluated that she had to be the inmate's mother. No way could a mother-in-law hug a man so closely as this woman is holding on to him. She has to be his mother.

3. I'm watching the young woman pace back and forth in anticipation of his release from this terrible institution. Her hair is long, sleek, and black. She wears a soft, white, cotton blouse and tight blue jeans. Her thighs are semi-thick and her ass is ever so pleasing to look at. I could have put a drink on her ass and it wouldn't have slipped off. She is so nicely shaped and has curves that last forever. Her black boots are shining in the early morning sun.

4. I am watching her as I would watch my own wife. The similarities are straining my memory. The young woman runs towards him as the inmate begins his walk across the street. Her arms are extended. They embrace and then kiss. He hugs his mother. As they walk away to the parking lot, I am noticing that she holds her arm in his cradled bicep *exactly the way my wife holds my arm* when we walk together. I can see the glimmers in their faces. They never took their eyes off of each other. I wanted this. I needed that. When am I going to get some? I am envisioning all of

it. My longing for love and lust has grown to explosive proportions. It boils and bubbles just beneath the surface.

5. I made it a point to relieve myself in sexual fantasy early in the mornings or during the lazy afternoons while most everybody slept. Still, to masturbate quickly, and hopefully in private, will never be enough to quench my thirst to drink from the fountains of love, which my wife could so readily supply. I'm feeling the need to be embraced and touched. I want to prolong my climax within the enduring madness of sensual play. Ah . . . *the art of making love will be mine to re-discover.*

6. I wonder if I can truly learn to forgive her for adultery; for her indiscretions. I knew sex with others could never mean as much to them as it did with me. I've always showed so much excitement in receiving such a delicatessen. Others may use it, but I am the one that adores it completely. Between us, it is never taken for granted and it is always appreciated. There is no way she could be *getting it* the way I gave it. She will have me again. *I will live to taste the tale!*

7. It has been, what seems like weeks, since writing Ohio for my job. I have not received any response. Worry has begun to itch my skin. This is a key necessity for righting a wrong and healing some old financial wounds. I will re-check that address and try again next week.

Friday Oct. 22nd, 2004

1. Friday night is on again baby! Time for conflicts and insanity on all sides. TV's blare loudly all night, workouts last up to 6 hours and the smell of food parties with soups, homemade pizzas, and burritos fill the air. And course, we will all listen to the noise of 50 men passing the time. Most of this noise is coming from story telling and rappers thumping on the walls, spitting out their lyrics. All of this, and more, *including the continuous fire cracking sounds of dominos being slapped down on the hard metal tables.* The echo creates a sharp ping each time someone slams his domino down with force. It goes on and on without end. There is no escape. **You cannot walk away to a quieter, more favorable place. There is no change of scenery here. It is all the same; dull, noisy, smelly, and unsightly. Nothing changes.**

2. I've got 40 days and 40 nights to go! Will this exodus back out to the free world be too much to bear? Can I endure this numbness of unbearable burdens as I have all these endless days and nights? The tension of having to fight has knocked at my door twice this week, leading me back into a state of urgency and anxiety. Physically, I am at the peak of my game. Better than I ever have been before. Still, I'm thinking about the potential for permanent injury while fighting. I'm not concerned about knocking knuckles with anyone in here. What *is* my concern, are the nasty fingernails some of these fuckers are growing at the end of their fingers; longer than most girls and sharper than knives. All it takes is one catch across and through my skin to leave scars on my body and poison in my blood. A poison that has become a multi-billion dollar industry. A poison that still has society reaching for a simple cure without complete success. Nope, that's not for me. **The chance of getting a nasty, diseased, fingernail in the eye is enough to deter me from spitting out egotistical, macho-dick, gestures back to someone that won't matter in my life anyway.** I'll take a knife in the heart, before I begin to suffer the lonely, prolonging, and painful death of dying with such a dreadful disease.

3. **I choose to remain in my own world. Sure, it would be easy to kick some dude's ass all over this dorm. But for what? So I could sleep with a towel around my**

125

neck for the next 40 nights. *Forget it*! I'll pass on that. I'll remain to keep the peace whenever I can.

4. I watch these dudes fighting with each other for the most insignificant, idiotic reasons *you couldn't think of.* It is, however, always nice to see the little bitch snitches, and the wanna-be bullies getting their ass kicked by the tough guys that don't put up with any show-off motherfuckers.

5. **Yep . . . I choose to remain as quiet as possible, and within my own group of fellow inmates that I communicate with. I make it a conscientious effort to avoid the rapture and anti-social currents of mounting conflicts within these walls. My attempt to remain uninvolved is sometimes disrupted by the unavoidable. And when that happens, I look around for allies . . . *and realize there are none*!**

6. I am so very tired of tasting the same feast of exaggerated stories. Every time I hear the old recordings, a new twist is edited into an already massive lie, giving the new edition an extended version with a much more climatic ending. I'm tired of listening to 25 year-old kids telling everyone about the six different sport bikes in their garage of the private lake house, that is only accessible by luxurious Hummers and Escalades. And of course, all of this was supposed have been acquired from selling a few hits of "X" or "bars" or some other profitable dope. I can't see the truth, or *"the brag"*, of telling such exaggerated stories. Sure, these great assets and possessions are easy to acquire through life's careers and good hard work. But I'm thinking the number of people in here, battling to convince everybody of their possessions and power in the free world, is disproportional to the amount of wealth on the street . . . and in the world. I look around and know that 90 out of every 100 inmates in here was living from "hand to mouth" on a day-to-day basis, while living in the free world. There's absolutely nothing wrong with that except that I have to hear lies to portray something different than is actually true. Of course, the information we receive in here, as everywhere, is only as reliable as it's source.

7. *There are 48 inmates in this dorm. The jail itself has a total of 640 inmates housed in this particular facility. I've seen bigger . . . much bigger! It is a world full of boneheads, potheads, "bar" heads, dope heads, cokeheads, and crack heads. I see "X" users, "tar" abusers, and speed freaks bouncing off the walls. Hammerheads, foam heads, and dick heads, are all meshed together in a sweltering rage of "fighting for your right" to get the fuck out of here!*

8. **They take it to the streets. They take it home, and they bring it to the house. They see you in the car, and meet you on the street. They introduce it to your friends and then, listen to them become fiends. They watch our families turn into enemies and chances are, at the end of the day, they'll watch you put yourself in jail tonight because of what you foolishly decided to put in your pockets today. *Do you really want to go to jail today*?**

Saturday Oct. 23rd, 2004

1. My body is in pain. I ache from several hard workouts. I'm also tending to a nagging pinched nerve in my back. *My mind is quicksand and I'm up to my eyeballs already.* I need to think my way out of this trap within my head. I need guidance in examining the problem. I need to find the solution to my dilemma. It is she. All of my pain is coming from *not knowing*. More of my pain is coming from being led on; a carrot dangling in front of me. She continues to hinder the healing process by hiding her intentions. She still actually believes that her tactics of silence, as a way of control, is camouflaged from what she is actually doing. It has become a transparent page, and I am reading these pages in disbelief. She is meticulously avoiding all of my questions. She is doing nothing to show any type of support: a few letters of broken promises and lies of her efforts gone badly. Nothing to make things right with my business has been completed. This only adds a new source of questionable actions in the history of our relationship.

2. My family has watched and listened to her lies and deception as she continuously ignores my requests for help. She has not taken my situation into consideration. And surely, she is not taking others into consideration by denying my family the info necessary to refund my customers. Soon it will be time for her to be held accountable for her actions, or should I say . . . *lack of it*! She finds it so easy to bring friends, lovers, and even strangers into our private life. She continuously lets others come between us and now, it has created new chapters of conflict. I wonder if this is even worth the infliction and torment anymore? I honestly believe I could have healed more peacefully if we had never corresponded during this time. Why does she even bother to write anymore? She has to make a choice! I want answers, and with these answers, I will be able to consider whether or not to stay on in this relationship. If she cannot be honest with me, I will not be able to test my faith of unconditional love.

3. It's better to know the truth of her abandonment now, instead of later . . . *no matter how hard it hurts*. I'm sure at this point, the less questions asked, the better. And I'll stop asking, just as soon as all my questions are answered.

4.   I know now, that I have a lot to bring to the table in this relationship, but I can't (or won't) if she will not help resolve questionable behavior. I need clarification. I need to know . . . *where do I stand?* She is consistently being too vague about everything. I am tired of filling in the blanks with wishful thinking. **If knowledge *"knows"*, and wisdom *"knows the difference"*, why am I still running on guesswork?**

5.   I am reading her last letter slowly and carefully. I am digging deeper down into her message. It makes me feel better to read about us. She reminds me of our better times. I love her madly. I know forgiveness from both sides will allow a freedom to love each other again.

Sunday Oct. 24th, 2004

1. I'm writing her son today to apologize for being away for so long. I hope she will read it to him *word for word,* but I assume, like most things, she will change the message to her own liking. I will express to him my desire to be the best daddy in the whole, wide, world. I will ask him to tell mommy that forgiveness from both sides is truly a means of putting all this anger and hatred behind us. I want to know she's not looking for another daddy for her son. *I want my family back*! I don't want to be in jail today.

2. I'm sick of being controlled by this dependence of her love for me. Looking back on it, I have gone through the worst a guy could imagine, but much of it has come from being a prisoner of abandoned love. It is the barbed wires fence that chokes my need to escape. Each movement slices deeper into my flesh as I try to adjust to different fables of deceit. It is the torment of waiting for help that never comes. The occasional correspondence only applies thin bandages to slow the bleeding of my aching heart. But it always leaves me seeking further attention, because the questions always outnumber the answers. I am feeling the never-ending wrath of despair, breaking me down and killing my will to live . . . over, and over, and over again.

3. **Back in the free world, I had been an empty, self-satisfying, heap of evil sin walking among the masses. Camouflaged in beautiful garments of style and wrapped in moments of lust and longing for whatever was within reach.**

4. **Now, I lay in puddles of self-pity and regret, soaking my headrest and dampening my skin to the point of saturation. I am a sponge, no longer able to absorb another moment of truth. And the truth being . . . I am alone in this nightmare with no identity for anyone to recognize me. All I have is the faith of being saved . . . *as soon as I die!* And even now, the death sentence I so desperately pray for, is being denied from me. I can't do it! I can't get one more manipulation of control to sway my giver to grant me a dying day. Why can't it be today . . . now?**

5. She is avoiding all concerns of my incarceration. She has abandoned all requests to make things right. She has aimed all of her anger towards others at my expense.

I have become her saliva. I wonder if she can taste the bitter, sweet, sting in her throat when she swallows?

6. I am looking to the future. It is bleak! I realize I will be wondering and struggling with questions that could last a lifetime. It brings forth, a heavy heart. I am so tired of fighting for it. Not even fantastic sex can be the replacement for a loving relationship between us. There have been so many wasted words of trying to hold it together. She has expressed so many exaggerated and manipulating false statements to win the shallow awards of people's sympathy in her favor. I have educated her with my letters. I have revealed to her wonderful words of passion that will never be expressed to her by another with such vigor and enthusiasm. I wonder if she'll pass them off as her own while winning the heart of another.

7. I am tired of crying for my own life, and surely, I shouldn't have to cry for hers. I have to find shelter from the idea of being in love with her. I have been hurt so much in the past. I have become so disappointed with her cowardness. She has blocked me out completely. Too many excuses. So many lies. Now, it's only a matter of time for her friends and *not* enough time for me.

8. Why can't she love me the way I want to be loved . . . *passionately*! I wonder if I can ever recover from losing her. I don't even want to. I want to always believe there will be that chance to renew our passion of love together. I want my innocence with her again: *the care-free, unrelenting, desire to give to each other without having to worry about what got left out.* Isn't this what she wants? To be loved by a man with so much compassion as what I possess.

9. I know I will have to leave the Island if I am not what she desires anymore. I've decided that if we are not going to be together when I get out, I *will* leave this place. For me, it's got to be *"all or nothing"*. And I want it all! I want all of her. I better check on my other three options.

10. This is an illusion: pretending to believe that she really wants me. I feel like a puppy in the kennels waiting for my master to take me home to my doghouse. I'd settle for any kind of house besides this one right now, especially since I don't even have a place to come home to right now, except this hell house. I have, in fact, no possessions to speak of, and frankly, it means nothing to me. I can retrieve all of it *and more* in time with my work. That's if I ever get back to it.

11. I'm looking out my window, high above the other jails across the street, and out beyond to the highways. I've become used to extending my sight beyond the perimeter. I don't even see the caged window in front of my face anymore. I have become a window gazer. For others, it is the torture they choose to avoid. For me, it helps pass the time in reflection and mediation. It allows me to create new designs in my life: a way of seeing clearer to paint a new picture of where I need to be in my life. Unfortunately, at some point, I have to turn my back around to see where I still am in this overly crowded, and sickening place called jail.

12. Tonight we are watching a perfectly full, lunar eclipse outside in the night. The full moon has passed directly in front of my window and has become overshadowed

by the earth. I can see the curvature of the earth's circumference reflecting on the moon's surface. Whoever said the earth was flat, obviously had never seen such a beautiful, astrological coincidence. The sky has been ominously dark for the past couple of hours. I can remember seeing a few eclipses in my lifetime, but never a full one like this lasting for so long. But then again, I'm in prison, and by now, we all know everything moves like molasses while in here. I watched the moon throughout the night. It became a large orange shadow beyond the reflection of the sun's rays, skirting the perimeters of the earth. I have remained in awe most of the evening.

13. How much more enjoyable it could be if I was sitting on my porch, or up on the "widow's peak" watching this anomaly with my wife and kids; watching, talking, laughing. Tonight, I have carnal hunger. I want to be ravished by her love. I envision receiving it all the time. I play out passionate conversations between us while we embrace and kiss . . . and make exquisite love. Only the way true soul mates make love; talking, laughing, feasting, encouraging, and nurturing each other's desires to satisfy our quest for perfect, lustful, moments of love.

14. This time in prison could have been endured so much easier with the genuine commitment and support of a faithful wife, but it is difficult to expect that of such a person who has been cheating family, friends, and loved ones, for her entire adolescent and adult life. The stories go way back. Too many to recall for this chapter. It would take another book to go there with it. And I'm not interested . . . I'm sure neither are you.

15. **Out from the gutters of this nasty, poisonous, and desolate hell, I have created something within me that will carry a lifetime of remembrance. How very fortunate I will be, when I leave this place.** *That's only if I ever do leave here.*

16. I'm looking at the pictures of her son. How beautiful he has become. How bright his smile is. Truly, he is well loved and nurtured. I wanted to instantly to be able to provide this same security for him. Seeing him, reminds me of how long I have been away. How quickly he has changed in such a short period of time. He looks good. No . . . he looks amazing! I can't believe I've only been in prison for 132 days; just over 4 months. My life has slowed to a crawl within these walls, while the rest of the world zips by at super-sonic speeds. Time is not on my side. All of a sudden, 35 more days in the hole appears to have the span of three more lifetimes. I'm slipping back down into the hole beneath the earth. *I am being smothered in the waste of my life.*

17. It's not so much the question of time, as it is about *how to pass the time.* How many inmates are letting this time pass them by, and how many won't allow the system to take this time away from them?

18. **I have become very curious about something. How many inmates have actually completed the unnerving task of taking their own lives? A man goes to prison for life, only to provide for the livelihood and well being of those given the task of watching over them. The very same people that are punishing and**

brutalizing them. What motivates a man to stay alive for the rest of his life term in a prison system, which allows for him to be physically, verbally, and psychologically, punished within the walls, after the judge has already punished him/her with time?

19. I assume the numbers of suicides per capita in prisons must be staggering, especially if they feel anything like I do. I can't imagine how bad it's going to get with the holidays approaching. Either I feel worse than most, or the rest of the inmates are just better at hiding it. So many restrictions in such a small confinement. It hurts so much now because I had lived so freely and uninhibited in the free world. So many times during this ordeal, I have wished and begged for this life to be over. But no easy remedy of death has come to light without first realizing; it will have to hurt worse than the conditions of this torturous hell itself. **It's not so much about suicide and ending my life in here, as it is to *eliminate* these angry, hateful, remorseful, feelings of self-pity and revenge.** The evidence is monumental, but I am helpless to verify my suspicions or prevent new ones from arising. This inability to act upon all that needs to be corrected is the prison within itself . . . within myself! I struggle with this war of many worlds within my own imprisonment. My incarceration lives on inside me as well as within these prison walls. *How could anyone want to come back after the first time?* But still . . . so many do.

20. **How many inmates act on the desire, to feel no more desires? To end the pain they have caused to others, and to themselves. How many were motivated by never giving the guards one more chance to get the better of them through wrongful, abusive, and aggressive acts? How many have followed through with voluntary death within the prison walls because their family members stopped following through and abandoned any hope of reconciliation or rehabilitation? How many took someone with them when they decided it would be their last act. These are the killers in here. These are the thoughts that go "bump in the night", and leave you banging your head against the walls every waking moment. It's more powerful than any weapon produced by man. This is the nature of your affliction. It's the time you spend thinking about what put you here . . . *and what you can do to get out!* The inner struggles of the spirit within my body clearly have absolute power over me.**

21. In here, I am suffering afflictions of many kinds. Out there, she has succumbed to temptations of every kind. We are caught in a dynamic conflict of winner and loser, good and evil, and life and death. Who knows what tomorrow will bring. For now, it is another day lost in my life, and another day gained for the system. *Today . . . I will choose life!*

22. I have received a second letter from my father. To see his written words are still foreign to me. He has become a compassionate father looking out for his son, his youngest one. Even with all my failures, he has still risen to the occasion of unconditional parental love. I feel it, even though his impression of me in dealing with the management of my own life is unfavorable. *All my life, I've been struggling*

to prove his wisdom wrong. And throughout all of my life, he continues to prove me wrong. Yet, he still remains. If nothing else good transpires in my life, I will at least follow in his steps by supporting my own kids with the unconditional love and compassion to accept them throughout their lives. No matter what the circumstances or the conditions of our relationships. I'm looking at her son's pictures some more. Different mothers, but identical features. Even at nine years apart. I can remember pictures of my own youth. The pictures of me as a child show such similarities to my own boys so many years later. I miss them so dearly. Too little, too late, I know. The strain of wanting to get out so I can be with them is over-burdening. I have to see them. I need to go home to them. I desperately want to get out of jail today.

23. I'm getting hungry. I'm going to prepare this evening's gourmet dinner now. It's the usual and the same as it ever is in here; tuna sandwiches and noodle soup. Try it for the next 150 days and see if you still look forward to eating it. I want to cook a spicy steak with all the trimmings. To order the menu at your favorite restaurant. To load up on Big Macs with fries and a large vanilla shake. Now those are the finer things in life to look forward to. Never again, will I be so ignorant of the rights and privileges of being a citizen again. *The smallest, most appreciated, things we take for granted have become the most desired and the most wanted things in our lives here.*

24. **Look around at your surroundings now. Are you in jail today? And if you are, is it bending your mind not being able to make the simplest of choices of, what to eat, where to sleep, how to dress, when to talk, or who to see? Wrap this thought around your head: If you're not in jail today, but have that nagging feeling you're about to be headed that way, you had better *do* whatever is necessary to *undo* whatever it is you've done . . . now! And if you still have no idea of what it's like to be in jail today after reading this, go down and visit an inmate. Find someone with a friend or loved one in the prison system and go see him/her in the confinements of this living hell. Then, multiply the time you spend there by infinity for each minute that passes. Get the picture? *Do you really want to go to jail today?***

Friday Oct. 29th, 2004

1. It's Friday again. This week has edged up on me. Here, it is always better to live in the Monday thru Friday mode, rather than in the Saturday and Sunday slush. I will be *"wading in the waiting"* for a visit that most likely will not come. I am thinking about the mail today, but doing this only brings more disappointment when it doesn't come.

2. I long to clear the air with her. I long to breathe clean air too. I want to find out if time will tell us if we are going to stand the test of time. I need confirmation. It is time to make our plans together and put our anger aside. We should at least, do this for the kids, if not for ourselves. I'm wondering about her remarks. What will happen after dinner on our first night together after my release? To know that she going to pick me up will not be enough. Life has to continue after the first day. The million-dollar question is: Will I be there to see it with her? Or will I just get to be a sample discarded after use? I am anxious to receive a visit this weekend. I'd like to find out where I stand with her. Maybe, she'll give me some insight in finding out who is laying down with her in her own life.

3. I just woke up from an afternoon nap with saliva running down my face. I've been dreaming that my dog, Rexie, is licking my face as I sit on the porch in front of the house. Ordinarily, in the free world, I would have stopped her. But not in this dream. This time, I just sat there and laughed as she finally got her fill and completely soaked my skin. I wiped the spit from my cheeks and lay there in my bunk. It is quiet. Unusual for this time of day. I do remember that several of the *"rowdies"* had just been released or transferred out of this dorm. I am lounging in the calmness and enjoying the warmth of the sun shining through my caged window.

4. I long to hear my name being called from the kitchen. *"Peter"*, she would say. I wouldn't answer because I knew she would eventually come into the room and lay beside me. She would touch me with her long, slender, silky fingers. I can feel her nails, softly stroking my hair and back. I will spend the rest of the day, daydreaming of her.

5. **My thoughts have taken over my sense of reality. I am engaging in full conversations with her . . . out loud! I am constantly playing out alternate scenarios. It is my daydream, but I can never get control of it. It always ends up with a tragic ending. I am praying for peace in my heart.**

Saturday Oct. 30th, 2004

1. Time is scraping by this morning. I'm trying *not* to look outside, but my feet keep dragging my body to the caged window. I'm clutching the bars, straining my eyes to see her. I never did. *So this it*, I'm thinking to myself. *Am I not worth one day's wages?* After six weeks of absence, she still couldn't give me 2 hours of her day. This had been my birthday request to her in one of my letters. The truth is . . . that I am no longer worth the slightest moment of her day. *I can't make you love me if you don't* . . .

2. From all the hundreds of thousands of dollars we spent on nothingness, she couldn't give up $100 dollars worth of wages to come and see me for my birthday. Her letters had said to me *"I'll be there for you every step of the way"* It had now become more like . . . *"hey, let me lead you astray with my lies and deception"*.

3. It is a beautiful day outside, but I cannot possibly enjoy such leisurely peacefulness with the rage surging through my heart. I want to hold her down and force her to listen to my wantingness. She feels nothing of the pain I have endured. The bunks are silent with everyone still sleeping. It is unusually calm. Last night after breakfast, the dorms fell immediately silent. Not a sound could be heard, but my own despair.

4. I do not want to let go of something so familiar. Even now, after turning my life around, she is refusing to respond to my pleas of truth. Am I not what she wants? It is the *"not knowing"* that continues to be the constant interruption and disruption within my life. My own mentality is lashing out against me. I wonder if she even misses *the idea* of me anymore?

5. Everybody is returning from working out in the yard. I should have gone for the health of it. Instead, I had stayed on my bunk hoping she would show. She hasn't yet. It is just another example of my wiliness to allow her to disrupt my routine . . . and my life! I am gazing out the window. Being on this side of the cage, epitomizes everything that has been taken away from me. I can see the baseball stadium to the right. The highway is running straight across my view. The park, where people are playing, is just beyond that. The sights, sounds, smell, and tastes, of freedom . . . *Priceless*! If only I could just reach out and touch it.

6. I have become worthless to her. I have lost out on a visit because of a $100 bucks worth of wages. She did not visit. I now regret sending her that abrupt letter. What else could I do to vent my concerns? She has no concerns for me, so it really doesn't matter. I've heard about men being abandoned by their wives, but I had never really considered the deep suffering it entails. It is a strange and unfamiliar flavor I cannot place. It is foreign to my palate. I'm trying not to cry today. I so badly want to be significant in her life again. I had been so important to her, and she had loved me genuinely right up to the day I came to prison. How can feelings change that fast? It doesn't feel genuine anymore. It doesn't show anymore. Nothing . . . or no one showed. Everything has just become words. Wasted words of a lying tongue. My days should have been filled with so much love and support. Instead, they are spurred with the sting of being stood up. She should have come to see me today; to talk, to laugh, to answer, to cry, and to consider. She should have come today to make (or undo) the plans we had together. Soul mates wouldn't be this cruel to each other.

7. I have become the Christian man she always wanted me to be. I found it in here without her (or anyone) trying to push it on me. My faith means everything to me. I have bettered myself in so many ways. My only frustration comes from her now. Her actions (or lack of them) are forcing me to abandon my hope. Is she trying to leave it up to me to sever the ties, because she is too cowardly to do so? Is she too afraid to write the words and make it official? What is she afraid of? What am I afraid of? My faith tells me, I have nothing more to be afraid of. But I am. I'm afraid of being without her.

8. She should have brought my son here to show off his Halloween costume. It could have been a joyous occasion, but instead, it has become horror in my heart for the day. Is there another man tending to the needs of my son. Is he making her feel incomplete? Did he take away from me, what I took away from her fiancé six years ago? I should have known it would end up like this. I fucked that woman every day for three months before she told her fiancé the truth abut us. She did the same to the guy before him. *I should have known.* And now it has come back to me. I guess this is the payback for all my own escapades during our six-year party. And now, another has taken from me what I had worked so hard for, and righteously earned. Will my punishment be a lifetime of regret and loneliness without her? Will there be no one to share in my re-birth? Will I stand alone in my glory?

9. *It is Saturday night. Are you out there tonight, masked in your disguise and hiding your face from the commitment of marriage? Are you cloaked in camouflage as you lust for another? Your refusal to take responsibility has created more questions and confusion, than answers. If this love of ours is to be lost in a memory, at least find the time to come forth . . . but just one more time. I am imprisoned in slavery for acceptance into your life. I am enduring a suffering beyond any solitary confinement. I cannot close my eyes to escape the inner torment chafing away at my soul. Assure me. Tell me you feel something . . . anything! Show me I'm wanted in your life. You*

know me now. I have expressed my true, loving, self, through my letters. I have put everything out there for you to see. Please take me! Please come forth. Bring me back in from the dark and take me back into the light of your life! I just caught myself talking aloud, but I don't even give a damn to who is listening anymore. *Only if it's her.*

10. The day room is too busy for mourning. I am fighting off the tears swelling in my eyes throughout the day. The rain outside is hitting the glass behind the caged window frames. It slashes at the window, striking at an angle, creating splices that appear to be cutting through the glass. Watching it, feels like a blade slicing cuts deep into my side. Some drops are smashing and exploding upon the glass from different directions. The drips that follow are to be my tears of loneliness. The day inches forward. My mood changes to mirror the dark clouds rolling in from the south. *I wonder if it is you that has sent these saddened clouds for me? Maybe you are sad too? Maybe you are longing for me like a lazy summer afternoon? Maybe, you miss napping under a slow, turning fan after making perfect, passionate, love. I wonder if you miss telling me what you're heart feels.*

11. **The sky has become gray, and the day is once again, timeless. The black and white shades of the afternoon has blocked out any movements in time. Dinner is the only clue that the earth is still spinning.** Would she ever be this sad for me, or does the hardening of her heart not allow for such emotional moisture to seep through. **I have become a sponge of sorrow, already saturated in confusion and desperation. I am locked on to this: time is standing still for me. I cannot conclude what to do. It is an endless loop inside my head. I wish I could fall asleep again. At least, I could gain 1-2 hours. I'm wondering what tomorrow will bring?** *SOS* . . . *same ole shit*!

12. It is 10pm count time. My heart keeps skipping beats irregularly. Sometimes, it goes into rapid fibrillation, like a vibration. It stings with each deep breath. It has been my concern for weeks now. It is said that stress is the number one killer. Maybe, these are the tell tale signs. How could this be even as I enjoy being in the best physical shape of my life? *Please God . . . I don't want to die here. Give me the honor and opportunity to love my wife, so she may feel the beauty of my soul . . . before I leave this earth*! I wish she could just acknowledge that I love her so much.

Tuesday Nov. 2nd, 2004

1. **It is my birthday**. I have already hummed "Happy Birthday" to myself. It was a Tuesday morning about this same time (7 am) in 1965 that I was born to two very proud parents and five jealous siblings. *Even if they didn't know it yet.* I was told I had been one of those *unexpected* and of course, *pleasant surprises.* "But of course". Well . . . it's 39 years later on the same Tuesday at 7 am. Only now, I'm lying awake in my steel frame bunk upon a fully torn, rock hard, mattress and . . . *I am in jail today.*

2. I can recall so many thoughtless decisions, which deviated me from the right path. **How could only a few key decisions create so many unwanted consequences**? I can tell you the specific morning of the exact place and year when the most significant change in my life occurred. I was only 11 years old. An age of lost innocence. It would take an entirely new book to tell you. Maybe you'll see it in my next one eh?

3. Right now, I'm staring outside at the soggy ground. It has not stopped raining for two days. I resolved to stay in bed this morning and reflect on 39 years gone by. My back failed me last night. My nerves are pinched. I am at the threshold of unbearable pain. I have basically been bed-ridden. I can find relief only as I lay on my stomach. It hurts to sit, stand, or even, just to move about. To write, would mean to "grin and bear it" with all the pain. *Just as I'm doing now.*

4. It is later. My bunk has been called for mail call. It is an unexpected and warm surprise. New books from my father; *Spanish Learning, Almanac 2005, and a novel.* My life has soared to eagle status. I cannot remember a day, even through childhood, that I have ever been so overwhelmed with joy to open my presents, even if they are being delivered in a plain, brown, shipping box. My father has remembered, and the timing is perfect. *Thank you Dad*! I will never forget my 39th birthday in jail today. Today, I will write my mother and welcome her home from one of her many trips. Today, I will also write my father and thank him for an unforgettable birthday. It is bitter sweet.

5. She also wrote me today. It is a birthday card from my son. I cannot hold back the tears as I drown myself in the verses of the song she has sent. It is from the song

True Colors. She has underlined the verse that says . . . *She'll be there for me.* My heart has been saved . . . again. She says she'll be there for me when I get out. I filled myself with her love when it arrived. And then later, I cursed her for waiting so long to write me. I can't help but wonder why it took so long. Maybe it's best I just settle for being accepted again. Maybe, It's time I just stop asking questions.

6.   Tonight, during my light workout, I did the stupidest thing. I twisted my back while sitting down at the edge of the bunk. I turned without pivoting. I have pinched my nerves hard . . . again! Now, my back is warped. The nerves sting and are pinching so terribly bad. I am unable to walk properly because the nerves are pinching against my spine. I have to struggle to make it up to the top bunk. Getting down off the bunk is much worse! This will delay my fitness goals. It will go on to last five more days. **Today is my birthday and I am in jail today.**

Wednesday Nov. 3rd, 2004

1. A struggle of wits has broken out between my "cellie" and I, regarding cleaning duties. He "called me out" and I stood firm (but crooked because of my back). I know I am the better fighter and I know I could put him down if needed. I also know that I made the right decision not to fight. I'm glad I did. I would have *instantly* regretted hitting him. He is my friend. Besides, it turns out that the guards were hiding around the corner, and were waiting to see how it was going to play itself out. We got through the argument without actually bare-knuckle fighting. That's pretty rare in these parts. I cannot imagine being put in the basement, isolated with no a/c for weeks at a time. I will continue to enjoy the privileges of my window view bunk under the sun. The incident did break a bond between us right up until the next Friday. On that night, he will cook others and myself a huge birthday pizza burrito: Best jailhouse dinner a man could ask for. *Thanks Joey!* I get to keep my bunk, and the game to rule that corner continues for 29 more days . . . *Almost!*

2. The weather is getting cooler as the fall season draws closer. The seasons are changing, as so am I. What will be the resulting outcome? I cannot begin to predict the right ending to a fresh start. So many scenarios criss-cross my scattered mind. I do know this: Not one of my hierarchies of immediate needs will be independently accessible upon my release. In other words, I will be completely dependent on someone in this world for the most simplest and basic needs; food, water, shelter, and clothes.

3. *Think about this*. **The path of the orbits of our galaxies can be predicted for hundreds of years to come. The ebb of the tides in every ocean can be measured before their time. And . . . life, in general, can be a series of predictions and calculations based on your ability to control your environment. But I cannot tell you what will happen, where I will go, or whom I will see, one second after leaving these prison walls.** I will be two hundred miles or so from any living relative, except for her. And of course, she has become too cowardly to even break off a clue of her intentions. I do, however, receive the occasional lie of . . . *being there for me.* For now, I'll keep reading those letters and pretend she really does care. I have become lost again and I'm having trouble finding that damn password for relief. Is there no end?

Thursday Nov. 4ᵗʰ, 2004

1.　*"39 Bunk"* has been sitting on his bed most of the day waiting to get jumped by some of the other inmates. He had left outstanding debts in the other dorm for borrowing food and mailing supplies. In here, it's all connected. We all have to answer to the entire organization of gang affiliates, no matter what section of where you reside. *Screw someone over in one place and you can bet, they'll be collecting in another place just down the hall.* I had recently exchanged disrespectful words with one gang member and insulted the little punk to the point of embarrassment Knowing full well that I could squash this kid and knock him into next week, I still had to work it out and smooth things over with him in order *not* to have the entire gang after me. They are spread out throughout the entire complex in different dorms. Most of these guys like and respect my stability and tone of character for the way I help inmates with their reading and/or writing. But I can tell you, if *I didn't work that conflict out, I would not have lasted one day in the rec yard during my workout session.* The boy is a good kid, but he tends to take advantage of being a part of the stronger entity of force by being a part the gang. That's the price we pay for "running solo", and that's the advantage of being part of the colors, signs, or whatever, while in a gang.

2.　Anyway, whenever this guy on *"39 bunk"* wasn't sitting up on his bunk, he was standing in the corner doing some shadow boxing, and trying to convince everybody he could fight off all his collectors. The tough guys just let him sweat it out for a while. At night, he tossed and turned continuously. His eyes were straining to both sides for the oncoming attack. I'm sure he wishes his eyes could move independently of each other. Just as he was about to be *raged* upon, he spilled his guts to the sergeant, and by the grace of God, this guard allowed him to be transferred. But knowing it wouldn't help, he attacked a "bitch" inmate and was immediately sent to isolation. He did it on purpose to protect himself from inmates in the other dorms. He had better stay there if he wants to live. I never saw him again. I guess I'll never get my stamp back from him either.

3.　My days are counting down toward the last month of incarceration. Most days are spent in my bunk under the warmth of the sunlight streaming through the cages. I read, write, and sleep. My workouts have been halted because of my back. I have to rest, or the swelling will never go down. I know that if it gets worse, I will have to seek medical attention, and that would result in being transferred back up north to the *hellish summer retreat*! Home of the dreaded "K" block. *Not a chance!* I'll puncture a lung and take a ride to the County Hospital before I return to that God-forsaken place.

4. I just want to go somewhere and write this book. I want to finish what I've started in peace and quiet. But that would make for boring reading? My most passionate feelings within this period have come from the panic and pain within my life. The fear inside creates inspirations to seek out many new outlooks on life that I have not yet considered. I am finding new ways of looking at old problems . . . and the solutions are much more productive. Many times, I try to just *"think and stare"* my life into an ideal conclusion. That never works though.

5. I'm longing for a place of peace to finish writing about this unforgettable nightmare. It has lasted much longer than the calendar recollects. I have re-discovered my passion for writing. I have also lived the worst fears of panic. It brings forth with it, questions, answers, revelations, and evolutions. But most of all, *writing has enabled me to pass the endless timetable of boredom.* It guides me in my quest to escape the suction that swallows so many down the drain. **I will never forget my history of suffering in this place. It will always be my reminder of *where I never want to be again*!** I'm ready to go home. I truly need to go somewhere by myself when I get out. I will never allow any woman to control me the way this ordeal has in the past. I need to live by myself for a very long time. I need to fellowship with other members of a church or some other organization. I will pray for the support of staying sober and responsible to myself. *I need to find my son Nicholas!*

6. **What I desire is to be loved by someone. I crave the softness of human touch, rather than the bone-crushing feel of bare knuckle fighting. I want to feel the arms of a woman around me, holding me tight and pressing her lips up against mine. I want to feel the moisture of her tongue in my mouth and the scent from her breath through my nostrils. I want to feel the heat, and taste the sweet, sweat of making love *to the one I love*.**

7. I miss my freedom. I miss the money. I miss the ability of making choices of where, or when, I want to go. I miss the Florida trips to see Nick and the Lake Tahoe trips to see my buddy Carlos. I want to visit my sister in Boston and party in Las Vegas. I miss having my bankcard. *I want it all back.*

8. **Past and Future . . . past and future**. My thoughts remain to be in the past and future throughout the day and night. I hate being in the present. I simply want to break free from the present. Hopefully, I will eventually reach a present time that won't bring with it, the same worries about the past and future. I want to end these worries about being able to walk away, end my grieving, being alone, and being able to move on without being lonely.

9. How will I establish my courage and re-generate my confidence? I've been weeping under covert conditions. I hide it well now. What I need is an uninhibited period of unrestrained crying aloud. A bawling so intense, it will leave me dehydrated. I have held it back for 5 months and it is becoming hard to stop the agony of this life gone by, from busting down the gates of remorse and pity any longer. How's that for feeling sorry for myself?

10. **I weep for all that I have given up by coming to jail. I couldn't care less what the conditions are any more. I have become hardened and callus to whatever is thrown my way. I just want to be near family. I'm tired of being alone among so many.**

Friday Nov. 5th, 2004

1. I'm waking up this morning to the perfect rays of sunlight in my face. It is warming my insides and giving me the same uninhibited, positive, outlook for the day. But even this euphoria can be forgotten within moments of waking from the nauseating sounds of the screaming guards. Sometimes, on good days, the serenity of calmness can last for hours before being rubbed out. But those days are few and far between.

2. Today is starting good. My back pain is easing a bit and I am actually able to get out of bed without severely stabbing my nerves. Walking is still much trouble. I have been watching what I think is the Red Planet next to the moon, and another bright star next to that for the past couple of days. I can see them outside my window on the horizon in the wee hours of the pre-morning, black sky. Now the sun has come up and I'm in the wake of reality again.

3. I'm thinking about being on the seawall in Galveston enjoying romance, fun, and laughter. But instead, I am caged behind these walls of imprisonment. I'm looking out the windows to the clouds. They are large and billowing upward toward the skies. There is so much light outside from the sun, but still, I remain in the darkness of my memories. I am reminding myself of that fateful night in Galveston; the transfer to County jails, the filthy conditions, the pain, the discomfort, the fights, the scorching heat, the blisters, boils, and bites. The summer and fall have come and gone. It has been a nightmarish living hell on earth. *Never to be forgotten . . . always to be avoided*!

4. I miss not having the weekends with my sons. I'm thinking about my wife being with someone else while I remain to be in prison. We should all be together. But we're not! Now, I'm getting angry and I'm sliding into agitation without pads to buffer the skid. So, I begin to think about everything else of nothing. I'm thinking about the guards; the physical and verbal abuse we put up with from the worst of the walking scum of the earth. I look beyond the unsightly characteristics of them and realize, very few of them could ever endure what they so easily dish out to us inmates. I know they could never eat one of their own servings of hatred. I have heard stories of how occasionally a guard would be pumping gas at a station and

an ex-inmate from prison would recognize them. The guard would get their face kicked in or their ribs broken. I can hear their pleas for mercy now! *"Please . . . please, I was just doing my job"* or *"but I've got a family to feed"*. These chicken-shit responses usually are responded to with a more severe ass whipping. It's good to hear of this retribution to the guards so they can be reminded of their actions. In here, we are never able to dispute the abuse of the guards physically without having new charges brought against us. We cannot even defend ourselves from the onslaught without being charged with a crime in return. Out in the free world though, it's *hit em back, and hit em hard*! Then . . . just walk away.

5.   Most guards live with one eye looking back over their shoulder. It is easy to predict the state of mind of many of the guards if they were to be discovered in the free world by an aggressive inmate. They wouldn't stand a chance of talking their own way out of such a brutal beating. I think of the guards slithering back into the ground after each shift. And there, they wait, until it is time to return back to the feeding ground of hatred and anger toward inmates. Their work is an excuse to vent all of their own real world inadequacies on us. Whatever they lack in their own lives, eats away at their insides while they are inside, here with us. They sit and wait for the shift to end just the same way we do. They sit and many times, do nothing. They are promoted and ranked on their ability to write-up, control, and punish inmates. So the norm is to create tension in order to find conflicts and inevitably, get noticed for being a "hard-ass" They go to great lengths to spit that scum from the gutters in the center of their face.

6.   **Occasionally, a responsible and respectful guard would enter the shift: One who has enough self worth in his own life. One that can maintain an obedient audience based entirely on the respect that they, themselves, give the inmates. This is when the most cooperation exists between guards and inmates. This is true based entirely on my experience. This is a time when the recognition of rules, regulation, policies, and procedures are followed enthusiastically, and without conflict. Both sides have a common interest: It's called *harmony*.**

7.   I can tell in an instant, the guards whom are straight forward and real. They command presence and they do their job of keeping order and peace as much as possible. I know this is a monumental task given the circumstances. Here, as in all prisons, there are inmates that will never reform and will always seek to destroy anything good within their reach. They are animals and will be reckoned with accordingly. They will continue to inflict their rage upon other inmates and guards whenever possible. This is the destruction of everybody's day . . . including the guards. Thus, it's no wonder why they become so bitter. I applause the few that are able to maintain their own self-worth as an individual. If they are fair minded and give respect . . . give it back.

8.   Here, however, the stress and strain of the day comes directly from the intolerance of ego-minded, bitter guards. They yell, scream, threaten, and create tension with such unnecessary aggression. Most of them belong here as inmates.

9.   My back continues to feel a little better as the day progresses. I'm hoping to start back up on some good intensive workouts. It is time to step up the pace for this last month. It's time to bounce back from the injured list. I will remain cautious. I should write Ohio again. I need that job.

10.   Friday's mail call. She knows where I am, but has chosen to loose me in here among the lost. She has created so much suspicion, mistrust, disappointment, and hatred, from all of her abandonment, lies, and inconsistencies. Once again, I am without promised mail. I guess I should forgive this lame excuse the way I have with all the other lies. I should really be thankful to her for leaving me in here to rot during my darkest hours . . . I means days . . . I mean months . . . It has become a time of complete exposure to my soul. And I have risen from the ranks. And now, finally, after 39 years, I find out what it means to be alone in the physical world. I have been stripped of all dignity and humility. Time has stood still for me in here. I'm beginning to believe it has stopped for me *out there too* . . . along time ago.

11.   In this facility, inmates are allowed one 5-minute phone call every thirty days . . . that's one phone call, once a month! Too bad if nobody answers. *Get back to your cell.* My mother tells me on the phone tonight that my wife has probably moved on without me. I'm thinking my mother knows something definite that I don't. Or maybe it's something that I still refuse to believe. For my wife, being free and single has become a whirlwind of games, fun, and power plays. I should relieve myself of this burden

12.   I was promised a visit from my wife tomorrow. It is anticipated, yet dreaded. To fare the inevitable: I will be abandoned. The outlook is smothered in grievance and disappointment. My heart is discontent with no relief in sight. As long as I remain to be dependent on her for love, I will always be left waiting for something that has not been fulfilled, *even after all this time!* It has alerted me to the bigger things to come.

13.   I'm thinking about the title of my next book. It will bring so much pleasure to my senses to reflect back on all the intimate encounters during my life, it is a much-needed change to bring happiness to my forgotten life.

14.   **It's Friday night; I wish I had answers to the burning questions of my future. I continuously formulate the infinite combinations of all the ways this ending will begin. Together, you as my reader, and I will discover for ourselves how these events will play out. I hope my journey doesn't take me to any more places that *I don't want to be*, but if it does, you'll be right there with me. If you want to take the time to come with me, I'll take the time to keep talking you through it. And together we'll make it. *What ever it takes*!**

15.   My "cellies" are throwing me a small, yet meaningful, birthday party. When I returned from my phone call, they were waiting with an awesome spread. It is the best pizza burrito I've ever sampled: It was made from noodle soup, chili, tuna, jalapenos, and various sauces. I am drinking my first soda in the last four and a half months. This is a most excellent experience for my buddies and I. I'm sure Joey

did it to renew his promise from a week ago. I too, will keep my promise to give him my lock and shower slippers when I leave: My release date is a month before his. Both ends are secure. Joey is a good man of his word. He has maintained his integrity in a world among liars and deceit. It maintains a bond between us. It's all part of the inmate trading post.

16. Tomorrow seems like an eternity away. I cannot grieve anymore, no matter what the outcome. Instead, I will attempt to maintain composure and confidence. I guess I really don't have a choice of incorrect behavior in here among the guards. I must remember that whatever happens, the sun will shine tomorrow, no matter how cloudy it gets. I am quiet now . . . here among the "brick house talk". Who's got what? When can I get it? And how do you want it? **I am longing for real conversations with people who aren't willing to cut my throat for my last tuna package.** Good night!

Saturday Nov.6th, 2004

1. My temperature is exploding into a blitz of fiery hatred. I never want to feel this way again. I can never let her do this to me again. Not even one more time. Has she no shame or dignity? I swear . . . I'll forever eat away at the two most critical things that count in her life. The two most important things that can last a lifetime . . . and beyond. These two things will die with her in her old age, and then, be re-born again in the stories of her grandchildren. It will be the shame that lasts for generations to come. **There are two things that count in this unforgiving world that we live: *It is our name, and our word*! There is no substitute for this in a person's life.**

2. *You are desperately trying to anger me to the point of lashing out so you can use it as an excuse to just let go without having to respond or offer any type of explanation. You will not succeed. What you can expect . . . are the worst things to come. I will spend my life taking them away from you, and in return, I will hand you back nothing but shame. This is terrible what you have done to me. Your life is filled with cowardness and shame. Hide . . . hide, I say. Hide yourself, for they will scoff at the very sight of you when I get through with your name.*

3. *I wish I could take you by the hand and lead you back into this cell to see me. You should have trusted me. Instead, you have chosen to deceive me about the things that I already know. Yes honey, I already know . . . and you know that I know. Still I remain. That's just a part of the eternal and unconditional love that I have offered you. That's what a loving friendship should mean: knowing the worst things about a person, and still being able to be their friend. And I know the worst of you. I will hold my tongue until it's time . . . until it's my time. I have learned well from the masters of patience and the authors of revenge.*

4. I am whirling in a haze of revenge, despair, pity, and sorrow. What the fuck happened today? *Again, you have denied me my right to see my son. Again, you have lied to me about visiting. Your son will know this about you. By my dying breath, I swear it! Money will never buy you proper breeding within your own family. My family and I show you luxuries you've never before enjoyed. We have given you eyes of greed for what you will always want. You will always be yellow with envy.*

5. Stress has elevated my risk of "snapping" here today. I need to be rescued. I shall attempt to replace my anger with the love of God. I'm trying to practice the philosophy and faith of knowing that *nothing's vital at stake . . . in the morning when I rise.* Think about it: Nothing that's worldly is better than the all powerful movement and motivation of God's word. This is the *Word* that supposed to bring contentment and release in the form of inner reflection. The words *"nothing vital's at stake . . . other than having God's presence with me in the morning when I awake"* is supposed to release me from all the insecurities of being accepted by others. Where will I find the strength to forgive and move on, after being led so far astray with false hope? I have been rejected, deceived, and tormented beyond human comprehension here on earth. *And it's all because I continue to live in my head with hopeless fantasies that you could be honorable in trying times. I have become the victim of your misgivings. There's a lesson learned here with all my torment:* **Pray for God to love you first . . . above everything or anyone else!**

6. *I should have left you in the other room a long time ago. Or maybe there, behind the garbage dumpster with that busboy from the restaurant, the night I got my ass kicked by the three dudes. I should have called it "quits" after the fifth drink. I might have stood half a chance. I should have left you when you left your fiancé for sex with me. Yes . . . I should have left you many times over. Instead, I am still enduring your promiscuous behavior and denying abuse. Yep . . . I'm sure you are happy to move on, now that you've used my very last muscle of effort to support you. You can attempt to justify your extramarital affairs and secret rendezvous' with false claims of abuse and anger, but none of your fabled stories hold merit for what you must do to hide your inability to manage an honest relationship. The legal consequences of your lack of compunction will haunt you for years to come. This is all too tragic. You will, one day, see what your lies have done to a man's life. I live for the day that you watch me die! I swear you will be witness to my death. Wasn't it enough for you to just come and sit with my son and I? At least you could have given me friendship, however temporary.*

7. *You lie, cheat, steal, and whore . . . and still, I love you. Who else, other than God, could love you and accept you without reservation the way I do? What about the poem you just sent me? You had underlined the part that says, "You'll be there for me". You've never been anywhere, but for yourself. And even then, only when it's convenient. This visit was supposed to be my birthday present.*

8. *I live in a place of lies. All I wanted was some truth. Is this what I will come out of prison to . . . deception? Actually, I'm already at the point of coming out to nothing and no one. It will be everywhere. I'm trying to think of one good thing to look forward to without having to struggle to maintain it. I thought my letters had encouraged you to be truthful and comfortable, even after I knew you had betrayed me.*

9. This is *betrayal* in its most abusive form. Is she so insecure, she cannot stand to face me? Does she tremble at being so overcome with shame and guilt? Or does

she feel nothing of anything? *No breeding bitch*! I am weeping uncontrollably. It is easy for my "cellies" to see why: I have prepared all week for her arrival. We have all gotten to know each other's lives. We know what moves us . . . and what shakes us up.

10. This whole God thing was supposed to help me feel good about life, now and everlasting. However, it has only brought forth endless torrential rains of pain and heartache. It has been one disappointment after another. I could spend the rest of my life . . . preparing for death. *Please don't prolong the end anymore*! This rejection has brought forth a living nightmare within the darkest hours of my life. When will I awake? **This has opened my eyes to the darkness of what suffering will mean for the rest of my days. Why should I prolong this agony any longer? Satan has come along for the ride into hell to see me crumble a torturous death of abandonment, loneliness, despair, and shame**.

11. I have prepared so much for you today; the poems, my son's portrait, my pressed clothes, all of it! It was supposed to be a date, but once again, and for the last time, it has become a disruption to my productive life. You will never understand the patience and prudence that has come to be a part of my life. It is a patient love and a longing heart. I have the belief that we were to be a family-even if it is an exception to the rule! I need a private moment to bring a cleansing to my soul. That, and a good workout to sweat my pathetic, pitiful, and lifeless body, back into shape.

12. Here's the irony of it: I'm working out for the health of it, knowing full well, *I'd rather be dead*. I cannot escape this wish. I don't even want to. There are no more pleasures in my life. Since finding God, it seems that I have experienced more self-destruction and inner turmoil than before. Maybe, He's still cleaning out the "attic" of all my skeletons and vices. *It's causing a big ruckus upstairs in my head!*

13. She keeps telling me to stay with God, but continues to lie to me about us staying together. She keeps telling me that we are family and she'll be there for me, but I can't see her. And it has been way too long since I have heard from her. She is raping me of my dignity and destroying my self-esteem. Over the years, and especially now, I have put everything of my soul into this relationship, only to be discarded by her for lust, greed, and false security.

14. *My tongue remains silent as the tidal wave of God's wrath comes down upon you. Eternity will wreak havoc for you and your family. Your pleas for mercy will never cease to evade you. I have prepared everything for this day, from nothing. I thought this was cherished and wanted by you. I made something worthwhile from nothingness and now, it's gone back to just that . . . nothing! I have slipped back into darkness. This is terrible for me to feel this way. Tell me, where do all of these angry, hateful, and constant revengeful acts come from? Why do you keep spreading lies to others, and to me? Why do you insist on speaking more lies when all you have to do is walk away? Is it necessary to keep me hanging on a string as your puppet?*

15.   **I can't breathe. I can't breathe. It's so hard to breathe now. Too many tears. I'm choking on the salt of my tears. I'm drowning, spitting, and gasping for air, but I can't breathe. I'm feeling this . . . here . . . now! I need a deep breath, but it won't come to me. I'm suffocating in it. I'm suffocating in it. It hurts. It really hurts so badly. I'm massaging my heart. It hurts. Will it stop? What will I think of last? What will I think of next? Is it her? No, it will be me! I'm not catching my breath. Where is it gone to? My chest stings. I am struggling to breathe. My lungs will not inflate. I can't breathe! I wish it would stop. Please God . . . make it stop. I don't want to feel this. I don't want to breathe . . . anymore. What will I see last? Will it be you? Will it be me? Please . . . please help me in my dying day. Take this pain away. Why am I still breathing? I'm trying to pass out. My eyes can't see. It is blurry. Hurry . . . blot it out! Do it! Do it now . . . erase this blindness. My brain is exploding! Feel this . . . hold my hand . . . I'm slipping, but I won't fall. I can't. Something won't let me. But it hurts inside. Let it go . . . please let this go. I'm so exhausted.** It's over now. I failed again. *I think the noose is too loose.* And what the hell was stopping my fall? I'll try again tomorrow. I wonder if she'll love me after watching me die.

16.   I will never rid myself of these feelings for I can never escape from myself, but only through deliverance. I want to permanently vacation in hell knowing it will be less torturous than this life. I don't believe a self-inflicted death is a cowardly thing to do anymore. It takes a lot of nerves (and courage) to succumb oneself to death; to know that life will continue without me to clutter it all up anymore. I'm just one less person for her to fuck over. I don't want to relieve this pain anymore. *It's the worst kind of "groundhog day" . . . over, and over, and all over again.* My best move here is to try to release her of my agony. My final step. She wants me out of her life and dead to her memory. So it should be done. She should be proud knowing she's driven me to death's doorstep. I will let her enjoy a front row seat. But first . . . I will inflict a humiliation for which there will be no escape. Far worse that what she has inflicted upon me. I will bring forth a life of shame and deceit for all to see. One that will continue for generations to come. And she won't even see it coming. I'll give her until tomorrow.

Sun. Nov. 7th, 2004

1. The door opened and the C.O. called *"45 Bunk"*. I was told my bunk was called three times before it reached upstairs. Even after confirmation it was for me, I was still in disbelief. It was already 11a.m. so knew it would probably be my dad, but deep down inside my hopeless, empty, shell, I prayed it would be her instead.

2. After going down stairs and stripping for check-in, I ventured out into the visitation room. It is nothing more than a garage to transport inmates to and from the jail. It is noisy and crowded. I looked for anyone familiar, but saw no one. Then, I heard the faint sound of my voice. It immediately brought forth a renewed sense of hope and humility. I don't even know how to act now. All my anger and volatile intents subsided as she hugged me with eagerness. Her lips planted firmly and passionately upon mine. We melted in each other's arms. We stood there holding each other tightly. All the while, we whispered wonderful expressions of love to each other. The guards practically had to tear us apart. She loves me; *I know so.* She wants me; *she says so.* She needs me; *I hope so.* We've come back to each other and I'm willing to do anything to keep her.

3. We sat closely to each other, holding hands and staring into each other's eyes. We made plans together; husband and wife plans. I'm so alive. I can literally feel my 5 O'clock shadow growing I'm so happy. *My blood tastes sweet for my heart has been dipped in honey.* I'm so in love again! Just hours ago, I'm laying in my bunk beckoning with God to answer my prayers. I am asking Him to let her come back into my life. Seconds, minutes, hours, days, and weeks, of praying for God to see into her heart, and caress it into compassion for this love lost. To be close, to listen, talk, and laugh. *Is it that God's prayers never fail, no matter how much doubt I may harbor?* **God's prayers** *are always answered in time. It's just that it comes on God's time . . . not mine. God has a funny way of showing His love to those that pray.* **It all comes in time. Be patient. I've got to learn to trust that patience in waiting for prayers to be answered.**

4. She looks delicious! Dressed up in new clothes. Her hair long, flowing, and silky, is beautiful. I am drowning in it. My tongue has spilled out across the table. We talked about love, patience, and our future happiness. *She swears to me that she has been*

faithful and will be waiting for me when I walk out those prison doors. At that time, it didn't even matter to me. I just wanted her back in my life. She says she never left. No one can imagine how wonderful it is to talk and laugh with her. She has brought forth much hope for us. I know there are issues to work through on both sides, but when we are together, nothing else matters. We immediately picked up on conversations in a way that said, "We never missed a beat". We hadn't lost that connection. Or at least I thought. Once again, the feeling of euphoria has blinded my sense of instinct and sense of realism.

5.   We began to talk about my options when I got out. Some of the options required me leaving for a while to generate income and then re-establish myself. She kept on telling me to take them and go. She kept suggesting to me that it would be best to leave and do this, rather than just come home and work at home. Was she pushing me away? Is there something . . . or someone there I'm not supposed to see? Why am I being asked to take other options over her? If she wasn't being faithful and wanted no more of me, why doesn't she just tell me and leave. Why doesn't she just tell me to quit trying and send me on my own path? If I have to, I will leave this woman that I love so much and go my own as a brokenhearted man. *But I'm taking this love with me, and she can't have it back. I will need it to survive what little life I have left. And then I will die. I'm tired of the ulterior motives behind this relationship.* She kept on drilling me about my options, telling me to take them. I wanted to trust her, believe her, and be happy with her. I love her and I want to feel loved by her. I shouldn't have to fight at every encounter to sustain her faith. What is she hanging on to? What is going to make her happy? I'm tired of being threatened with abandonment each time I have a difference of opinion with her.

Mon. Nov. 8th, 2004

1. I cannot displace all this anger and despair I'm feeling inside. My seams are going to burst into a fiery ending of a violent death. My thoughts are locked on the constant equating of circumstances and scenarios.
2. I received my mother's mail today. She has come back from her vacation tired, but happy. **She reminds me of the hardest decisions yet to come. They are the ones that I have the responsibility of making back in the free world. She reminds me that the hardest decisions would be the most rewarding ones. She has also reminded me that some of the easiest decisions will be the most damaging.** The ones that will send me back here.
3. What will I do?
4. How will I be received?
5. Where will I live?
6. When will I recover from my ordeal?
7. How will I support my livelihood?
8. Why did all have to happen?
9. I have endless questions of infinite possibilities. Not one of them had a finality of surety. Not one . . . except that God is my savior, and all I had to do was believe. I'm trying, By God . . . *I'm trying.* Even amidst the mystery of his power, and all the infinitesimal of his love, I struggle to maintain my faith in the almighty. I'm praying that he will guide me back to a point of prosperity in my life

Tues. Nov. 9th, 2004

1. I don't even hold a card in my hand. How can I play this hand when no cards are even being dealt to me? I'm constantly trying to arrange her day in my head. All of her lunches, dinners, and dates with friends and lovers. I am a prisoner, and she is the social hour. Of all the money spent on her, she has only once returned money to me in here. It was the $25 dollars that was mine anyway. If she knew what $5 dollars could have bought; soups for three weeks. It never came to be. I should never assume it would happen in the future either. Surely, she could never deviate from her own spending . . . ever!

2. My release. Where will I go? I cannot spend what I don't have. I think I should go it alone. I think it's going to get worse before it gets any better. How can I be quiet and absent about the abandonment of our marriage? I know everybody has been bombarding her about a new life without me. Maybe, we aren't capable of healing together. Maybe, it is better to go separate ways.

3. I know if I leave, I would stay gone and never come back. I would, as I always have, continue to fit in wherever I could. I tell you what I really need . . . sex, good hard-core sex! She keeps on talking about the loyalty of her friends of not messing with her man. I think of all the days and nights she didn't show up and her friends did. If I told her the truth about her friends, her head would swell. So many times, I left with someone right in front of her friends. So many times I left with her friends! The clubs, houses, rooftops, pools, and the seawall. Why hadn't any of them told her? I'm still trying to figure that one out. It's like a brown paper bag being delivered to the doorstep. Nobody's claiming it, somebody always wants it, and everybody's doing it, but nobody's talking about it!

4. I wish she hadn't lied to me about sending that letter. It's the same letter she keeps telling me she sent. But she hasn't. It only takes 2 days to arrive. How long has it been? Once again, I have been brushed off. She comes to reel me in and enthrall me with laughter and passion. She interrogates me for my past and my intentions, and then leaves me in wonderment of what the fuck just gave way; my soul, my trust, my friendship, and fellowship, and of course, my love. *How easy has it become for you to lie without a remnant of consideration for my genuine feelings.* I hate these

feeling that I have for her. There is too much contempt in my heart. But I know all she has to say is, *"stay"* and I will. Passion; *man's greatest incentive.*

5. I'm so confused of her intentions. I need guidance. **What does God want me to do? Even after meditating and praying for hours, days, weeks, and months, I'm still unsure. What does He really want me to do? Nothing has been specifically addressed to me. How will I know if I'm doing the right thing? I have searched inward, time and time again. All of my imagined scenarios end in tragedy. A life lost! A love gone. I cry in my sleep and weep within my soul constantly.**

6. *I am in here alone within my soul, among the liars, deceivers, cheaters, druggies, drunks, thieves, and all other predators of sin. I'm trying to convince myself this is not where I belong. But still I'm here . . . now, on my knees, scrubbing the shit stained floors of this filthy dorm. Is this how I am to rejoice my cherished well being? I have been robbed of my future. You haven't been here for me, except within the context of lies and deception. Your life is different now and you can't even come to terms with having to answer to a husband or any type of commitment with me. I have no recollection of truth in your heart anymore. You will have to create new memories of truth and integrity for me to conjure up a shred of belief in you. I'm not sure you are capable. I hurt so badly about this now. You've said over and over that when I come out, you would be there to help me. But that has been traded for lunches, dinners, clubbing, and new clothes. I remember spending everything on us. I spent every penny I had on us for new decorations, clothes, dinners, clubs, and even whores for your pleasure. The traveling, the SUV's the homes . . . all of it was for you. I pounded the pavement for six years all so you could be comfortable. And now that I've given you the education you need, you swing from the branches to new opportunities. You are the monkey that swings from one branch to another but never letting go of one branch until its grasp is firm upon the next one. And now I have nothing, and that's exactly what I've gotten from you. Can I ever come to believe that you will actually help me?* I had to keep my anger at a minimum and be careful not to lash out. I knew I had to get my clothes and my driver's license, and other particulars. I weep openly now, for a love and a life that I'll never get to keep. My body is a lifeless mass of flesh without her. I have been dead too long. I'm going back to the only place I can now. She should know my love is infinite because of the things I know she has done to hurt our relationship. But still, I love her.

7. *I wanted to win you over to show you that this much love actually exists in a person. I have prayed you could return this love. Instead, you've given me a bitter, sour, taste of unwanted reality: the realization that you will do anything to maintain all lifelines leading to your success, and that you have no particular care how other people's lives are being disrupted in the process. How can I ever trust you to support me for my next two years when in fact, you lie about every thing now? I honestly thought that you missed me and am mourning for my life. I realize now, this mind set is foolish. It is evident now after talking to you, you've been living and loving the single life. And all this while you've been leading me on to believe*

you are preparing our future in the free world. You've offered to be there for me the way I've been completely there for you, but you have not fulfilled any of your lies of deceit.

8. *As I scrub the toilets, sinks, and showers (a daily chore), I ask myself . . . what the hell are you doing right now? I am in an endless loop with thoughts of what you are going to do to deceive me next. I am looking down a septic tank sewer hole scrubbing shit. Meanwhile, you're out sipping drinks and talking shit to whoever has to listen. You've been allowing yourself to be taken in by whoever compliments you. Your self worth runs only as deep as that make-up needed to hide your true colors . . . and it appears to be taupe in color. You will spend the rest of your life applying a new face every time you find someone else willing to give you the approval necessary to boost your low self-esteem. You are chained and bound by the opinions of others. It profiles the impression that you have of yourself. It is what matters most to you. I know you can never be faithful to any one person. It's not in your nature. You kept on telling me that it was your sister who was molested by your grandfather, but I think it was you. You are constantly seeking others approval and acceptance through your deviant sexual promiscuity. Can you really tell me I'm wrong? I wish you could've trusted how understanding I can be. But you can't! You've never loved like I have. How come you couldn't give me the chance to show you? Everybody in your past has cheated on you, so you believe faithfulness is not possible. The first step of being there for your husband is showing up. Now you're using the fact we never walked the isle as an excuse for not showing up and telling me where I stand. We have lived together for 6 years with a child, and now you refuse to acknowledge it just so you can justify your infidelity. Please just stop living this lie to me. Why can't you cleanse your soul and come back to me in truth? Will it take a tragedy? I should hope not.*

9. Here now, I'm reaching a moment of clarity. I should follow my heart and instinct and take my own advice . . . and God's too! It's time to start again. Somewhere else. Maybe back to a small town. It won't be much, but it's honest and true. I'll see to that. In regards to the lies she was spoon-feeding me, maybe it will easier to let go now. It's probably that I'll just miss the sex and not her. But the way I've come to be here, I realize the sex means nothing without a good companion. I need to break free from this spell. What to do . . . what to do.

10. It's so simple to communicate. To take but just a moment to jot a few lines every other day to allow for some hope, instead of having to wait for months just to hear lies and false claims. *I've written hundreds of pages abundant of love and prayers to you. You have never responded to my compassionate calling or questions of concerns. What you have given me is all negatively questionable.* In contrast, my parents have consistently sent me pictures of friends and family. They are considerate in their time to share and show an interest in my well being and progress.

11. *It is going to be difficult for us to be together now. It goes against your influences and mine. My family has been here for me . . . so much more than you, my wife I*

don't believe you are missing me and you have failed to show anything of the sort. How shameful this is for you. I will not share your son while you are allowing other men to be a part of your life. Your lies are transparent. This cannot take me in anymore. I must move on! I've given so much to this, and now this is how I am being repaid; lied to, stolen from, and cheated on. I thought I had earned the right to have a trusting family. **No matter how good of a provider one can be; no matter how great of a lover you are; and no matter how well you think the relationship is going, if the spouse has the weakness of falling prey to cheating, he or she will do It. There's nothing to stop it.** The only thing I can believe now is that she is lying. It is the only thing that is consistent.

12. I feel like a dog, waiting and longing for her to come by at feeding time, only to get there and throw me a hollow bone.

13. *I hope this prayer helps me . . . and you too!*

"For I know the plans I have for you" declares the Lord.
"Plans to prosper you and not to harm you,
Plans to give you hope and a future.
Then you will call upon me and come and pray to me,
And I will listen to you. You will seek me and find me
When you seek me with all your heart."
Jeremiah 29: 11-13

Wed. Nov. 10, 2004

1. I have prayed and prayed, but really never knowing what my answers will be or when they will come. I have had to rely on His timing, sometimes with extreme pain within my patience. However, He has kept me in His presence. I couldn't have survived so far without it.

2. She has not kept me close to her own presence. *You have not kept me in your presence. Instead, you have spread lies about how I have become a burden in your life. Let me make it easy for you. It is time to let go. I know you don't have what it takes to maintain a healthy, faithful relationship.* I thought that I had earned her respect but now, I dare not consider it! She is not deserving of it! She left me a long time ago, but has been too cowardly to admit it. She has driven me away. She has worked hard at it and now, has finally succeeded.

3. *It is here among the liars, cheaters, and sinners that I know this is the place where you belong. If everybody knew the truth, it would be you here down on your knees, scrubbing the shit of 50 men off the toilets. Still, I find myself strong enough to rejoice for my cherished well-being. It is here . . . you have lost me. Once again, you have found yourself in the middle of ungodly sins and worldly worthiness. So wake up and carry yourself through the day telling all your lies to those that will listen, and then slither back into the ground.*

4. Now, the message is clear. *I'm a fool for believing you anymore. This is the last disruption of my life. Save your idle, lame, excuses, for your so-called "non-existent" fuck buddies. You will never lay your hands on me again.* **A wife, with another man swimming inside of her, has the same relevance as a crack smoking whore. Both are nothing more than a brief place to unload a quick shot of immediate pleasure.** *The men you attempt to please are pulling up their pants as they open the door to scurry away into the night. Your life will not be my life. Okay, that's it. Don't waste another moment in thought about me. I say, you're free to go now. I think you've been gone along time now. I have tried to heal the hurt, but it was impossible to do by myself.* **God and I kept praying for your return, but you kept lying to us.**

Sat. Nov. 13th, 2004

1. Morning. I have conscientiously prepared for this day. I watch in elation and envy, the wives, brothers, sisters, mothers, and fathers of inmates come from all over the state to see their loved ones. I knew she wasn't coming. I wanted to avoid these ill feelings of neglect so I laid in my bunk praying and meditating on spiritual readings. I am trying to relax my body into complete calmness. It is working. I am always amazed at how calm the heart and soul can become with God's prayer. I have suffered minimum damage so far, but the day is young. Through my readings, I am discovering the desire to heal our family. To tie the bind of love, forgiveness, and trust between us.

2. I prayed God could keep her in my prayers. I prayed for her to give her soul to God, her love to me, her life to our child, and her passion to her work. I wonder if she recognizes how compassionate I have become? I wonder if she even wants it. *Please God, I selfishly ask you to bring her back into my life and family. I love her so much.* Can't she see this? I don't think I've ever wanted or needed anyone so much in my life. Except for my son, Nicholas, I've never felt the urge to be so accepted. It is consuming my every waking moment. I've wanted her since the day I met her. She, for me too. But it seems she doesn't want me anymore. I remember when she needed me. It was all about wanting back then. It seems it's different now. Since I can't be there in the immediate form, she has reached out to hold onto someone else she feels will support her. Doesn't she realize this is only temporary and I'll be released soon? Is she hoping I'll never get out? Is she hindering the help of my release to see that I *don't* get out? She must feel that for what she's done to me, I'll never get the chance to recover. But she is so wrong. **I'll be back, bigger, better, and stronger. And hell of a lot smarter too. Also, I will be much more protective of what I give or what I should expect.**

160

Sun. Nov. 14th, 2004

1. Outside is freezing. I am periodically watching them down below, huddled in small groups, patiently awaiting their names to be called for visitation with inmates. Hundreds of family members taking hours out of the day to wait in the windy, wet, and chilly air. They are standing around or sitting on the cold steel benches. Waiting . . . tending to their loved ones or contending with the rude, impatient, guard's apathetic attitudes of a day interrupted, but still, *they waited*. They wait and wait, only to be met by inconceivably ruder guards while sitting on picnic tables with loved ones in the cold chill of the morning air. But still, they come, and they come with love and support. Many never miss a weekend. They would be there all the time, *every weekend*. And they would come from far away. **They came to fellowship and give hope. They came to ask the same question that every family asks an inmate. Why does it have to be like this? Are you ready to come home and put all this behind you now? When will you break from this circle of crime and punishment? How can we help you change? What will be the replacement? Who will guide you? Will it continue to be God? How long will it last? Aren't you so tired of being sick and tired that the change will be a permanent one? Can you break free from this failure and despair!**

2. My cellie called me to the window at 3:30 pm. I knew it was to just to see someone else's spouse. I wasn't really interested but I went anyway. I looked down just as she turned toward the building. Her head was covered in a sweater hood. She wore black pants and tennis shoes. She has arrived . . . and so had I! My blood is racing through my veins at lightening speed. My son has also come to see me. He is bundled in his Russian style hat and coat. My appreciation of this absolutely, unexpected surprise visit is infinite.

3. We talked through all the emotions of love, anger, resentment, failure, longing, wanting and receiving. Forgiveness and hope was my theme for the day. Hers are words taken from my own letters. Why couldn't I have been released earlier? Through it all, she makes it very clear to me that she will wait. I am to be given the chance to make things better. To prove myself worthy of being what my endless letters have described and promised. Dedicated to make it happen, happiness is the

goal and I am the lead offensive player. The ball had finally come back to me. And now that it is in my possession, I had to score . . . and score big! She tells me she wants me to be there for her. I love what she wants.

4. *She emphasizes that she has, in fact, sent that letter from a week ago.* I wanted to believe this, but it is too far fetched now. She tells me to win her back. I keep telling myself she loves me. I will look forward to her letter tomorrow.

Mon. Nov. 15th, 2004

1. *My promised letter from her never arrived.* My mother's did. It is post marked from Friday before. Just three days ago. This can only mean the letter has not even been written. I choose to forget the truth and hang on to her lies instead. Remembering the lies of love and compassion are easier to accept than the truths of filth that ooze from her lips.

Tues. Nov. 16th, 2004

1. I'm trying to remain calm about her coming back into my life. *Or was it that my life had come back to her?* I hoped she could keep her spirits up about us. I prayed to God not to take her away from me again. I truly did not want her to forget the love we share. I miss my kids. They needed me and I wanted them close to me again. **I've come to realize something time and time again. My entire time spent in jail did not mean a thing of pain or suffering except for the time spent away from her and my son Nicholas. It has been my hellish nightmare within these prison walls, and still, the sun has not risen for me yet.** It remains to be dark in my heart at all times. However, I do not believe my recovery, if any, would have come to light in real terms if she had not abandoned me the way she has done. I don't know why she keeps hanging on loosely but won't let go. Here, I have learned to be alone. Here, I have been led astray. Here, I have to survive the outside looking in and the wantingness of needing to look to the outside for hope. Even when there is none because of the deceptive practices of those that wish to bring me down further. She has left me in the imprisonment of my soul. And from that empty, dark, hull of selfishness, sin, and abuse, I have created a God loving, health conscious, family minded, and goal-oriented person. *Hey! I think I'm becoming a pretty decent guy after all.*

2. I do know that I'll be licking the scars of this time in my life for many years to come. I wonder why she had decided to come back now, after leaving me alone for so long. How do I know she won't do it again? She wants me to concentrate on loving her the way she wants to be loved again. I can do that.

3. *Looking back on it now, God has, and still is, answering all of my prayers in matters of family, safety, health, forgiveness, and hope. Through my prayers, I have learned how wonderful the power of prayer and fellowship can mean to a broken heart and hopeless faith. It has restored great creativity to my mindset in ways of personal thinking. The fortune of being saved is priceless. Through prayer, I have crawled and scraped my way from begging for death, to finding a way to realign my life with such a powerful force, never to be doubted, even in the worst of challenging fears. It is the almighty force and presence of God's love. And it can be found in*

each one of us. All you have to do is sincerely seek . . . and you shall find. However, it's not a quick come and go. God has a distinct way of answering prayers on his own time, and it's never a moment too soon or ever too late. It's only interpreted that way if you have not yet started. Don't wait for a tragic event to turn your life upside down before finding this infinite strength to see yourself through it all. It's God's plan. Start preparing today.

4.   I'm thinking about my own personal government in terms of God, health, family, and work. Work . . . yes it's about that time to get out of here and start working again. Just a couple more weeks now. To make money, pay some bills, and save some money for the future. I'll end up paying for all these fines and warrants that have surfaced while I have been in here. If she could have just handed over all that information on customer deliveries. I don't know why she refused to aid my parents. She kept making excuses for getting them the info needed to complete those deliveries or offer refunds. Everybody began filing criminal charges against me. It was impossible to play guesswork with this while in prison. *She really must have wanted me to stay here and do more time.* It's getting that time to make things right now. My father did actually find some of those customers and gave refunds but the damage had been done at other locations.

5.   It's Tuesday night, and I'm yet to receive any mail. It takes only one day—two days top—from the Island. How very disappointing. Love continues to be blind, and I've become bruised all over from bumping into lies. Once again, as I write these words, I realize she remains to keep me in the darkness of her lies. What a fool I continue to be.

Wed. Nov. 17th, 2004

1. The first words out of her mouth had better be "*I'm sorry . . . I lied to you about sending a letter already. I meant to, but I have not sent it even after I said I did.*"

2. It has been since 11/06/04 that she said my letter was on its way. How easy the slime drips from her tongue. Even now, during her second visitation with me, she still tried to reinforce her lies. But once again, forgot to follow through. She doesn't even have to apologize anymore. It would be worthless. I don't think I'll be getting in the car with her. It looks like I won't be getting back in her life either.

3. Here, mail call is called "*suicide watch*". When the communication lines are supposed to be open between two people, the anticipation is ten fold for the letters to arrive. The letters did arrive . . . but not from her. Thank God for real family that cares enough to take the time. I knew if I sat around and waited for her letters that she had supposedly sent, I'd be dead and buried already.

4. If only the lies were gone from this abandonment. The realization of rejection in truth is far nobler to contend with, than the deception of lies while in a desolate and isolated place. This whole fucking thing has become a lie. It is the only history I know between us now.

5. Even for me now, my hand tires of precious expressions shared to someone who undoubtedly discards my outpour of love into the crack of a broken drawer. A drawer, which remains off its rollers. And now, through the narrow slit between the frame and drawer, mail goes into the darkness, where it will remain for three winter's gone by.

6. Maybe, it's finally time to fess up to what's really happening out there. We are wasting each other's time. I'm trying to hang on to a love lost. She, on the other hand, is trying to keep her hooks in me while she finds a replacement. I don't actually believe it has all been a waste of time. At least I have found the outlet of writing to pass the time here. I've definitely found out some things about others and myself. My undying efforts to bring this family together were not enough to show a promising future and a happy home. Surely, it's what I wanted. It's not what she wants.

7. This could've been accepted from the start. Instead, the mentality of lying, cheating, stealing, and deception had to accompany her departure. The act of forgiveness

has been lost in the sludge of premeditated acts of betrayal. *Tough fucking luck for me.* I should have known a woman who leaves her fiancé three months after starting her affair, would eventually do the same to me. Most likely, it will be her statistic throughout her lifetime. It took me one hour of the afternoon to seduce her after meeting her. And now what's going around has come around. Now she's doing it to me. If she only knew how long it's been going on around her now and since we met, her head would explode! No sense in telling her. It will be my silent celebration. They do walk among her. Unbelievably, they choose not to speak. I guess the friendship means something enough, not to destroy a bond . . . and a reputation. They were all as easy as her. Maybe if she didn't go around boosting of my capabilities, they never would have approached. They use to come up to me and say, "Hey, we heard about you (from her). Can we see if it's true?" *"You bet,"* I'd say . . . *"here in the club, or should we take it upstairs."* Some nights, we never made it off the couches in the lounge of the clubs.

8.   Still, with all the running around, there was much love between us. I thought we still could have showed strength in our relationship during the tough times. In the past, we endured considerable setbacks in life, career, custody, and courts. We seemed to have gotten through it all successfully. These trial and revelations bonded us in a way that nothing could come between us. Now the money's gone and she didn't think I was making it out of here, so she begins her quest to latch onto the next closest *"cash cow"*. Anything with a puise, I guess.

9.   I thought that's what love was for; to show strength and unity during times of trouble. She hasn't shown me shit. But rather, just ruthless lies aimed at severing my jugular. I've poured out my heart to her only to see my life being poured back out in heartache.

10. She always pushed the cliché that it is the little things that count. But she fails to see the big picture. She concentrates on following a script so particular, that she forgets this is about life's, *dynamic continuous.* It's not just a play-by-play act, or a word for word script. Sure, the little things count, but let's not forget about the forest that surrounds the trees eh! There are no words to describe how disappointed I am.

11. Yep, it's all been a waste of efforts to keep this together. It has been so easy for her to go on with her life, and so very difficult to give back any whatsoever time to me. I know how easy it is for her, because I remember just how easy it was for me.

12. Why does she keep telling me she'll send dollars so I can get commissary. She had come to visit the other day and loudly boasted of the way she would send money each week. She said this just as she looked over to see if others were listening to us in the visitation room. I never saw a penny and probably will never see so much as a dollar of my own money that she is spending. How cheap. How lame. Amazing . . . so much scum in one body. *Spreading lies of hope to a despairing man in a desolate place.*

13. Words will only be wasted on deaf ears now. Both of us are wrong now. One of us is right. It doesn't matter who is wrong or right. But I know whom is the snake slithering in the grass back to her hole.

14. I had remembering feeling so wonderful when she came to visit. But this, like her visits and her letters, were short-lived bursts of emotional elation. It's worse than dope: The downside is always a hard crash and burn.

15. *You have taken my love and heartfelt somber humbleness, and placed it on a shelf away from your own heart while you sample other sweets to see which is your favorite.*

16. I remember during the visit you asked me to come home and be there for you again. You asked me to wait on you, by cooking, cleaning, tending, serving, fucking, and playing daddy for your kid. I thought to myself *"what the fuck is that . . . are you asking for me to be your boy toy?"* You want me . . . you don't want this . . . where the fuck is this going? *I've been torn by your inconsistencies.* This won't do anymore! *You are riding by on a roller coaster of emotions that is preventing us from growing, trusting, planning, and resolving to bring our lives back together. It has been during these worst of recent times; the tests of love were put into play. We failed miserably! We failed to even score in this last set. And now, you have torn the ties that bind*

17. Thoughts of coming back into civilization is bringing forth burdening anxieties. I don't have any of the right answers for the questions looming over me. What to do? Where to go? I continue to pray in faith my answers will be shown to me. I know now, more jail time looms over me. She had supported the prosecution all this time with false accusations. She knows nothing of forgiveness and loyalty. *I still have not received your letter that you said was sent over two weeks ago. Now, that's not just lying . . . that's stupid lying! You are unable to even confess your own sins and deception to yourself in private. How pathetic.*

18. **I am writing a letter of my intentions. This is now the hardest letter of my life, for it releases me from the personal quest to bring this family back together**. *The lies have been easy for you to speak. The suspicions lay too deep. The inconsistencies are the only constant. Agony has consumed my heart of all that remains. The flow of love has ceased to run through my veins. The last drip has dropped. Any more acceptance of such a one sided vision of our lives has become a fantasy of the past. This letter will allow you to release yourself from this burden I have placed on your commitment to me. The one that you've been lying to me about. The one that you've been telling me you will wait for. No longer do you have to love me out of pity, and no longer will you have to weigh the circumstances of every encounter with me. Nor will I.*

19. I've been thinking about what I'll do with my life when I get out of prison. There are no answers of surety? What I'm not going to do is wait around in a new loft hoping you'll show up every three or four days. That's not going to happen. In real life terms, I can't let that happen ever again. My short vision of wisdom, tells me it would be a quick, but long, two steps back into quick sand. I would be stuck in a rut with no forward motion. I would sink into my grave if I continued to wait for such sludge to surround me. I've been living the crusade that "love conquers

DO YOU WANT TO GO TO JAIL TODAY?

all". I've been fighting off the reality of what's really going on. I have failed to act accordingly to the signs of deception existing within this forgotten relationship. It has taken away any rational sense of well being within me. I am in constant defense of her accusations as an excuse to ignore me. It is a weapon of expertise that she has perfected. She has forgotten the most important thing though, and that's to *change tactics more frequently*. She continuously uses it so much now; it's easier than reading a book to predict it. *I guess the best way to avoid it is to just stop listening. And the best way to beat it is to focus my life toward my own goals now.* Work . . . save. Work . . . save. And oh yes . . . *work and save some good money.* Lot's of it! I knew if I remained in the same industry, I could immediately start earning good money again. Over the last decade, I have spent a fortune on nothingness. This will never happen again. I must keep the strength of "*never*" in my life. There's going to be a lot of "*never again*" in my daily routine. **Never will I be so casual of the money leaving my pockets. Never will I be so insecure about not spending my last bit of money to impress someone. Never will I ever feel insecure about money I don't spend. Never will I lie to myself and think someone could love me when I have nothing left to bring to the table.**

Thurs. Nov. 18th, 2004

1. 15 days to go. What to do . . . what to do? I have become deaf for the most part. Everything is just an echo now. I know my ears need those drops, but I dread going down to the nurse in fear of being transferred back up to the North unit. The stinging and ringing in my ears is shredding my sanity. I am trying to yawn and maneuver my mouth constantly to find relief. Months and months of being exposed to yelling, and banging, and crashing of lockers in cement rooms crammed with metal bunks. I've probably lost hearing anyway, even without the ear infection.

2. I can be standing three feet in front of someone talking to me. I just keeping nodding in agreement, but never really interpreting the message. The noise has a way of deviating the sound of someone's voice coming at you. Within this noise vacuum, words become incomprehensible. There are 50 men trying to spit out their stories of lies, and words of power. The decibel levels reach concert status without the thump of the beat. It is never-ending. It never stops. I pass out in exhaustion from having to hear it pounding in my ears, and wreaking havoc on my mind.

3. I can sit in my corner bunk looking out among the scene. I can hear and observe 50 men conversing to each other in groups (or to themselves) and not understand a single word or recognize the story of one conversation because of the hardening echo bouncing continuously. It is maddening to the mind.

4. Sure, it is easy to distinguish what voice belongs to whomever, but it is impossible to decipher the words through the echoes of yelling, screaming, cursing, laughter, whining, and crashing. The blaring of the two TV's at full volume on opposite ends of the day room for 14-18 hours a day doesn't render escape from this situation. Adding to that, people arguing for the channel rights. *"Oh God, somebody turn that UPN channel off"*. And when will they tire of watching Jerry Springer?

5. I would not have believed it if somebody had described this to me. Fights and arguments for the most fucked up shows on TV. Nobody could have even tried to convince me. But it's true, and it's happening right now as you read these words. It's probably happening in every single jail system in the nation; people going deaf from noise pollution.

6. Dealing with this 24/7 for the last several months has truly taken its toll on my eardrums. Maybe it's best that I cannot hear the things I don't want to hear anymore. The noise levels will remain a constant painful reminder of the surroundings of which I have to endure and dwell within.

7. It is easy to fall into a pattern of thinking to yourself, listening to yourself, and talking to yourself. It is easy to realize a little insanity in all of us. There are those of us who will contain it, and those of us who will be controlled by it. *Makes for a splendid day in jail, don't you think!*

8. **The revolving door gives this arena an unpredictability, which never allows for a non-stressful night. There is always conflict amidst the new neighbors and the "old timers". "*Across town*" is just to close. Conversations turn into cursing grudge matches. The cursing becomes character attacks. And the attacks turn physical quickly . . . and decisively.**

9. The rain has been coming down hard for 2 days. I can see it coming down, splashing hard against the windows and down below in the puddles of the parking lot. I can see it at night reflecting against the light as streaks across the night sky. The rain keeps coming and it's all I can see. But I cannot hear it through the thick glass supported by the heavy cement walls. The rain has become my silent movie; to watch it, to see it, but not to hear it. And with the lightening, comes my blinding light show.

10. I am stopping to workout with "*the crew*"; two black fellows, a Mexican, and myself. The four of us have accomplished much in the ways of strength and endurance. Sets of 50 come easy. I can run without concern for how long or how far. *I love being in the best shape of my life.*

11. I'm thinking about these months that have come to pass. I'm thinking about how it is better and how it is worse. I have lost my wife, but gained so much more. **What I've gained is not yet clear because I've lost everything in my life. What I stand to gain now will be my new life's journey. And it *is* going to be a brand new life. One of no regretful days. Soon, it will be peaking over the horizon . . . where the skies meet the earth. But where, or when I'll get to live it as a free man, I do not know yet. It is visible, but not yet seen. It's called HOPE!**

12. I thought that friendship, love, and forgiveness, could have made an awesome difference in our lives. It is obvious that "*none of the above*" matters to her and my renewed sense of commitment means nothing. Without any dialogue from her now, I'm convinced there is too much standing between us. She has created too much history between us and for herself. Her abandonment, infidelity, and defamation, has KO'ed any chance of trusting her. No matter how hard I tried.

13. How on earth did this get so complicated so damn fast? All events have led up to a casual night gone awry. It had been the spiral that dropped off into oblivion, confusion, desolation and despair.

14. We had made each other so happy and now, she's not even able enough to apologize for a simple lie. I should have known. She looked to the left when she said she wrote me that letter so long ago. She always looks to the left when she lies.

15.	Damn, I can't wait to get laid. Maybe, that's all of it. Maybe it's just the need to be held and caressed. Maybe, anybody will do, just as always. Maybe, just to catch the eyeful glance from a woman wanting my attention would be enough to cure the lonely blues. Maybe, that's all it's going to take to cure this lost love. That very moment will cure my endless sense of rejection. I'll make sure of it!

16.	I love being in the best shape of my life!

17.	Mail call has come and gone. Still, I have received no mail from her. I did, however, receive my father's blessings. I checked the postage. It had taken a whole week to arrive. It has arrived on a day that I will receive no other mail from anybody else. I can loosen the noose from around my neck a little further today. Dad's words are firm and the message is clear. I am not alone and the family is expressing their love and concern for me from around the globe; from all corners of the family globe that is. I can feel it. *It gives hope . . .* and options.

18.	Throughout the day, I'm thinking of God's promises and His guidance in love and forgiveness. My prayers have been answered even without me knowing it yet. Those prayers that cannot be reached in faithful vision will be left for Him to decide when the time is right. I've decided to believe in Him always and without fail in all aspects of my life. To rejoice Him always and even more so when in troubled times. That's when the faith in his protection matters most.

19.	This is not the punishment of God that has brought me to this hellish venue. This is Satan and the evil forces surrounding his agenda that are trying to chip away at my faith. I have no time for this tonight. I cannot falter in my consistencies of a belief, which allows for infinite love and acceptance.

20.	**In my life, all my emotional pain has come from the desire to be loved and accepted by women. And I've gone way out of my way to see that it happens. Sex, spending, and sacrifices . . . all at my own expense. So today, and for all my life continuous, all my glory will continue to thrive in the arms of the faith of God. This is what it has come to in my pathetic life; while the world can turn it's back on me in every possible aspect of life, I am to know that I will remain to be fully pleasing and fully accepted by God.**

Fri. Nov. 19, 2004

1. I am laying in the bunk this morning watching the watching the sun come up over the horizon. I can calculate exactly where it will become visible as its rays peak through the early morning clouds: A new canvass painted fresh daily, just for me. All to remind me of the miracle of the day to come. Orange ribbons of clouds streak the sky in brilliant radiance. It never lasts long enough. I am watching the first commercial airliners rising into the sky, far off in the distance. Their metal hulls are reflecting like mirrors from the sun's rays. It's hard to imagine, while in here, there is actually life going on in that metal tube. People snacking, drinking coffee, talking, laughing, working, and . . . living!

2. The birds are busy this morning. I can see them far away and right up close. All movement from them ventures north across my window. Some stop on the wires, others under the warm lights. All the time, chit chatting along the way. It seems that they, like the school buses on the highway, are headed for class.

3. I remember she and I used to take my son, Nicholas, to school every morning. I wonder if we'll ever get to take the other one to school together. Will we ever sit in his class together, or take pictures, or eat lunch together? If I could only trust her, I could tell her something.

4. The sky looks warm today. The sun will shine. This is the first day, in many pasts that I did not get up to work out today. *I should have gotten up today, but I didn't.* And now I'm going to regret it for the next thirteen days. Right up until my release.

5. Still, there is no mail today. My letter of departure must have fit her schedule well. It fits perfectly well into her cowardly scheme of abandonment. I have given her the easy way out. And myself!

Sat. Nov. 20th, 2004

1. It's been raining all day. I know she's not coming today. I've slept until dinner and now I've awoken to the Saturday night blues. I know I'd rather be sitting in my living room watching my son play with his toys. Maybe stroking my wife's hair and reading a book. To be snug up beside her. A simple night once taken for granted is now so very longed for. Now, it is far away . . . *so far away*.

2. What does God want from me? Did He put me here, or was it the devil? I can't remember. I can't stand this living in suspicion any longer. It is such a waste of time and space in my head. These suspicions (however true) are living rent free in my head and I can't eliminate the torture of it all.

3. I'm so tired of the count calls. *"On your bunk"* is relentlessly being yelled at us each time it is count call. We sit for hours sometimes, waiting for human inventory to be counted. This is done six to eight times a day.

4. I worked out after dinner. I slept most of the night to escape the reality of the present questions, which burned my mind into a scorching fire of anger.

5. Where is she tonight? *Dressed up, sexed out, and lying her marriage away in the silky sensations of a chocolate martini.* Two is all it takes for her to grab onto whatever has a pulse and a dick. Bitch, whore, lezzy, slut, hooker . . . babe.

Wed. Nov. 24th, 2004

1. Today is going to be a really bad day. Today, my routine, boredom, and familiar surrounding are going to be uprooted and rotated into a spiral heading straight for the dungeons of a furnace that has no escape. Never in my life did I believe that this mousetrap could turn so nasty so close to my release. It's about to go beyond the scope of what I think is punishment.

2. It's 5 pm. And they've just called me out to the sergeant's office. I never had a clue about the seriousness of its nature. I have been charged with an "*out of place*" case. No big deal. This will be my first "*case*" against me since arriving in this unit. I read the report. It simply states that I was in one place, instead of another during a role call.

3. This is a charge from the other day when I got caught lying on my rented bunk. I thought the restrictions were going to be probated, and I was just getting a warning. But this is prison and there is no compassion for the convicted. I have just received 15 days of restrictions for recreation (workouts), commissary, cell, and visitation.

4. It means I am to be sent down below into the burning basement without any A/C, for 15 days without any extra food, no workouts, no readings (supposedly), and no visitors. It means that I will not leave that cell for any reason. I have been given isolation. *Damn, what the hell just happened here*? 8 days before my release, my civil liberties have been stripped

5. I will no longer be able to workout, or eat, or even see the light of day for the next 8 days. At least I'll be leaving before the restrictions are over. But I will be here until the end of my prison tour.

6. So much for impressing my wife and family of my good behavior. I will become dehydrated in the heat exhaustive cell. I will lose so much weight from not being able to have late night carbohydrates; soups and tunas. No more TV, no more reading/writing, no more workouts, no more anything. Just sit there and wait for time to dissolve into the moments.

7. What I've got is fifteen minutes to eat what I can, and pack up three months of sanctuary (my notes and my books). My "cellie" stuffed my torn mattress with pastries, while I stuffed my face with the rest of the "*sweet things*". And then it was downstairs to the dungeon.

8. Mattress in one hand, and two mesh bags in the other—laden with books. Books, which were quickly taken away. I panicked inside as they took all my tablets of notes away from me and stuffed them in a closet with all the other bags from other isolated prisoners. I kept my daily prayer book and snuck one literary piece that I passed off as a religious piece.

9. I found my bunk and cleaned the remnants of the last resident.

10. There are 24 bunks separated into 3 sections: 8 bunks to a section, each sharing only one commode . . . 3 feet from the bunk. Each section is divided by wire mesh. Eating will be done standing and holding onto the food tray. Or, if you wish, right on your bunk.

11. I am immediately reminded that this is the place where troublemakers are sent. Several inmates are showcasing swollen faces and black eyes. I notice a few of them from my dorm. They have already settled into their boredom and apathy. I am locked up . . . in *"lock up"*. I managed to bring a couple of pens in and I am writing notes on book pages and legal form papers, which are allowed to pass through.

12. The heat is immediately consuming me. This dungeon in the ground has no ventilation at all. There is no movement of air. We are breathing in each other's exhale. Damn . . . when will they get it right? It's always too cold or too hot . . . and it's always too stale. It's always guaranteed to be uncomfortable with as many unpleasant sights, sounds, and sick people, as you can imagine for your UN—enjoyable stay.

13. I read my old mail from my mother. *"Hope"* is the message. She tells me to keep my spirits up. She asks about my so-called wife. I wonder if that worthless sack of whore has informed my mother of her decision to move on. I wonder if she tells my mother of her complete and utter refusal to admit her lies and deceit. I heard she's running out of money and she's been calling all my family members for more money. How pathetically low of her. And how very funny she has become to my family for even trying to get more than what she has already received. *Rust, now rots my blood of the love I used to feel.* I have resolved myself to going it alone.

14. I will keep the line of forgiveness open. If she does want me to come home, I'll know soon enough. For now, I cannot let this poison consume my waking hours. Not in here. Not in this sauna bath of isolation. **I will never fall asleep in this confinement. The heat is too thick. The filth too nasty. The waiting too deafening. I will only pass out from exhaustion as my body breaks down each time. It will be the torturous death of ten lifetimes to endure 8 days of anger and betrayal down here. If I remain angry, it will surely eat away at my soul from the inside out. Working out will be hard in the poisonous air. It is thick and still. The place is sour in smell and burns the nostrils. Everything about this place is stal**e.

15. We are only allowed out of the cage to shower at 6am. We are let out one at a time for about 4-5 minutes. Always being yelled at to hurry. I lay on the bunk in a semi-conscious state. Any sense of reality has become distorted. I have become glazed over with disbelief.

Thurs. Nov. 25th, 2004

1. It's 4am. Time for chow. I was let out of the cage to the commons area to pick up my breakfast bag and ordered back to my cell. I ate on my bed. Two hours later, and its time for showers. Maybe this would be a good time to workout: between breakfast and showers. "*I can't*". I'll loose too much weight if I cannot eat extra foods at night. This 2000-calorie a day diet from the jail is not enough to sustain my metabolism with workouts. Most of the calories come from "*sweet things*".

2. Five minutes to shower in a double stall while the other guy shaves his face. I have no time to groom in front of a mirror and go back to my bunk. I read my daily book and crashed into some far away mind zone.

3. I awoke to the sound of chow. **It is Thanksgiving Day.** Can you imagine what this feast will be?

4. Same process. Line up to be released out to commons area, collect tray, and take it back to the bunk. There are no tables to eat on. **Here on this celebrative day, I give thanks. I'm standing in my boxers and shower shoes at the end of my bunk, 3 feet from the shitter, shoving mashed potatoes, stuffing, and a tiny chicken breast down my throat. The trays were ordered back under the cage 4 minutes into starting the grub session. I didn't get to finish the sweet potatoes or pecan pie slice. I shoved them into the filthy mattress for later.**

5. Back at my mother's beautiful home in the hill country, I'm sure the festival of chatter and cooking had begun already. All the kids (nieces and nephews), including my son, Nicholas, will be running around and playing, while all the adults, my brothers and sisters, are sharing stories of their home life, work, and travel. The stories, only the healthy, wealthy, and wise can share.

6. I wonder where my wife will be sharing her time today. Will she be cooking for someone else today? Is he tending to the needs of her child?

7. **In this desolate place of punishment, I am thanking God for my health, strength, and energy. I am praying for my blessings. I am remembering my past and meditating in the future to come. It is getting time to be released. It is time to**

leave all the foolishness behind and practice becoming healthy, wealthy, and wise, for myself. To earn my birthright.

8. I lay in my bunk constantly turning over to reduce the sweat factor. It soaks right through from the mattress. It is a constant struggle to get comfortable. I never will reach the satisfaction of being content. How can I get through this day with the minimum of suffering? *I can't!* The lessons of this place remain on maximum overdrive. I am marinating in the wonderment of *"what ifs"*.

9. As Thanksgiving comes to a close, the revelations in my mind, tell me to embrace this day like no other. It is a day of infinite thanks for being able to survive this long. It is a day of absolute resolution and humbleness to my life lost. It transpires a generation of suffering from a multitude of bad decisions. One of them, being allowed to become co-dependant upon a deceitful lover. One who has never had the vision of moving forward together? Rather, a maggot infested mind, hell bent on deviating my resources for her own agenda.

10. A rebirth of my life has begun many times, but only with the fainted resemblance of vigor. Soon, I'll give thanks with a new kind of vengeance. A well thought out plan: one with goals and sacrifices. I reside in here, among the stench of sweat, dirt, odors, and foulness so unbearably hard to cope with and yet, I still find myself alive with the desire to create a life of calmness, stability, and sweet riches.

11. I just worked out within the stale heat of my cage. I have achieved a personal best. *Amazing what the mind can convince you to do.*

12. Seven days to go. Then I can begin the rest of my life.

13. This place is terrible. I hate it! I can never return. This is what has been handed down to me as a reminder of what it's like to be in *"lock up"*. Upstairs, I had become relatively comfortable in my surroundings. It had become just bearable and at least, the anticipation of being released soon, would ease my anxieties. Also, the possessions of choice were more readily available to pass the time; games, books, showers, food, visitations, etc. Here, I am reminded of the bare necessities and it is rotten to the core with every breath.

14. This time spent down here will require endurance, patience, stamina, and a preoccupation of the time within my mind. I am going to live with it . . . *or I will die in it!* I have already chosen to put on my mental health helmet. This is going to require some serious *"living in my head"*.

15. I miss my books. I found others stashed away in here. One in particular. It changed my life, my attitude, my altitude, and complete sense of well being the moment I opened it. I remember flipping it open to no particular page, and what jumped out at me was 5 months of agitation and insecurity gone . . . in a split second. It became the welcome mat that binds me to the free world. It is the reason my writings have become a book. It immediately put my life in perspective and placed me back in the race for success. I read it once, and then read it again and still, I read it some more. **I will be coming out a cool, calm, and confident man. I am healthy, motivated,**

goal oriented, and spiritual in my nature. I am ready to achieve, and I know how to achieve great success. My sufferings of the unknown have prepared me for this book. I deserve it . . . I've earned it! This place no longer smells. With each page turned, the book has become my endless breath of fresh air.

Fri. Nov. 26th, 2004

1. My head is pounding constantly from the sleep and read routine in my bed. There is nowhere else to go but to stand next to my bunk. Besides, it is difficult to move around in the heated, stale air. I will remain committed to the calmness within my heart. I wished I knew I was being loved honorably. I wish it were true what the letters keep saying over and over. How she'll be there for me upon my release. I desperately wanted love from her . . . from anyone. I needed sex. Filthy, passionate, hard core sex. I'll provide the romance later. I wonder if she'll show herself.

2. I've become so confused. It has become difficult for me to write. I know what has to be done, but I have absolutely no resources to start. I do not have one resource to call my own except me, myself, and I; charming, articulate, and motivated. Will that be enough? Not without a plan. Everything needs plans, so I had better make a list.

3. Find Nick! Pay tickets, find a new job, and get a new home. This is literally from the bottom of the ground up! Right now, I am spending my time reading, writing, sleeping, and the occasional workout in the evening when the sun goes down to cool the building. It makes no difference though; midnight in this hellhole is never without it's hot breath of air.

4. I have no pants, only boxers, so I cannot run for exercise. The humidity is way too thick to even consider it anyway. I am constantly struggling to get a breath of circulated air to cool my lungs. It never comes. I can wait for six days . . . 18 meals . . . 144 hours . . . infinite nightmares. I'm thinking, "*hang in there, or hang yourself*", which ever comes first.

5. Who will be there for me? Who will it be? Mom . . . Dad . . . Her . . . The police? Where will I go? How will I get there? What will they say? How am I going to be received?

6. **I have lost all forms of independence in here. I am completely lost in dependency. At the moment, I'm suffering from lack of food, no sleep, and too many improper conditions to mention. Upon my release to the outside, I am anticipating no food, no shelter, no clothes, no anything. The most basic of all needs has been stripped from my grasp. All that has been so easy to obtain and taken for granted, has now become so very far away.**

7. I am motivated though. I wish I had a woman to kick start it all.

8. **I want to make a better lasting difference.** I don't want to be a memory. It makes me think about how I will live my life now. To stop . . . and think . . . before I get in the car, go to the office, go to a bar, drive home.

9. **How do you live your life? Are the activities or events of the day leading up to a crime? Do you hit your wife? Yell at the waitress? Pound someone in the face for looking you for more than a split second? Are you doping up? Do you steal, rob, and rape? Is it working? Does it make you happy to be so angry all of the time? Are you going to end up here? Are you already here? Are you afraid? You better be.**

10. It's coming to an abrupt end for you unless you find the change that deviates you from the end of a crooked road. **Find the straight and narrow road of health, wealth, and function, and your rewards will be broad and plentiful.** Remain focused in your quest to add vitality to your life! *Read that sentence again!* Find that change in your life before it's too late! Allow that change to bring happiness in your life.

11. *Do you want to go to jail today?* Consider all of the activities and events in your life that lead you to a crime. Consider the conditions . . . the time . . . the loss of everything . . . and the violence. Why would you ever want to come to a place where individuals who enjoy the power of their position take all civil liberties from you with the wave of a hand? They are trained and required to fulfill the need to inflict pain, violence, inconvenience, and whatever else is terrible and unforgivable in a world without pity or compassion.

12. **A judge has sentenced you to jail for committing a crime. Now you must do the time, but the real punishment begins at exactly the moment of entering these walls. It is an eye for an eye already. And it's understood. It's the way society gets back at you for committing crimes in the free world; by placing you in a crime ridden, criminal infested, nest of predators.** You will be subjected to being robbed, raped, beaten, and preyed upon by other criminals and worse, the guards. The guards are the dogs of this domestic war on crime, hired by the state to remind you of your crime . . . day in and day out, and sometimes for years to come.

13. Time is only part of the required repayment fee. This is a place where inmates govern the conditions, which will allow you to function and survive. You may be required to abide, or pay with getting your head beaten and your ass kicked. These are the added punishments of your crimes.

14. **Do you really want to be in jail today?**

15. *Consider this*: A place where you are reminded with violence and pain that comes in waves . . . and by the numbers! This is a place that will not discriminate because of age, race, ethnic background, or sexual preference. You cannot leave here because you want to go home to momma. Nor will you ever control the actions or inflictions that the guards or inmates can, and will place on you. It is a place of constant yelling and screaming of the worst kind. The kind that reminds you, *that it could be you!*

Here is a place where complaints are laughed at when heard, but never listened to and rarely, are they ever corrected.

16.	**Compare pictures of yourself from years past. Place them side-by-side in a row. Before and after. What do you see? Does it look like a life going down the path of destruction? Is it a cycle of unnecessary self-infliction.**

17.	Today, after almost three decades, I have finally come to terms with what it takes to succeed beyond the daily scope of just surviving.

18.	I no longer smoke or dope. I exercise with vigor and enthusiasm. I will plan my day and work my plan. I will execute it with direction and excitement. I will not harm anyone, unless protecting myself. My imagination is vivid. My influence will be positive. I will keep myself in a safe environment. I will constantly seek higher ground. I will live below my means. I will live a life that progresses toward those goals . . . *everyday.*

Wed. Dec. 1ˢᵗ, 2004

1. And the hours of the days are transformed back into the time of eternity. The intervals of thoughts of getting out have become infinitely entwined. There is no break from the endless loop that leads me toward time, *but less than a split second ahead into the future*. **Time whispers forward as the noise explodes continuously in my head.** This dorm far exceeds the torment of C block during the past summer months.

2. I'm trying to think of tomorrow, *but it doesn't look like today will end*. Time intervals are so short. It leads me to believe that I'll never leave. A new wave of fighters has entered the isolation block. I'm afraid to be here anymore. I'm afraid of what awaits me tomorrow . . . or rather, what won't be waiting for me.

3. The lights have been on for the entire duration of my stay down here. My bunk is directly below the long, Florissant tubes. They run the length of the bed. There is no escape. I cannot cover up under my sheet, for I will suffocate in the already thick, fumes of nausea. How could anyone ever want to come after the very first time? I am continuously hungry. I can never get that sense of enjoyment that a good healthy meal provides. I try to save what little I can, but it doesn't tie the hunger knots until the next rationed meal.

4. Her letters have never come while being down here in this septic tank. She has left me alone so many nights. So many hours, days, weeks, and months of continuously waiting for her to write or visit. It's funny how things come full circle. In the free world, there was so many nights that I waited for her to come and visit. So many times she waited on me to show and even when I did, I was looking for a way to leave. There was no consistency in time shared together. So many nights I waited on her. So many nights, her friends came to wait on me instead. I wonder if she knew about these late night visits. I do miss her now though. I miss her friends too. Or is it just all the good sex that they readily provided.

5. She is oblivious to the pain I have endured; insensitive and unnerved by my incarceration. The disloyalty has torn away at everything we had. The lies have been multiplied by her deceit. She has become less than the dust of the earth. Thoughts of us have become foreign to me. I do, in fact, feel much love for her still, but I

find myself incapable of expressing this love without first feeling the burn of hatred instead. Everything of her seems less important and insignificant in the scheme of things now.

6. Down here, in the gallows of N dorm, I discovered another book stashed away. It has, in fact, saved me from the torturous ticking of time. It has brought a new sense of right way thinking. It has relieved me from my insecurities and added self-confidence back into my esteem. From the moment I opened it, I found proof of my good fortune, and it immediately became my greatest asset. It revealed to me the one thing . . . *the only thing,* which I could control; my thoughts! It is here I developed a new state of mind, and a superior state of altitude. One that elevated me to a level of self-confidence that I had not experienced in years. My mind released millions of flashes of visual interpretations as I gobbled up the pages. I read it quickly. Then I read it again . . . slowly. I am still looking at it today for quick references.

7. I have retrained my brain for success. This time, I'll keep what I earn. Never again could I see it fit to squander riches and labor, only to have another put their teeth into it. It would be nice to date a professional. One that earns her own way. This, I could share. *An equality of sponsorship within a relationship.*

8. Being here in this has ultimately rejuvenated my desire to succeed. I am constantly repeating my goals for reinforcement. I have maintained my character; I have suppressed my personality; and I have expanded my intelligence considerably, while being in jail. **Holding back my good nature and charm has been the hardest. It's difficult to present yourself as happy and good-natured in a place like this. Depression has plagued me to the point of begging for death throughout the months. Most of it came from not believing she would wait, and then always being reeled back in, to the tune of hope.**

9. I'm thinking about what I've lost, which is completely everything. For me, it has become everything of nothing; the car, trucks, lofts, furniture, money, clothes, and so called friends. Some of it meant everything; loosing my son Nicholas and not knowing where he resides or even if he's okay is the hardest matter to deal with on a daily basis.

10. *And now that I've made it to the end of this terrible ordeal,* I have lost the willingness for death to come a knocking. Instead, **I feel I have earned the right and privilege to go on with my life as a free man.** A completely, free man. Free from the wrath of another to burden my mind, time, and soul. Not to mention my pocket book.

11. **I'm thinking about all that I've gained. It is good, acceptable and perfect. It is the love of God in my life again. Here, He shall remain for the rest of my years and on to eternity. I have retrained my brain from the ground up . . . from scratching the surface, to minding my success.**

12. I've been rehearsing my lines for months. Thousands of hours spent playing out the day that I will be released. It has been a theatrical bend of plays, never once being the same twice. I wonder how I will be received; as a father to her child, a husband to her, or as an outcast to society. I want to know what she wants.

13. She will deny her part in this. She will pretend to forget this abandonment. She will forget these events by attempting to create a new false history. She will pretend to be unaware of the suffering I have endured while waiting for her untimely letters and visits. And now, I'm sure she will act confused. Confused of what to do now that I'm out. I received a letter from my mother. My mother said my (ex) wife would be here to pick me up . . . *if I'm released!*

14. *This immediately tells me there's a chance I won't be going home tomorrow!* This also tells me that she knows something we all don't. If there are tickets outstanding, I will be transported to that place of holding: To another jail or city. This also tells me she never did anything to apply for time served for these tickets or new charges while I have been here. This is just one more kick below the belt from a lying, deceiving, conniving, leach that has decided to swing from someone else's branch of support. But not before using and abusing all that remains of me. She can have the rest of the old me. I've got a new one of me. And it's something like she'll never get a piece of.

15. It is a simple process. Call to inform another *place of hold* that I am an inmate already and we would like to apply my time being served for these simple tickets. This is so that I can be released on the scheduled date of departure . . . *tomorrow! It is that simple of a process.*

16. Well . . . this is how a man has to realize a love lost. I pray it becomes a life realized. No longer do I have faith of a woman standing behind her man in good times and bad. Will I ever love again? I don't want to begin to think I ever could. It has all become a lie to me. *"I'll be there for you"* has now just become *"what's in it for me?"* Being in love shouldn't have to mean begging for it. It shouldn't have to mean being lied to, and criticized for accusations that cannot be defended properly. She will conjure up false accusations to create a justification for her complete and utter deception and abandonment. She has been a criminal hiding behind this bad boy image of mine. My public life has overshadowed the criminal acts of her crooked mind. I have hid all her pitfalls and embarrassment from the world. And now she has created a false hope and is telling fraudulent stories to create an uninvolved history. How easy it has been for her to be with someone else. Someone who, in fact, is just seeking the rewards of listening for a while. That reward being . . . getting laid.

17. I have tried to reach into something so beloved, she couldn't ever possibly find again. Although she may pretend, she will never find the comfort we both shared with each other over the years. There's no longer the need to know who's right and who's wrong. I don't know what's real and what's not anymore.

18. I figure I've been feeding her the best of steak and sushi for the past 6 years and now it's gone. It's likely she'd be open to taking scraps up off the floor if she had to. Anything to keep the tune of pretending to be full. I have hunted and foraged for food and shelter for us for 6 long years, never once complaining about going out there and pounding the pavement to make a buck so she could be comfortable. And

185

after 6 years of such, this is how I am repaid. How many times did she write and visit to tell me was sending money so I could order commissary to eat? About the same amount of times that nothing showed up in my trust fund. Complete and utter lies and abandonment. I have been the silver back champion ape in my industry; daddy war bucks baby! For six years, she never once went to earn an independent dollar utilizing her non-existent skills. Only now . . . now that I've gotten her through the school of nursing, she has decided to be in isolation away from me.

19.   Everything she had; the clothes, money, vehicles, home, and furniture . . . everything came from the fruits of my labor. My family introduced her to luxuries she will never know again. We have opened her eyes to the best money can buy, and now she longs for what she doesn't have. Everything she has enjoyed comes from us. All that she has seen has been shown to her through our eyes. She will forever be in need of what she can only wish she has in her possession. Her life remains full of envy.

20.   **It is chow time . . . for the last time! It is 4am chow. I am eating here for the last time. I can't believe it! My time here will be done in a few hours. Release is scheduled for 8 am. I will not rest. I am pacing back and forth. It is mind boggling to begin to realize I have made it to this end.** Finally, *life will begin once again*! All inmates are being too nice to me for they are looking for my possessions to be handed down. Toothpastes, soaps, shower shoes, anything of extraordinary value. I will disburse them to the fellows I had support with. The guys who, I know are real on the outside too. The guys who didn't get in the way of me allowing myself to pass the time the way I wanted to . . . which is exactly that, *my own way*!

21.   **It is the morning of Thursday December 2ⁿᵈ, 2004. I am scheduled to be released from prison today.** I have not made any phone calls other than a 5 minute one, a month ago. I have not received any recent letters from my so-called wife, and I do not know who will be waiting for me when those doors are swung open. I am sitting in the commons area looking back into the wire-meshed cells.

22.   I'm looking back at the people that made it good, and the others that brought havoc and confusion to an already instable environment.

23.   It is my turn to shower now. It will be the last time to shower in this nasty, confined, no mirrored hellhole. No longer will I have to wear my shower shoes to protect me from what grows below in the drain holes. No longer will I have to tolerate loud mouthed, crude and obnoxious, guards screaming filth from that pie hole in the middle their face for me to get out of the shower. It is time to go home and scrub six months of grime and dirt from my body. I can't wait to use my body scrubber with a full bottle of body wash. I will soak my head in Head and Shoulders shampoo for an hour. I want to feel the cool crisp burn of it cleansing my scalp.

24.   I have no free world clothes. I told my mother to tell her to bring some for me. I heard if they were no one there to get me, I would be given Salvation Army donations. Whatever works to get me into whatever clothes that will get me out of here.

25.   How will I be received? By who? *I am being set free into a lost world of the unknown.* My mind has been cleansed of many poisons that wreaked havoc on my life. Only

now, the poisonous snake chews on my curiosity. My anxieties are swelling in my heart. I will explode soon, if I am not released. So many words of sorrow, anger, fear, and wonderment are circulating around my every thought.

26. It is time. My name has been called to shower. Oh shit . . . I'm being called over to the sergeant. What is it? Am I being given the thumbs up to follow the guard up the stairs to the waiting room? Huh . . . some fucking waiting room! It's just another nasty cell, no more than four feet by six feet, in which about five us will wait in anticipation for the next four hours while the system checks on "inmate holds". We'll see what happens soon. Hopefully, *I'll see you on the outside*!

Thurs. Dec. 2nd, 2004

1. I am showering in here for the last time. The cold water from the useless showerhead does nothing to wash away the taste of salt from my tears. **The wonderment of being released has been stripped away from the clutches of my eternal hope. I am struggling to grasp whatever notion of belief that I have that I could actually be going home today. It wasn't happening. It is shredding the life away from me. My organs are collapsing within my now frail shell. The tears of my sadness and despair are burning deep within the cuts of my heart.** I have been sacrificed yet still, again, so that she may not confront the time with me that she still readily is trying to avoid.

2. A hold has been placed on me for something so simple as a speeding ticket. All that was required was a phone call to allow this time here to be used as time served for that violation. *She never did it*, as requested. Just another ploy to buy more time to do whatever it is that she is doing.

3. My tears are falling upon the shower floor. I do not care who can see this. It does not matter. *Even the shower spray cannot camouflage my tears of sadness.* I can hear the guards screaming at me to get out of the shower. They are angry and threatening. They are telling me to pack my shit and get ready to be transported. What little possessions I have, are ready to go . . . *but to where?* I'm sure, to another place called "*hell*". **And hell is the place that becomes the nightmares of our realities. It is called Jail.**

4. I am not going home today. I am being transferred to another jail today. The guard has opened the big locker to where isolation inmates have all their stuff packed. I can see my bag there . . . untouched since I put them there 8 days ago. I am happy. It contains all of what you've read up until that time 8 days ago. It is neatly packed in mesh bags, hidden within the entire collection of books that mom and dad sent me over the months. That yellow whore (my so called wife) never once sent me any purchased literature. Only lies . . . only sorry, pathetic, words of untruthful, and cowardly lies.

5. I do not know where I'm going today. I know I'm not going home. And at the end of this anticipated long day . . . *I will still be in jail today.* For you, as the reader, knowing the way that I am feeling right now . . . *do you really want to go jail today?*

I am waiting in this coffin to be transferred to another suffocating and intoxicating waiting room.

6.   The pathetic, weak, sergeants are harassing me as I go through the check out process. The nasty looking and pathetically slow, speaking female guards actually believe their lives are more important than ours, just because we're inmates. I can only shudder at the thought of going home to them at night. Now that's got to be a nightmare of gigantic proportions.

7.   I am being led out into the garage area that also serves as the visitation room. It is sunny and hot already. There is a policeman waiting for me with ankle shackles and handcuffs. He tell me three things; if there is someone coming to help me escape on route, *he will kill me*; if I myself try to escape, *he will kill me*; and if I attempt to hurt him in any way, *he will kill me*. The line sounded so old that I knew he had to have been practicing it all morning. What a way to wake up!

8.   As he walked me out into the street and across the road to where his squad car was, I looked around to see loved ones waiting for the other inmates who were being released today. I cannot see her. Again, it is a lie that I must endure. She had told my mother she would be picking me up. The only way she shouldn't have been here is because she already knew I wouldn't be released to the free world today. My mother and everybody else knew this was to be my release date. My parents could have easily taken care of that silly ticket, but that bitch hid it from them. And now I'm being transferred hours farther away.

9.   I am placed in the back of the car shackled and cuffed. My belongings are shoved in the trunk. He tells me, we are going to pick up another inmate in a town 2 hours away, before I will be transferred to my new jail town.

10.   The ride is long and degrading. Every single car we pass has eyes of curiosity looking in to see the convict. That would be me. I was actually hoping I would have been an ex—con by now. She saw to it that I would remain an inmate in a far away town.

11.   It could have been so easy to solve the hold on me before my time in the state facility was over. Now I'm traveling East to a distant, redneck, and hillbilly town. After waiting for hours in another town, we are ready to hit the road again.

12.   Upon arriving here in this small town hick cell, I am immediately concerned to see that the jail, courthouse, precinct, and city hall are all under one roof. It's a tell tale sign of one-man jury's. I'm sure the judge and prosecutors are neighborly drinking buddies. The guards are apathetic. Most went to high school together. They make the minimum of money and hold the lowest regard for any other person in the penal system. Their concerns are whose fucking whom within the daily soap opera hallways, and how drunk they got on the weekend. This facility houses the lawbreakers who got caught passing through this crappy little Texas town. They catch the drug runners and speeders with warrants. The speed traps net them like a web on the highways. The police create huge revenues for the town by pulling over everyone and anything that moves down that highway.

13. I can feel the vibes in my bones upon entering this crooked little town. The guards are ignoring every possible situation of interaction with inmates. The waiting cell has guys in it that have been sitting there for days. The judge passes through this town for court day, once a month. The conditions are subhuman. I am stripped, given scrubs, and led down a hallway towards the back of the building.

14. I cannot believe I am here to do more time for such a trivial matter. This thieving town has found a way to capture me while already incarcerated, and they will keep me here to earn more state funding. They will place me in a dorm cell with about 6-7 other inmates. **The place smells like it is below sea level . . . way below. The stale, humid air is creating drips from the walls. I am sweating intensely although I am not moving. The tables and floors are filthy. The shower stall is unbearably primitive. It has massive amounts of fungus and other growth on the floor and curtain. The food is slop and infested with live prey. I am eating on the picnic style tables while eyeing the rat, which is eyeing my food. *I will eat it if it comes near.* The TV blares down the corridor style dorm. There is no escape from the noise.**

15. I speak to men that have found comfort in the "*three hots and a cot*". They have become numb to life outside. They do not seem to care. I cannot be like them. Whatever life they think they had now has no bearing on their lives. I have to get out of here now! All it takes is a payment. I will call my father.

16. My father cannot believe this had not been taken care of sooner. She has avoided every possible solution to my release and now I am in the worst of all transfers that I have endured. This one takes the cake . . . and it is rotten to the core. How can I breath in such foulness, listening to these no rule disrespecting punk bitch boys all night. It would be easy to put two down quickly. And with a little effort, I would have three begging for mercy. But I cannot confront 6-7 at a time. My throat would be slit tonight. *But that would be good right about now.*

17. I'm listening to the guards tell the others it will be a couple of months before the judge will see inmates on cases. What the fuck happening to the rights of having a speedy trial. Oh, I forgot . . . *this is the shit hole jailhouse in the middle of Anawac, Texas.*

18. They avoid such regular court dates to establish really nice account receivables from the state funding for inmates in jail. The price we pay so the crooked officials can line their pockets. The judge is a slug. He is nothing more than a "bar fly" in a hut hole on the outskirts of town. The correctional officers (ha) are young, imbeciles no more educated than your kid brother in grade school. It's a dangerous kind of place to see such gun toting, trigger happy, egotistical punks with the power of a badge.

19. It is a week later. Somehow my father has convinced her to pick me up when he pays my fine and posts a bond. This turned out to be a useless waste of time and money. I had earned money for the state by sitting here for a week. Still, my father paid the required fine. It should have just been time served. The night she is to arrive to pick me up, a background check is done on any other holds. Of course,

as no luck would have it, my ex has filed on me for not paying my child support while in prison for the last seven months. I'm now speaking about the mother of Nick. Go figure. She wants me in jail for not paying child support while I am in prison.

20. I am about to be released. I am on the phone with my mother and she is holding another phone talking to my wife. She is in the front lobby of the jail yelling at the guards. She is trying to get them to let me go, now that my father has paid the necessary fines. They will not let me go, and send her on her way.

21. I am weeping uncontrollably on the phone with my mother. So very close . . . what was so very near to my final release . . . has now become so very far and distant. I am beyond despair. I had actually heard her voice for the first time in several months. She had come to get me. She is here . . . or at least *was* here for me. I cannot even listen as the two guards come to tell me that I am free to go from here, but will be held over until an officer comes for me out of San Antonio. It is over 4 hours away . . . 6 in traffic. I know I will not be leaving for a few days now.

22. **Intolerable inmates are making this an unstable environment. I am in near conflict with everyone. I can kill now. I can feel it. I'm blistered inside from the rage that fuels my head and heart. Nobody will take my domain! Not in here . . . not anywhere!**

23. It is the morning after I don't know how many days. The guards feed me double meals and ask if they can do anything for me before I am about to be transferred to still, yet another prison. They do this just before asking who's talking about what in the dorms, and if I'm willing to talk about any suspicious activities going on in the cells. As if . . . I'm not inclined to tell these parasite cops anything they want to hear. No matter how fucked up the inmate is in here or anywhere, *I choose to give no cop the pleasure of" informing" on someone just so they can practice their GI Joe skills in undercover crack downs*. They can figure it out themselves. I was basically asked to "Rat" out any persons in the cells before I leave this town to go to another. Yea, wouldn't that be comforting to know bullshit like that would follow me to another prison? *No thanks.*

24. So, once again, I am being shackled and cuffed for the long journey into the far away places of hell that I have become so familiar with in recent months.

Thurs. Dec. 9ᵗʰ, 2004

1. And now it's back to the Bexar County Jail facility. Check in is a zoo. Hundreds of drunks, druggies, and space cadets of all ages, race, and odors are lying about, waiting for check in.

2. I see a dude from college that I used to know. We have a mutual life long friend, Daniel. Rick is now a correctional officer. I'm watching him as I am watching all the correctional officers. Maybe it was because I knew Rick that I'm noticing he is actually being civil and respectful to those who are complying with his commands. Yep! He is definitely managing his temper and job objective well. I'm watching the other guards. There are a lot of women guards here too. The men are constantly blasting bullshit out of their mouths to showboat the position power that maintains their livelihood. This place is quieter than all the other places. The inmates seem to be better controlled through voice commands. I'll find out why in just a little while.

3. I'm enduring the second transfer since being released from the state facility. I realize now that I will be paying for each crime separately. She could have executed this a long time ago. All of these fines, bonds, and time served could have been avoided through honest communication. And now, my family has to pay for all these fines and bonds separately just to get me to the next place of hell that has a hold on me. She had not put one foot forward to alert of us any charges that had arisen while I suffered in this incarceration. Instead, she avoided all that was to be done so that I would sit here and there . . . and everywhere else she could get me to be incarcerated. It is true. She doesn't want me to get out. She has her life now. It doesn't involve me anymore . . . it doesn't have to. She has stood upon my shoulders to get all that she can for her own agenda. And now, she refuses to give any acknowledgement of our marriage at all.

4. I have finally reached my cell after an exhausting day of tests, sitting, odors, yelling, and "*johnnies*". These are the dry, stale, and squashed sandwiches we are served over and over until we actually get upstairs to our assigned areas.

5. It is somewhere in the early morning hours when the large metal door is opened to reveal my next place of the unknown. What a beautiful sight to behold. I cannot

believe what I'm looking at right now. *It is a burden undone.* Temporary sanctuary from a living hellish nightmare that refuses to end. What I'm looking at is complete isolation. But this cell is different from what I've ever seen before. I'm looking in through the open door and I am in elation. The cots are raised. The walls are clean, as is the floor. There is a bed, a table, and cleaning supplies . . . real cleaning bottles of disinfectant and rags. I am blessed with a private toilet. And the most amazing, luxurious, comfort that I could ever ask for, especially after enduring the many months of constant noise pollution. It is the fact that I will sleep alone and wake up alone in a cell alone that pleases me. *A soundproof room with no "cellies".* I will not have to hear the agony of snoring echoing off the cement walls. It angers me to listen to this for hours on end . . . for months past! There will be no cursing, belching, farting, or unrecognized grunting within the wee hours of any time while I remain to be in this room. Unless it comes from me. There is space to work out. I have a table to write my endless hours away. The best part is that there is no TV blaring out mindless couple conflicts throughout the day. I can, however, at my discretion, ask for my door to be opened and go downstairs to a day room full of couches, to watch an evening show. There is an outside area where I can go to run (on the spot) or just sit and shot the breeze with others under the stars. It feels good to look outside. The night air is cool and crisp. *This is the Cadillac bar of all cells I've visited while on tour throughout the Texas penal system.*

6. My mind is at ease. My door is opened during chow time. I go downstairs to get food and drink and then, take it back to the confinements of my own privacy. No one to beg, borrow, or steal, whatever it is that I'm eating.

7. This is my 8th vision of jail since being incarcerated less than six months ago. I am embracing this isolation. The silence is welcomed. I have not broken down the way I thought I would. I just want to get through this time here and be home for Christmas. I want to make it out of here for the holidays. I want to go back to work.

8. I am finding out that lack of contact means lack of medical services too. It's no different than anywhere else though. In prison, there is a waiting time . . . and a *"don't give a damn what you're suffering time".* It reminds an inmate . . . "I wish I wasn't in jail today".

9. Memories of getting into my own shower have me missing the comforts of home. I want the days of having to gather up all my shower utensils and supplies just to go downstairs and take a shower in cold water to be gone. I miss my body scrubbers and wash. I want to get a shower without having to continuously press two different buttons for hot and cold water.

10. It's nice to have the day room open. Outside, we can go under the stars. I can feel the night air. I ran for an hour filling my lungs with fresh oxygen. The cleansing was welcomed. My body is strong, my muscles toned, and my blood cells without toxins.

11. I'm wondering what the pivotal point to which she decided to abandon me. I hear she's now trying to embarrass me with my own friends by spreading made up

rumors. Such a lack of loyalty. It is the poison that tears at our society; the lack of loyalty to those whom we supposedly love. Liars and cheaters.

12.   I am praying to God for His blessings during this tour of jails. It should be the last. I am praying for Him to keep me safe, strong, and alert; patient to endure this time; and content to help me accept this situation as it unfolds. Would this, in fact, be the last stop before going home? Were there any more holds on me? Did she create more problems for me so that she could continue her life without the responsibility of her marriage? *How will it play out?*

13.   I am in my own cell. I can, at random, clean, wash, scrub, and wipe my floors, walls, toilet, and/or sink. What a feeling to sit and enjoy "movements" and not have to hurry for the next 8 guys wishing for the same. This is far better than any of the other systems I had visited . . . especially Chambers County Jail. That one is the scum of all jails.

14.   I just went down to the Med. Ward. I was denied medication for an ailing problem that has inflicted it's own kind of stinging pain upon me; constipation. I think it's from lack of decent water and too much starch, I went to med ward and as I was coming back, I saw a real water fountain for employees. Nobody was around so I stood at it and downed at least 2 quarts of that cool refreshing giver of life; fresh water. Mmm . . . . never tasted so good! When I got back, I ate the little food that I had saved from breakfast and lunch. It is three pieces of dry bread. It was delicious.

15.   *Where are the dreams of being a family again? These thoughts have been my friend for the duration of my tours. I slept with it. It woke me up and got me out of bed in the mornings. It had me reading, writing, praying, working out, and eating right. It even had me walking away from confrontations, because I knew it would have made you proud. All of these functions were the motivating forces of my living dream; to be a family again.*

16.   *Houston, TX. The forth-largest city in America. I was lost in the wicked belly of its prison system. Within these walls, I have wiped clean from myself, the scum of the earth; the worst that the world has to offer. I have watched, and many times fought off, this breeding ground of people conforming to the untruthful and deceitful marinating of daily survival. I rose above it. I blocked it from coming into my own arena. The thrill of victory has come from believing that I would be anything worthwhile to you. The desire of winning you over and close to my heart has been the fuel that conquered all my selfish and egotistical ways. I have suppressed all that I am to survive this place. I have given myself completely to you. I have resigned myself from everything that is worthless to propel myself into a healthy, mindful, and loving person. It was this desire to keep your heart and mind close to me that never let my persistence to survive this ordeal falter. The passion to be loved by you sent my world into a complete overhaul. I did this many times for you. All my actions led to the desires of being received by you. All motivations led to the same hope; the wishful anticipation of a letter of*

faithfulness from you. But there is no desire in you to strengthen our passion to be together. It is a letter I will never receive.

17. The continuous quest to win her over has provided me with both, the many trials of struggle and the rewards of excitement during the quest to better myself. Only now, the finish line will not be my wife waiting there for me. In fact, I no longer have man's greatest passion, that being a woman, as my audience. No, from here on out, the lustful drive of being accepted by someone else no longer cultivates my drive to succeed in surviving prison . . . and in life itself. The lustful needs that drive man can no longer be the one source of relentless improvement.

18. For the first time in my life, I have to draw on the strength I see looking back at me from the dull and battered stainless steel reflection on the wall. This time, I've got to be there for me . . . first! I know my family is looking on and they have communicated their support, but the progress to win is all mine to fulfill and continuously self-check. I cannot fail. I will not falter, and I surely will not go quietly in the night.

19. *My struggle remains.* I will continue my passionate interpretations of life, as I now know it to be. It has become good habit now, and it will continue to see me through the best of times. I am no longer afraid of rejection. I've had enough for ten lifetimes. No longer will I have to listen to the rebellious lies and created alibis of deception and false hope from another trying to keep me down. I am immune! Rejection does not scare me, and intimidation has no value within my frame of existence.

20. *Life as I knew it, ceased to exist when I came to prison many months ago.* The love of my life also ceased to exist. It just took a long time for it to sink in. Maybe the longing would have ended a long time ago if she hadn't played all the lying games. She continuously threw me a line with each distant letter. It is, truly, a love lost . . . and a life gained! For this life, I will always give thanks.

21. *I am in disbelief of the letter I have received from you. You speak of my mother being senile and my father, an old crippled man. How dare you spew this malicious content from that whoring mouth of yours? For what? To break free from your cowardness of communicating any more pertinent information concerning my release? Let me remind you of your continuous remarks you make about your own mother and father.*

22. *As for my mother, she is truly the greatest woman I've ever known. Her integrity as a mother, homemaker, professional, and adventurer, will always far exceed anything close to what you could ever dream of accomplishing. Her life has been full of multiple accomplishments. Her source of good nature is unrivaled. You, yourself, have been touched by her generosity beyond your own world. She enjoys a life you could never comprehend. You don't have the breeding for it. We tried to show you, but money and luxury in your hands slips through the snake oil coating your skin.*

23. *Even now, at 70 plus years, my mother still enjoys the likes of trekking the Southern tip glaciers of the Antarctica; camel riding across the desert of Arabia; sleeping*

with the lions of the Serengeti in Africa, and so much more. She has provided you with love, generosity and compassion your own mother wouldn't know how to do. Now . . . what is it you have to say about my mother? That's right! Not a damn thing. You are not worthy enough to mention her name in a circle.

24. *And as for my father? He has dedicated his life to the improvement of medicine. You attempt to degrade him in order to not answer his calling to you for information about my business. You do this as an excuse to abandon responsibility. At 70 plus years, he still attends symposiums for the latest cutting edge technological advances in medicine. A physician of over 50 years, and you attempt to belittle his intelligence?*

25. *It is your nature to scoff at what you do not comprehend. I remember you trying to tell me about your Dean of Nursing and how she didn't know what you did because you thought she was out of touch. Your sense of what's for the good of everybody only circulates in that selfish mind of yours for your own gain.*

26. *There is a limit of disagreement with professors and superiors. You have not found it yet. Someone will be there soon to put your pathetic life in place very soon now. Maybe not today or tomorrow . . . but soon. You are quick to say he's dying. How could that be a benefit to you without believing you was going to be a part of his legacy? And still, you will try to rob from the grave. Not a Chance!*

27. *Look in your living room at the already dead man sitting on the couch 14 hours a day. What has he done to change the world other than pull a few fish from the sea? Oh I forgot . . . he's raising your kid, because nobody else wants it! Even you, from what your friends are saying; you're out every night and gone on the weekends. And so you continuously seek any other baby sitter you can find to avoid the responsibilities of being a selfless, loving, and consistent parent . . . Now, what was that you were saying about my parents?*

Sat. Dec. 11, 2004

1. I've just had breakfast; pancakes, cereal, and milk. The quietness of the morning is most welcoming. I am in complete solitude. I am a sponge for thoughts coming to my head. There is nothing more to do here but write and when I'm not doing that, I can read what others have written. **I am speaking aloud to myself in full conversations; listening to myself, talking to myself, answering myself. I play out these conversations and even choose the words of my company. I can never get them to end the way I want though. Nothing changes.**

2. There are two bunks in here so the threat of the guards placing someone else in here is always looming over me. I do not want to share this cell with anyone other than myself, and my own company of friends (and enemies) that I have created. Having one more would be too many faces to contend with.

3. She and I had a conversation over the phone. Finally . . . after all this time of writing hundreds of pages of letters to her, I am about to get it straight. I had asked her if she was, in fact, still waiting for me as she had stated, and she replied, *"waiting for what?"* That response had immediately put an end to a devotional promise to myself of the commitment I had for her. A wall of lead had risen between us now. I remember dropping to one knee as the shock wave rippled through my body. My dream of us being a family died when she said that. At that moment, I lost a dear friend, lover, and companion. The fantasy was gone. Everything in the fight to bring it back together became worthless, and I became an empty shell. She had erased the memory of us.

4. So . . . all the letters of commitment from her had been a lie! The disbelief had been overwhelming. She said it sarcastically in front of her friends. I could hear them in the background. She had just made me a public fool. Now, this is the final act of betrayal I can tolerate. It's time to add up all those hidden treasures of dirt on her, and let the world know what it means to be a scum whore and traitor.

5. She has been pounding at the gates of hell to tell her story to whoever was in hearing distance. *And now, I will speak once—loudly, so the whole community not only hears, but they are able to listen and understand the unnecessary lies you have*

197

told. I will make it their business to know what kind of person that lives among them.

6. I am able to make phone calls on a calling card. I started to ask around. She is breeding hatred from so many people in my life. She has attempted to get my own family to turn against me by siding with her justification to move on. Of course it's easy for her to move on, now that I have completely financed her last six years. Now she has a new job coming up and has made some hospital friends. I'm sure people are sick of listening to her lash out in anger in hopes of gaining the notoriety of nobleness.

7. What has been said to my parents has had a reverse effect. They are standing by me 100% in my quest to move on without her. They are telling me to stop pondering and let it go. They have better plans for me. **The best things about real family and friends are that they know the worst things about a person and they still continue to be by your side. That's unconditional! That's the spirit of true love.**

8. It's difficult to determine how long I sleep for in here. I know I have not slept for longer than 4 hours at any one time while being in prison. Not once in 6 months! There is not enough time between count times, talking, meals, yelling, lights, etc. But this is a new kind of jail. It is one that seeps isolation into your veins. For me, this kind of newness is the most precious gift I could ask for. It is quiet time . . . complete privacy and silence. Once, in the wee hours of the morning during a shift change, a guard will open the flap to check for life and immediately close the flap again. That's it!

9. Masturbation has quickly become a pleasure again. I am able to fully enjoy my fantasies. After it is over, I no longer desire her anymore. I use thoughts of what she does to me for that only reason now. Brief memories of lust are all she is good for now. I don't even want to talk to her anymore. The thought of communicating sickens me. Why should I?

10. All my tears, fears, cries, and screams. All my regrets and remorse's of these circumstances was faced, fought, and resolved through the motivation of the belief that she would be waiting. It was the glimmer of hope I had painstakingly hung on to. And now it's just me.

11. I was offered dope today in jail. I said "*yes*", and then I immediately said "*no*". I got sick just thinking about it. "No use in starting now". I'll never have to say yes again. *Not one good thing . . . not one . . . not anything of value of anything good can come from it.*

12. I enjoyed another good workout. I listen to the "*rascals*" talk their bullshit. How pathetic it is to hear these young bucks talk of things they have no earthly idea about. It's all made up in hopes the next person will not know any better.

13. **I crave human affection. To be held and embraced. To feel human hands . . . loving human hands, wrapped around my body . . . pulling in me close. To feel the warmth of skin against my own. To listen to the soft breathing in my ear.**

To feel another heart beating against my own. Damn, I must be lonely to come up with needs like this! But it's true. I do need affection. I am alone and I have become so very lonely in my world. I read letters of hope and love from mom and dad over and over in my isolated cell. The day of release remains to be seen. There is no light at the end of the despairing tunnel.

14. I have been to so many jails and different units within them in the past six months. All of the jails have different degrees of guard involvement. Some have minimal contact (during meals only) being only 30 seconds at a time. Other units have guards on you 24/7, every moment of the day. There seems to be less tension among the inmates and over all when they are not present. It also means having to struggle harder to get medical facility or other liberties. It's kind of an *"out of sight, out of mind"*, world.

15. Being here is the most tolerant place so far. The dayroom is quiet. I workout at leisure. I am in complete solitude at my discretion, just by closing the cell door. I am able to clean my room, use my own toilet, sweep my own floor, and wash my scrubs and under garments in the sink. However small it is, I still have privacy and silence. The meals are weak though. The food is delivered in Styrofoam trays. *I measure the quality of my meals by weight. Anything to fill a void. It gives new meaning to sucking the syrup from the Styrofoam containers*. Just a few extra calories to keep up appearances. It's never enough to get that sense of satisfaction. I miss the luxury of raiding my own fridge or pantry for all my favorite foods.

16. **I am alone in here, only with the faith of God by my side. It is a silent celebration. I have no arguments of the validity of facts that support, or don't support the Bible. It is not necessary. The science that supports God's existence and the visual aspects of my imagination of my belief in this faith of my higher power is enough to follow the Word. And the Word is good. It has brought new dimensions of endless possibilities to my life. It has awaked within me, a dead spirit. One that soars through infinite intelligence and abundant energy. The Word brings forth a mighty sword of power that allows nothing to stand in the way of success in my life. It has brought the desire and persistence to achieve anything that I can imagine. It has shown me how to live life . . . every minute of it!**

17. I am prepared to fight the good fight. I will not be denied the opportunity to step back into the ring. **I will beat this evilness surrounding my life**. Every thought is immediately followed by it's physical equivalent. *Start thinking like a Christian, and you'll soon be acting like one!*

18. I have to sit by idle while my parents scramble to undo things to come. *You could have easily prevented my extra days in jail just by handing over info. Instead, you have withheld information pertinent to my release in hopes of keeping me in jail longer. All you had to do was be honest and say "goodbye". But you had to rub salt on open wounds. We all see your motivation of moving on. No longer do you need my money, for now you are about to start working and earning your own money. And*

all this time, you've been fishing for some one to listen to your twisted justification. Your lies are transparent and your friends are blind. Even your own mother refuses to believe the atrocities of what you have done. Never will she ever truly know the dark side of your life, for she is too afraid to listen. She can only turn a deaf ear and continue to pray for your forgiveness from Christ. It is only I that knows what you are capable of maliciously doing to another person. It has marked a pattern in your life to betray and use people. But I will have my day. I will win the day for me. I will win the day from you. And I will have my way with you.

Sun. Dec. 12th, 2004

1. My heart has remained so discontent all these months due to all the lies about monies sent, faithfulness, abandonment, being with others, and over all, the lack of consistency of her words and actions. What is to be gained by all of her callus and intentional misleading? My stay here, and for the last six months, could have been so easy if I did not have to endure all the unfilled obligations and the lying tongue of an unfaithful wife. The wickedness of her deceit has been manipulated on through to my own friends. What I'm hearing is burning my ass beyond belief. She is using the simplest of tactics by pitting my friends against each other . . . and me. She is pitching untrue statements and spurting made up rumors to spread a little panic among the sure and easy.

2. None of my timetables with her were realized. *It could have been so much easier to have just walked away and left me to myself.* But instead, she chose to drag me into the fires of false hope and anticipation. I have suffered disappointment ten times over from relying on what never transpires. And now, I have finally succumbed to the realization, I would have to leave the lust of a woman behind as my motivator. I will have to achieve the hardest goals of my life by myself first. I had always believed she would be there for me. But she chose not to wait for just six months . . . even after six years. Being back with her and family had me digging my heels in for even more self-improvement.

3. Since being in prison, all I've been doing is working on heeling and strengthening this relationship. All she's been doing is tearing it down . . . piece-by-piece, day-by-day, and lie-by-lie. Every event and spoken promise becomes a struggle to believe. I wait in the suspension of time praying she will be truthful to her words to me. The letters continue to give hope and conjunction to us. She gives me hope and tells me to hang in there until it's over. She will be waiting on me when I come home. How can I not embrace such words of encouragement in a place like this, which gives no compassion? Deep down inside, my heart knows it is too late. Still, I am propelled to keep an open heart and a hopeful prayer of our reunion.

Thurs. Dec. 16th, 2004

1. I'm lying in my bunk surrounded by 48 other inmates. I ended up getting transferred out of my secluded sanctuary of privacy. And now, I'm mixing it up with all the drudgery that I've come to hate so much. Gone, is my personal schedule of eating, sleeping, reading, writing, working out, and relaxing. No longer is it possible to walk and talk myself through the nights. No longer can I leave, but even a cookie crumb out on the bunk, *for the dogs of war and crime attack without warning.*

2. This dorm is far worse than the state facility I had despised so much. Once again, just like at State, my bunk lay directly below the air conditioning unit. But this time, there was no paying someone for a different bunk. I couldn't even lie in the bed to read without having to cover every inch of my body. The shivers of my skin never cease to stop. This place is always so cold . . . so very cold. I hate it. I can't see out to the world. There are no windows. There is no life in here other than the endless incomprehensible noise, lights, and 24 hour guards. Everything out of their mouth is vulgar and shallow.

3. I am lying in my bunk awake tonight . . . all night. I weep uncontrollably under the filthy blanket. This place has a new meaning of the word suffering. A new wave of emotions has hit home to my heart and soul.

4. *My lungs are screaming a silent cry. My mouth hovers open, but I'm trying not to make a sound.* The tunnel of despair remains endless and dark. I cannot see the light. *My thoughts are begging God to talk to me,* but I hear no words and cannot see His vision. He died on the cross. *His suffering is way beyond my interpretations of pain and loss.* His agony remains distant from my own. I am dwelling within the threshold of begging for death. Will it ever end? Could it ever stop? *Please God, show me your Son's death was not in vain. Tell me there is salvation from this desolation through the faith of prayer.* Selfishly, I am begging Him to accept my pain as His own.

5. Court has come and gone today. My mother sat in the back. She has been here for four days in a row, rallying for me. She has paid my past due child support. The judge is hard and stern. I waited last in line to stand before him. I listened as he sentenced inmates to months in prison, and fines beyond their capabilities. I

am on display for all the citizens who come to see their loved ones in jail today. It is the shame of my presence. I am presented as an inmate for all those to see my delinquency. The judge demands my compliance and I abide. *My mother stands close, never faltering . . . not once*! My theft cases have become crimes because my so-called wife never provided information to give refunds for deliveries not made. It is her wish to see me rot in hell. I will see to it that I stand tall as she falls from the false graces she has so eloquently forged. It is only 9 days till Christmas. I was told to expect to celebrate it here. *The noose quickly grips my neck tightly. I am struggling to breathe, only really wishing I couldn't*!

6. **And now, here lies some more truth**. However insignificant, it remains pivotal to my realizations of where I must never venture again. I know that the premise of losing everything to drugs is true. **Understand that no matter how small, how infrequent, or how casual of a user you are, the subtle changes are masked in transparency. However unacceptable, untraceable, unsuspecting, and deniable it remains at this very moment, it will always be too late to anticipate its final blow.** My life, wife, kids, reputation, job, career, and future, has become a whirlwind of terminating chaos.

7. My mother's strength is unwavering and she remains steadfast in her quest to get me released.

8. The morning has been way too long. Hundreds of inmates are herded everyday across the street under the courthouse to a waiting area. There, we remain for hours till herded upstairs to an appointed courtroom. The process begins at 5 am and doesn't end until the afternoon. There is no escape from the barrage of endless bragging of crimes. Inmates raise their voices to extreme rock concert levels. It is unbearable. My head pounds from the echoing of hundreds of intolerable voices.

9. I am back to the bunk. It is no wider than 2 feet. The mattress is paper thin and rock hard. It is no cleaner than any other jail. Here, the TV blares out all day. I remain to be starving between meals. I keep missing commissary. The meals are light. Workouts are not allowed here. Breaking a sweat would be met with "kiddy corner" write-ups resulting in more denial of privileges. The guards are pathetic in their quest to impress superiors with more write-ups. Most are nothing more than "*out of place*" when role call is counted. Or maybe it was because an inmate talked too loud or was seen trading food. Simple shit. Nothing more than anything to keep the weak and feeble-minded guards from dozing off during their shift. Most sleep anyway. Nothing they do to me could equate to anything more than what has already been done to me.

10. I had mom pick up all my written notes from up until now. I signed them out to her. Now they are in a safe place. It has been a massive burden upon my shoulders knowing that the guards could have, in fact, picked up all my possessions up and mistakenly "*lost*" them. They'll wish they had after reading these enlightenments of their character and integrity. I don't believe any of them think about a person taking the time to record the filth that these guards spew from their mouths. It

probably won't make a difference up on Capital Hill. These pages are never meant to influence any law.

11. **What this book _is_ hoping to do is reinforce your ideals and daily routines to the point where you know . . . you don't want to be in jail today. That's all!**

Fri. Dec. 17th, 2004

1. I'm looking at my mother. I can see it in her eyes during our visits. She is exhausted. My incarceration has consumed her life. I will never complain again of being here. She is literally spending her retirement money on my child support and commissary so that I can eat.

2. I think back on it. When she was getting ready for work at 5 am on any given day, I had been preparing for bed from a night of drinking, and doping. I did this for years without thinking twice of it. Up until 4-5 am and working from 12—5 pm. Then doing it all over again. I never really saw it as getting in the way of anything until now.

3. But I am convincing myself that God has better things for me. So does my mother. My mother has, in fact put her own life on hold. Her home life, interrupted, because I relentlessly begged her to get me released so that I could get home to save my family. She must have known something I didn't. *Everybody knew the something that I didn't.*

4. My medication was prescribed. It is paid for . . . and nobody can find it. And nobody gives a shit!

5. I made up a schedule of expenses; business and personal. It's time to pay back some debts. Discipline and prudence will be my sweet revenge. If money is why she left to be with another, then I'll make ten times what she does.

6. **What does it mean to lose everything? Not being able to go home. Not even having a house to call home. No car, no clothes, no budget, job, or prescribed income of any sort. No reserves of any kind to fall back on. Knowing that as you walk out these big metal doors, not a soul who cares will be waiting for you. You will be walking out alone. It is the fear of being alone in the free world must have some wishing they'd never leave. That's not me. I'm ready to go. Have been for a long time now. Since the tenth day, I've been preparing myself for something so much better than what I had or thought was good. Good in anything has now just become mediocre to me. New standards have been built upon for me to propel myself into an expanded life of better quality.**

7.	Remember when we used to be able to be greeted right at the gate when we got off the plane after a trip? Somebody we love was always there waiting to see us. Cheers and laughter always accompanied hugs and kisses. Now, it is the norm to walk the terminal toward where the baggage is, to see our loved ones waiting for us. There is an anticipation of your kids running to you. Your wife looking for you and wrapping her arms around you as you come to her. Maybe, it's your friends "high-fiving" you. It's a given, when family and friends are plentiful.

8.	As I understand it to be, after flying around in this nasty cage for 6 months, my wife and kids won't be there to greet me. There will be no job, no food, no clothes, or transportation of any kind to earn my keep with. Maybe, it's best that I just stay in jail today . . . and tomorrow. It would be easy to knock the guards teeth into the back of their skull for a free world case against me. That would leave me in here for a good long time. Then, I could just enjoy all the irresponsibility's of life on the inside. Always being served . . . never seeking success. Do you know what it means to have everything taken away from you? Walk in my shoes for just one day. **Do you want to go to jail today?**

9.	My fortune and my future have been robbed. Stripped away at a moments notice.

10.	I got my commissary today, but I slept too late to eat it. Now, I'll be awake all night wishing I had gotten up earlier to stuff my face with better food. It's time to read. Anything to pass the time. It's getting hard to absorb even just one page without my thoughts venturing back to the free world. I'd rather be spooning with my wife. But she's probably spooning another meal ticket right now. I'm looking at her letters of love and support. Such betrayal.

11.	*I want to give you a lesson from God if I may. I pray for you to realize that you don't have to lie, cheat, steal, and deceive people in order to be accepted. Here is a chance for you to discover that God loves you unconditionally for not what you do (good or bad), but rather, for whom you are (a creation of God). Find God. Ask Him to receive you in your wickedness. Ask him to forgive you for your lies and deception. Having everything taken away from me has given me the very sense of security of knowing that nothing's vital at stake tomorrow (nothing else matters), other than God walks with me, and remains in my life each day that I awake. If you can get this, you'll realize that you don't have to lie to get people's acceptance or likes of others. You don't have to lash out in deception to hurt me anymore. And you don't have to drag other's down with you when you cheat, lie, and steal, for money and companionship. Stop being a whore!*

12.	*You are constantly trying to deviate everyone from remembering your own past. It is littered with filth. Still, I've accepted you without hiding in shame. Even when people approached me to warn me of your likes. I still remained by your side. But now you have found another branch to swing upon. What ever it takes eh!*

Sat. Dec. 18ᵗʰ, 2004

1. So many questions are coming at me. They are multiplying exponentially. I am angry all of the time. *You constantly remind everyone to forget your checkered past by putting mine out there for everyone to see. I will never let them forget about what you have done to disrupt this family and to deny your son the rights of his father. My son will know the truth . . . even if it is by my dying breath.*

2. The S.E.R.T. team hit the bunks hard today. They rush in with all their protective gear and harass inmates by stripping us and leaving us in the day room for hours. We sit in freezing temperatures for hours as they go through our lockers. All of our belongings are thrown into a common pile for us to separate after they leave. It's done to showboat their power over unarmed inmates. Most inmates are complacent and non violent. However the message is that guards can, and will, kick your face in . . . *by the force of many.* **They are quick to mention that it is within their right of the law to beat and repeat any beatings they feel is necessary to satisfy their cravings of violence.** None of them could begin to show aggression in the free world. They are overweight, and unfit. The loudest ones are the little women who feel it is necessary to take out their frustrations on male inmates. Must be their history of being rejected by men. I'd be pissed too if I was so ugly . . . inside and out!

Sun. Dec. 19th, 2004

1. Specific details of this hellish incarceration have been eroded into general memory. Now that the clock is here in the dorm, the nights have become so much longer. **I watch the clock tick away by the seconds . . . by the seconds of each minute, of every hour that tediously inches forward into the night.** I never get to sleep for more than 4 hours at a time anyway, so the days are multiplied by 6 times, each and everyday.

2. What am I still doing here? I'm wasting free airtime . . . and space! Someone . . . anyone . . . please let me out! Let me go! Damn, this is the drudgery of idol time.

3. I'm thinking of my mother and the suffering she has endured while I remain to be a prisoner. I'm thinking of the time, energy, money, and love she has put forth to help my broken soul.

4. My wife was supposed to have waited! I prayed for it continuously, and I did all the right things to enforce it. *Everything I'm doing is moving toward the good of this relationship. All the letters, visits, inspirations, and motivations were nothing more than chimes blowing in the wind. I was the last to know, and even now, I still don't know the true meaning of the extent of your deception. What happened to us? What happened to soul mates? It had been so natural between us. It was to be us. But since I've been gone, you've been practicing a different agenda.*

5. "I found a picture of you . . . those were the happiest days of my life". (Pretenders)

6. **Tonight is the six-month anniversary of my incarceration. It has lasted too many lifetimes. My pain far exceeds the dates of absence. I will never recover from the loss of my wife. I cannot bear to witness one more day without her. It is the imprisonment of my mind. My anger would cease to exist with one word of love from her. My unconditional love extends to forgiveness on all sides. If I could just reach her. Talk to her. I want to express to her the health and wealth of my recovery.**

7. But I have lost her. She keeps probing into the past, while I kept setting our sights on the recovery of our future. *I fucked it all up. I gave it all away. And so did she.*

Mon. Dec. 20th, 2004

1. I am constantly disoriented. The pain of self-pity is hammering away at my heart. Will I die of heartache or a heart attack? *Which ever is easier please*? Just get it over with already. I'm thinking about how many times I've wished for death. How many prayers have been answered and how many got lost in the mix of forgotten faith. The prayers that were answered seem less important than the ones that got away. I guess the same would be true if the opposite was in effect.

2. Lack of sleep . . . and food, leaves me constantly weak and dizzy. What is the fate of my Christmas? Will I have to dream another bad dream? Will I be devastated once again by the transfer to another facility?

3. All of this has placed so much strain on the ties that bind our family. It is difficult to defend from the sidelines of these prison walls.

4. **I am left incapacitated with the overwhelming emotions of despair and misery. Lost in a struggle to maintain any sense of value within my own life. A sense of being left for dead. Abandoned in the bowels of hell's dungeon. Too weak to maintain any mental health. I willed for someone to take my life. I wish for it to be quick and painless.**

5. I'm tired of the same colors.

6. I do not belong here. I have never felt the connection the way others do in here. I never wanted to. I've only wanted to survive. I don't know if I will. I hope I don't make another breath. It lasts too long.

7. I can remember vividly all the feelings I have encountered during the earlier and middle stages of my incarceration. The way I would feel the skips of my beating heart from the abrupt notions of her giving in to lustful actions. I physically felt my body tense and jerk. I had visions of her with another. My dreams were so real. My anger burned. The stress applied pressure. It bore down upon me. Somehow, between us, I knew even without communicating it. These are not the suspicions of a paranoid mind. These are the likes of knowing because of the closeness we shared for so many years.

8. I'm thinking about all the times I woke up with my mind wrapped around her guilt and pleasure of being with another. I felt her guilt of giving in to shallow one liners

and deep martinis. I cursed her pleasure of being with another. I could smell another man swimming inside of her. I know my instincts are true. My notions are real. It rumbles throughout the night within my bunk. It is the imprisonment of my soul.

9. I know now what it means to love . . . to truly love the one you're with . . . and if this is the result of a love lost, I will never want to love again.

10. It is enough to want to escape. I could. I know how. The pros and cons of it tear at me to get out and stop her. If I went there, they would be there to capture me. I just wanted to watch her from a distance. Surely they'd be watching me from a further distance. 15 years automatic for attempted escape. And after that, every fantasy of being with her would cease to exist. I hope I get to her fuck again. Just once more. Easy to do. It always has been too. Could I still have my way with her, even while she's with another? Absolutely! I'll see to it. Mark these words. Mark them now. Someday . . . someway, *I will have her again.* Even if it is for just one day.

11. **I am writing this letter to you now**. It will be just two days from Christmas when you will receive it.

12. *Once again I am feeling the lies of your breath burn deep into my soul. We were to be together for Christmas. We were to remain together for life . . . forever. So many unanswered questions linger in my mind. What happened to us? We were supposed to become partners in this life, rather than enemies in this tragedy. It appears that you have left me from a long time ago; since the first weeks of my incarceration.*

13. *Why did you continue to support me with your promises, letters, and visits? I hung on to every word of support and dedication from you. And in return, I decided to embark on a complete overhaul of what remained of my life. I've made good on every aspect of what I set out to do. All you have left are words unfulfilled. I'm finding out that all of this has been a lie. Just lies to get me to hang on so to keep your options open. I've become nothing more than a net to fall on in case your solo and deceitful plans fall through and dissolve. But why? The words "wait for what" remain scorched into my memory. Shockwaves rang through my body that night. I am still in disbelief.*

14. *Everything I had become in here has been completely motivated by one thing . . . in receiving your so-called renewed love. In here, I have become a responsible, patient, Christian man, a loving parent, and a creative human being. I've learned a new language, studied and composed a lucrative business venture, and generally learned how to live again, instead of trying to die. There are too many specifics to cover, but I do know this; I thought you were waiting for me. You promised me that you were waiting.*

15. *Your actions have displayed a different heart. One that has no conscience for what you have done to my life. What was it? What changed your heart? What turned you yellow? Your actions show no remorse, conscience, or compassion for the love of people in general. As a new nurse, I find it hard to believe peoples lives will be dependant on your thoughts. God help them! You are self indulgent and rotten to the core. Your heart bleeds for all that you don't have. I've given you everything*

you've never had before. And now I have nothing, because you have taken, and given nothing in return. What happened to it all? Please explain all my unanswered questions. Why, after all this time, do you continue to lead me on?

16. *It is hard to let go of anything in such a place. Tell me to leave you . . . and I will. Continue these letters of promise and I'll believe, because it gives hope. Am I to continue to believe in this hope of our reunion? Why have you continued to withhold information that is pertinent to my release? Why did you accuse me of a crime I did not commit? You and I both know the truth so well. You did this because you "thought" you knew what was going on. If you really knew what was going on, your head would explode! But you don't. But you pretend that you do. But you don't!*

Wed. Dec. 22nd, 2004

1. It is the worst kind of feeling knowing that nobody is listening. She would actually have to take the responsibility of being human. I know she loves to talk and boast to all those within an earshot away.

2. I just want to talk to someone alive, and free, and healthy. I need to hear from someone that is actually interested in me! I'm constantly exhausted from being forever frustrated. Bitterness, confusion, and anger continue to swirl around in my head on an endless loop. I am here with everyone doing the same thing, but I am alone and disconnected, except for a few, short, brief, moments to talk.

3. I'm immersed in the constant pity of feeling sorry for myself. I'm slipping into a coma of self-regret and remorse. How pitiful I have become. My thoughts cannot clear. I cannot find words to formulate these unfocused visions. I reach for them, but cannot put my fingers on them . . . or my mind.

4. She doesn't know me anymore. We had made plans to always be together. Now, we are playing on our own agenda.

5. Inmates could be talking to me and I would just walk in a haze of semi-trance. Confusion remains.

6. I went to the phone after eating. I did not know I had to wait until trays were gone. I had just barely picked up the phone when the guard said "*no*". I stopped and walked away. Nothing more about it until a half hour later, when he approaches to tell me that I'm receiving 5 days of all restrictions for picking up the phone. I never had a chance to dial one number before he had told me to get off the phone. Now I have no phones, no commissary, no visits, and no books. It is 3 days before Christmas. They do this for self-indulgence of petty shit merits on their scorecard. They love to hear the sound of their voice. He is talking to me, but I am not recording anything he is saying. Nothing is registering. I am not coping. I pay attention to nothing but my own self-imprisonment.

7. *Another hold has been placed on me to go back to the original place of entry into this long and arduous journey.* I will be heading back to Galveston. It is where she is now. I will be just blocks away from the house where she resides. Sheltered by her parents. It is the 10th day of my hold. My time here is supposed to be done.

Why the hell am I still here? Let's hurry to get to the next stop so I can clear those charges too. I will have to wait for an officer from there to drive the 4-hour trip to pick me up. They'll do anything to get inmates back to their turf to generate money to line their pockets.

8. I'm doing everything I can to get me through the night. I'm hanging on . . . but to what? What is this I'm dreaming about? I dreamt I was leaving here, and jail forever. It is the first time I've dreamt of leaving. All other dreams have had me in the thick of it. Is it a sign? I must be dreaming. I'm fighting to hang on physically . . . mentally!

9. It wouldn't do any good to question my faith. I've resolved it to remain constant.

10. **I wanted our bond to be the steel reinforcement supporting my mental stability, but instead, all it did was bring a false dependency. I'm going out of my mind. And so this is what it means to be co-dependant; completely at the mercy of another's companionship for the sake of completion? I must escape this net! I am caught in a trap of false motivations and unbelievable resolutions. An endless loop of circle conversations in a push-n-pull struggle to reach finality.**

11. And now, I'm thinking of the lack of loyalty she even has for her son now. To abandon his right to allow me to be the daddy in his life. She has replaced me with foreign blood. Her hopes are to support this child with another man's love and money. So be it. Would it really be as pure as mine? A real father to his blood related child? Is there any comparison to the genuine likeness?

12. **What happens when our own parents die? Who will be there in the end for each other? Who will be there to fill the shoes of your family? Will it be "till death do we part?" Who will we have to truly love after our family passes? Will it be you? Shouldn't it be you? Don't you want it to be you?**

13. *I want to forgive you for all that has happened, but I can longer endure the patience of it all. I have to let God take over now. After all, I'm only human. So from this point forward, I'll leave the capacity to forgive in God's hands. I'm no longer capable.*

14. *Never can I forget the feelings of abandonment. Nor, will I ever forget the lies handed down to me during this time of despairing need. I was the last to know. You fed me sweet lies of support and hope. You deceived me into believing you would wait, but all the while, you nurtured the lust of letting another man's waste swim inside of you.*

15. *Amazingly you would come to visit me, dressed in your new fancy clothes, promising to send me money to eat and money for hygiene supplies. In six months, your generosity has afforded me $25 dollars of my own money. In six months, that is what you have sent! My parents have picked up the pieces of what remains of me since your terrible strain of having to send me back a small piece of the fortune I have given to you. Do you know what $5 dollars of commissary could have provided me? Soaps, soups, and snacks for a week!*

16. *Your disloyalty runs deep into your friends, co-workers, teachers, and even your own parents. If they could only hear the things you have said of them all.*

Thurs. Dec. 23rd, 2004

1. *It wasn't supposed to end like this. I've been putting back together, the pieces of a great life to come. You've been tearing yourself away from all that you knew me to be. You forgot to come to know me again . . . now, the way it is now. I did everything for myself out of love for you. I guess I acted too late. Maybe it's better I did wait. Who could have known you would do it like this.*

2. *Loving you was my sole motivation; my one source of command. To be a family again. I could not have accomplished anything in here without the belief of my dream to mend all the pain. I've done so much for myself. The daily drudgery of each goal being to bring happiness back into our lives. I have lost you. Maybe, I never had you.*

3. *I've dropped so many hints of wanting to tell you truths. I just can't do it through letters to you while in prison. I've been waiting to come clean on a couple of things. To make things right . . . no matter how wrong it was. I guess there is no need to now. Not at 4 am in the morning anyway.*

4. **I have no concept of this being a Merry Christmas: The hustle bustle, music, colors, crowds, snow, or anything that could possibly bring happiness in this place. The little hints I see in the newspapers, or on the commercials only slice cuts deeper into my desire to be home. Gadget sales on TV only remind me of what I should be buying for the kids to spread holiday cheer.**

5. It is two days before Christmas. I just missed the last request for booking to let me go. There will be no cop coming to pick me up for transfer to Galveston. There is no way I'll be going any where near the completion of my prison sentence. I don't even know when this sentence will end anymore. I will remain here, in this dungeon, for the celebration of the birth of Christ. My family will not be happy. My mother is torn. She has endlessly tried to resolve each conflict of interest preventing me from being released. Now, it is out of her hands.

6. It is always so cold in here. I fill my plastic, stadium cup with hot water just to hold it with my hands. I do this to warm my hands and spread whatever warmth I can throughout my body. It works. I am on restriction now. I cannot even drink my water bottles or hot chocolate even though they are paid for already.

7. Is it here I will celebrate the birth of Christ, while I remain to be an imprisoned man? Is it here I will lift up my arms to the lord and feast upon his generous love and compassion? Is it here, I will find the strength of his power to carry me on with my spirit lifted up high for him to shine His light into my soul? Is this the mercy of Christ within my life? Is this the hand of my free will or the destiny of the Lord? What is to become of me? When will enough be enough?

8. For all my life from these days forward, I will remain without my lost love. Be still my beating heart, for there can be no reason for life without the love to carry me through to a greater purpose. I am truly lost without her. It has been the foremost reason to survive these places of hell. I thought the heaven of her presence would be waiting. I thought the softness of her skin could keep me warm. I had hoped the scent of her breath would whisper sweet nothings into my ear. I am wrong.

9. **This is my burial.** I have experienced this death many countless times since coming to jail.

10. **I would pull the sheet over my head. The rise would provide for an air pocket. It becomes my make shift coffin. I can lay here, in silence, and play out my dying whispers just as the last traces of molecules of air vanish beyond my lips. I wait for the ground to cave in, and the dirt to forever seal my failures inside so nobody else can see them. I cannot envision one more success or moment of happiness to seep into my dying body. Freedom has become a foreign tribal language, which I cannot decipher. It will never be discovered as long as the tribe eludes my grasp. And now that the mysterious tribe has gone into the thicket of the brush, my freedom from this suffocating death will never be realized. *The exhale of my breath, becomes the stench of my death.***

11. I cannot put my thoughts together anymore. I can't seem to make sense of it all. Nothing registers.

12. This place is a breeding ground for bacterial growth and viral diseases. Unsanitary conditions are harbored and spread through lack of goodwill or common sense. Inmates are washing spoons that they use to feed us in the shower stalls. They reuse cups. Everybody is continuously grabbing, scratching, and itching themselves. Yet still, they want to shake your hands. Most seem uninterested in defending themselves against contamination. Others are just ignorant to the related factors of spreading germs. And still others, well . . . they are deliberate in their quest to communicate their death wish on anyone within reach.

13. I am going through transfer after transfer. There have been times when I would wake up not even remembering which prison I was in at that moment. In isolation, I could go for days without knowing where I was. When I would ask the guards, they would just laugh it off. Sometimes, I would go all day without realizing the location had changed. It was all the same hell to me, just a different location. I am reliving memories of a lost place on an endless ride of despair.

14. *This is how you have honored the father of your first living child. Finally, after so many abortions. With so many killings of the fetus, you decide to have a child.*

And this is how you will honor this boy; by abandoning, deceiving, and lying to his father; by accusing his father of crimes uncommitted; and by stealing from him. You, yourself, hide in shame, as I am publicly humiliated. This is the way you have dishonored me.

15. *And for the rest of your days, there will be no stopping the circumference of reminders coming back to bite you in the ass. It will come back around.*

Fri. Dec. 24th, 2004

1. After lunch is finished I am to pack my belongings. It is 11:30 am. I am being uprooted again. I am one of five inmates to be transferred out of here to the main jail from the annex. *I just made trustee.* Damn . . . the very word that conotates the worst to come; washing dirty drawers or dirty dishes. What's the difference? Either way, it's going to suck-big time! My hours will be 2 am to 8 am. Well . . . this fits my schedule since I'm awake into the wee hours of the morning anyway. But I'd rather be writing.

2. I was led down into long halls and passageways to reach my new Christmas residence. I walked into a breath of fresh, warm air. But it was quickly taken away from me as I poked my head out the open door to look outside.

3. The dorm was less restrictive; open policy on watching TV. We were able to choose from a large collection of books. Each bed had a private table desk at the end; great for eating, writing, and reading. I hid behind the beams to workout. I began to stuff my pillowcase with huge books to do curls. Overall, the place is warmer. It's got college dorm style beds, with shelves and a desk. There are private showers, sinks, hot and cold water, comfortable chairs, and the environment is so much quieter. It's quieter because the guards are not in our faces. They are reading or watching TV with us. They are not control freaks so there is no conflict here. The less the guards interact, the more civil the environment! It's also a well-behaved place because nobody wants to give up places like this while in prison. Sure, I'll scrub shit for six hours a day out there, so I can enjoy the next eighteen in here. I sat back on a chair and indulged myself on the new Spiderman 2 movie on DVD.

4. I received mail from her son today: she actually is the one to send it to me for him. She says nothing of herself. She did leave the scent of perfume in the letter. It's what a whore would do for her pimp. Nothing more. She obviously has embarked on a journey to forget the man that gave her everything. It's probably the only way to avoid the pain every time she looks in the mirror.

5. I am residing in a dark place that no one else can see-not even me! I am trying to feel my way out by groping into the black, thick, stale air. I still have not reached anything long after the panic has set in. That's the worse part of not seeing what's before

217

you; not feeling the walls of stability around yourself. It's a kind of suspension. I remember what seems so long ago on that terrible night. When I thought it could get no worse, the stench of abuse had filled the air. Being witness to that nightmare began a timetable of suffering that will extend far beyond my lifetime. *It will remain with my children because one day, they too, will know the truth of your cowardness of not allowing a father to do his duty and perform his role as a daddy. They will know how quick you are to trade off men as easy as monkeys in a camp. It will die with you as an old lady, and be reborn again in the stories of your grandchildren. These lies that spewed from the gutters of that septic tank in the middle of your face will live on in your children's children. They will know you . . . through my words.*

6. *You should have waited. You should not have led me on. You should have let me go . . . along time ago!*

7. *I remember that night in June so long ago. The very next day, you let my son, Nicholas go. You immediately broke up the family and sent him back to where he didn't want to be. You stripped him from his brother. And you took any notion of being a faithful wife, and threw it out the window. It's what you do easiest. Whore yourself out to the next contender. And there always will be another "Johnson" looking to get some of the action baby!*

8. *I just didn't think it would happen so fast. I gave you six years. You couldn't give me six months. As a matter of fact, you didn't even wait sixty days. Even with your other "fiancé" before me. It only took you one day of knowing me to have you slobbering in my bed for more. And even back then, it took you three months to tell him. I guess what came around then, has come around now. And it will come to the next guy too. It's been coming around to you for along time now. Just ask your friends. You will never enjoy them the way I have.*

Sat. Dec. 25th, 2004

1. I was awakened at 1:40 am this morning. I was led downstairs to the kitchen with about 10 others. I am to stand in an assembly line of food trays being slid past me on rollers. Here, we all take our turns throwing food into the tray as it slides by our section. We are to feed over 3000 inmates for breakfast. The place is cold, wet, and filthy. *There are places in this massive kitchen that have been abandoned all together. Growth of "whatever" lies about in the corners, under tables, and in food storage.* Nobody gives a shit because nobody cares for inmates . . . especially the food supervisors. Some of the equipment has lain dormant for years.

2. After the trays are sent out, we get to eat our two trays; that's supposed to be the incentive of feeding people. We get one extra tray to fill the void of continuous hunger.

3. After feeding time, we begin the longest 4 hours of my life. It is freezing in here. I have rubber boots with holes in them. I have no socks on. The rest of the hours are spent mopping and more mopping. There is no end to it. I mop and re-mop. Only to be told to do it again because someone drags and spills dirty water and food across the floors just as I'm finishing. We scrub trays and place them into the washing machine. It is so cluttered with food; most trays come out full of food stains and cleaning residue. We wait for hours in the cold to be placed back into our dorms. It is past 10 am when we arrive back to hot showers and a bunk.

4. *This is the morning of my Christmas . . . without you. You promised we would be together this morning and for all time. I'm thinking about why I'm still here. You ignored all of what was supposed to be done for my release. You took months to send important papers to help past due deliveries and refunds. It has taken months of persuading you to help my parents find the information. And now, I'm hearing that you have sent X-mas cards out to my family from your son, soliciting money for gifts. This has to be the lowest form of crime that I know; stealing from those that have already given. Please send the money back to them. You are not worthy of corresponding with them. Communicating with them can only bring back thoughts of your irresponsibility and rogue behavior.*

5. I'm listening to this kid sing to the "*Stairway to Heaven*" song. He doesn't know who sings it though. How young does that make him?

6. For lunch today, I am eating ham, mashed potatoes, and cake. For Christmas dinner, it's a bologna sandwich and lemonade. After, I enjoyed a good workout.

7. What is my family doing? They are celebrating the best of what Christmas has to offer; great food, good fun, loving family, and the power of Christ's presence. There is no loneliness in the house today where my brothers and sisters celebrate this holiday occasion. Are the kids playing in the snow? Will they say a prayer for me? **If you were in jail today, you would like to believe that someone is always thinking of you. They probably are: it is the burden we place on loved ones when we come to jail. This is definitely not the time of year to be in jail today! No time ever is good for such a place.**

8. Everybody, but me (knock 3x), is coughing and spitting up phlegm. Everybody is hacking away at their illnesses. I'm tired of sweeping away everybody's filth from my bunk area.

9. And now it will come to pass, my child is born to a single mother whore. He has become a bastard child. It would be safe to say, *he will live a quality life*, however, the past will rise up to meet him. It will remind him of his mother's cowardly acts and blatant disregard for family values. This is a woman of deception, lies, deceit, and thievery.

10. Even now, she continues to deny any wrongdoing. I so desperately want her to answer my questions. I already know already she can tell me whatever she feels will keep her clean from the dirt she expels. Lying has become her truth. She is so desperately seeking to find out the truth of something I know. She will play whatever role she thinks I want her to be to get that truth. But nothing can be resolved. Between us, it's all become a lie. It always has been.

11. In these six years, you have spoken of me as the best of this, and the greatest of that. You describe me as competitive, good looking, and outstanding in so many ways. You gave me public praise of my hard work and courage for what I do as your provider. I have been a family man, friend, and lover to you. You praise me for being the pivotal point of our home; the anchor that grounded stability. I gave you a livelihood you had never experienced before me. All of me has been on public display in a positive way, right up until you walked out on me. And now, for all time, I have become the crutch of your agonizing sessions of airing all of your dirty laundry for everyone to see, smell, and hear. It is within the wake of the filth spewing from the gutters of that septic tank in the middle of your face, I have been tormented by, lied to, cheated on, betrayed to, stolen from, and incarcerated in . . . all on your behalf. You have been fighting at the gates of hell to tell your story to whoever had to suffer the torrential drenches of the actress turn tricks into tears.

12. **Today is my day. For I seek justice for all men. And as they read on, I know they will rejoice in silent celebration, knowing that finally a man seeks to reclaim his name. This one's for all the hard working, devoted men and women with**

loving, trusting, and supportive spouses. Hold each other tight. Take a bow and know that the family unit is the thread that holds society together. To sever that knot, sends homes into chaos . . . just as I'm doing here today.

13. Lack of loyalty tears away the fabric of businesses; it eats away at friendships; and it dissolves relationships. In all, it destroys everything of value, as we know it.

14. *For six years, I pounded the pavement, living on only commissions. I was out there in the mix of it. I braved the elements of everyday rain, sleet, and snow. I've trekked through the blistering sun and the freezing rain. All to keep earning money so you could decorate our home with furnishings, wear pretty clothes, enjoy fanciful dinners, and dance the night away in clubs. I have provided you with luxury vehicles to drive and vacations to remember. Never once, did I complain to you about your lack of ambition to move a muscle to earn a living. I moved through all the "no" sales. I relentlessly leaned into it and conquered the "sale" so you could afford "the sales". I did it for you . . . for us. Because I loved you. Because I love you still. That's what eternally means. Loving without conditional circumstances. But your proximity of love to me has been directly proportional to the thickness of my wallet . . . and my pants!*

15. *I have forgiven you for so many events in our life . . . since the beginning of our relationship. An unconditional love defines a love based on what you are, an imperfect person, rather than what you do, or the things you've done.*

16. *You've been fighting at the gates of hell, screaming your story to all those that choose to endure hearing it. Now, I'm here to speak it once, loudly, so everyone listens, and more importantly, understands.*

17. **You should have waited. Not only for what you can see on me, but also, for what you can see within me. I miss you. I miss all the things we did, and the places we were. I wish you would find me again. You would be pleasantly surprised.**

Wed. Dec. 29th, 2004

1. I have been in court today. More bullpens. More waiting. More listening to sentences, strategies, and complaints, from inmates who want to convince the system their case against the charges brought against them are valid. I listen to the prosecutors give out prison sentences randomly. *Have a lawyer . . . get some probation. Don't have a lawyer . . . do some time.* The court files read through inmate cases as fast as flipping through a book.

2. She came to see me this morning during visitation hours. Always probing for past suspicions. She talks in circles, never actually answering clearing. We sit in a private room separated by thick glass. I am weeping uncontrollably. **I am reaching but I cannot touch. I place my hand against the glass partition. It does nothing to warm my body through this imagination of touch.** She seems to be detached from me. She complains about so many unheard of things from the past. She tells me she has a *"friend"* who is getting her though the pain. What a crock! She asks me if I will have my own money when I get out. She says she doesn't have any for me. She is wearing a new outfit. She seems to forget I am a moneymaker . . . and I always will be. She has spent all my money, and the money of others who donated to the fundraiser we were working on at the time of my arrest.

3. *She has spoken to my son, Nicholas.* He's here in Houston living with his mother now. He's not happy. He wants to come down to the Island to see me. His mother won't let him. *I miss him. He knows this already.*

4. *I'm thinking of all the places of interests; the people, the museums, in all those cities I brought you to over the years.*

5. I ordered a normal sized toothbrush. It is my first long toothbrush in over six months. I no longer have to stick my hand inside my mouth to get to scrub my molars. It is a good feeling. Actually, the feeling is liberating!

Fri. Dec. 31ˢᵗ, 2004

1. It has been six months and 13 days upon entering the system. I am in Galveston. *The place where it all began.* I'm standing in total disgust of the filth and stench of my now familiar surroundings. I have stood here before. I am standing in the 3J block. It is the medical ward where the nurse placed me on that unforgiving night. The painful memories of what seems to be ten years ago, has flooded back into my life. It now claws at my heart to see this again. Has it only been 193 days ago that I stood in this 8-cell block, listening to all the "crazies" screaming and hollering? I looked down the hallway to the Number #2 cell. I could not see in it from where I was standing, but I knew what was there. I didn't have to look any farther. I sat in the dayroom staring at the blue screen of the TV. I am daydreaming. The TV is playing back the sequence of events that took place during those 14 days of insanity.

2. **I'm watching this dude in the No# 6 cell. He is on his hands and knees sweeping the floor under the bunk and around the toilet. He is using his hands to sweep up the filth. Now he is licking the palms of his hands to clean the dirt off. He keeps making his bed over and over. He is pitching cards onto the bed; jacks always first. He is going back and forth between these functions all the while that I'm sitting . . . waiting . . . watching.**

3. The nurse finally called me in to the ward to be seen. She is beautiful; bronze skin, with long, black, hair. She speaks with full lips and seductive bed eyes. *My hormones raged*! I immediately looked for a place to relieve myself, but could not find one. I will hold the memory of her face and the scent of her perfume in my mind until it is time.

4. **On the way out, I looked into those cages once more. I had promised myself beyond any belief that I would ever return to such a place. I had promised myself would never set foot in this hell hole again. I was wrong. 193 days later, I am standing in a place I thought I had long escaped. I came here once. And now I've been here twice . . . even though I haven't left the system yet. There will not be a third time.**

5. The sharp stench of urine and stale, musty air remains with me once again as I ascend up the elevator to the dorm pods.

6. I am back in my dorm. It is 8 am. It is the last day of the year.
7. It has been 48 days since feeling the embrace of arms around my body. I will actually look forward to court proceedings knowing that I would get to feel the hands of that cute female guard gliding her hands up and down my legs, arms, and body. My favorite is always when she grasps my chest and runs her hand down my stomach. She does it slow and gracefully. She knows that I like it. She does it just for me. Better than she would for her own husband. My body aches for compassion.
8. I have finally received my stamps and letters. I immediately broke down to write her. I am asking her for friendship and a chance to be a daddy to her child. Why am I doing this? At this particular moment in time, I am missing her terribly. Then, thoughts of hatred begin to streak through my heart.
9. This is my 11th pod within the 7th district in 193 days. I'm thinking I've got one more to go. But that's a lost hope.
10. My mother is ill. It all came to a head the other day. She does not comprehend the suffering I am feeling in this place. She thinks I'm playing a part. I know nobody could begin to realize the devastations of being rejected by my wife. It is mine to hold. My family must have known about my wife leaving me a long time ago. It was still fresh in my mind . . . and my heart. Why was I the last to know? What to do? What to do?
11. My mother had tried to come yesterday. I am ridden with guilt. She had left her house in San Antonio at 6 am, but turned back, due to the fog. I didn't want her to drive 4-5 hours for a twenty minute visit and then, have to turn around and go home; *A ten hour drive for a twenty minute visit.* These are the sacrifices she wills herself to do for her son. It has taken its toll on her. It has taken its toll on everyone, especially my mother.
12. Mom and her husband had just spent a month in Thailand and surrounding areas. They just missed the floods from the earthquake. So many have died amidst the flooding and devastation. It could have been my mother. They are suffering in that land now, more than I could ever imagine. I will not complain today. How can I? Even though, I know three simple steps would be the light at the end of the tunnel. Three steps, two phone calls, and one motion, and the doors would swing open to release me to freedom. But that's not going to happen today. Not today, tomorrow, or the next day. Still, I will not complain. *At least not for a few more minutes.*
13. **My wife will be in the arms of another tonight. It is New Year's Eve. She is sharing her dreams of the future with someone who could not possibly love her the way I do. It will never mean as much to him as it does to me. The impossibility of not reaching her carries with it the burden of struggle so great, it leaves me impaled against the floor. It takes my breath away. My lungs are crushed, and I am unable to inhale. How do I keep the hope of this letter reaching her?**
14. What should be foreign in sight and sounds soon becomes familiar, bearable, and tolerable. But, never accepted! Here inside, I feel disconnected. It didn't matter

how involved I became among the talkers or within a conversation with someone specific. I never felt the enjoyment of any memory of conversation. It always ended up to *"why am I still here?"* My concentration never lasted that long anyway. All the times I was having conversation with an inmate, I would be wishing I were talking to her instead. This feeling of wishful thinking never went away . . . never! I longed to hear her laugh. I wanted to hold her hands. I dreamed of making love. To take a drive along the beach, or just to go eat lunch at a fast food restaurant would have been nice. **These are the certain things you never think about when you're not in jail. Come here, and they immediately become the very things you have take for granted. Are you prepared to come to jail today? Nobody ever is.**

15. I wonder if she'll write back? I wonder if she'll visit? I wonder if I'll ever see her again? I've lost my property, my clothes, and my pictures. Photos that I cherish so much. Will she give it all away? *"Sold"* . . . to the greediest motherfucker wiling to pay her the most amount of money. She has sold herself for a buck. Now she has sold her soul for less. But how she has lost so much more.

16. I'm listening to endless arguments of nothingness: Cookies to go, dominoes slamming. Who couldn't light the dope? Why wasn't such and such not offered another joint? Why did he split it in two and sell them when he finally did get one? Endless loops of struggle to have recognition for who we are.

17. *And these are the days to pass.* Always wondering, never knowing, but oh . . . so very predictable now! The facts remain. I am here. I am not leaving. And I have no idea when I will be leaving. It's been like this for months. It's been the *"not knowing"* that has left me in peril. *There has been no beginning and end.* I never know when I'll be transferred or just left here to rot within these so-called walls of justice. All the while, **I've been climbing the walls, searching for sanity. Waiting for answers, and trying to survive. Searching for an end that never seems to realize. Attempting to pass the moments of another minute, hour, and day with each breath.**

18. The clouds finally broke above my head to reveal the blue skies through the window. I see blue . . . clear, blue, beautiful skies. I've been waiting for days to see the sun shining through. I'm gazing at the local beach sky and wondering . . . "is she out there?" I'm tired of looking at the same old taupe color in here. I want to see colors.

19. The window spans 3x6 feet above my head. It is enough to catch the occasional bird flying or to see the clouds lazily drift across my path of sight. I lay underneath it looking up. **I am dreaming of our lives with memories in sight.**

Sat. Jan. 1ˢᵗ, 2005

1. The night passed into a new year last night while I slept on my bunk. It hadn't even occurred to me to stay awake for such an event. The thoughts of celebrations were too distant. But ironically, the party was only 2 blocks away. I had actually spent the last year of my life celebrating every night with bad boys, bitches, bands, and bars. Just two blocks away. Only a stone's throw away. Yet, I know nobody, but nobody, could hear my silent cries for love and compassion. No matter how loud I screamed.

2. Is she there with them now? Is her body close to his? Is her heart here with me? I played tackle and block throughout the night, until I fell asleep. My dreams are better these days, though I don't really remember them. I just know it doesn't hurt as much to wake up. That always changes throughout the day with my afternoon crashes.

3. **I'm thinking about all the celebrations; cheers to each other, kisses between lovers, toasts among friends. In general, it's a celebration of life among the free. How many will keep their resolutions? How many will continue their promises in the dark throughout the year? Who is lying? How many are dying? How many went to jail last night? How many are sitting in jail right now? How many are headed that way today? How many thought of the consequences before they acted upon the impulse to break the law? Did you get singled out and sent to jail today? Sorry if you did. It's always the case of "wrong place at the wrong time" isn't it? If only this. If only that.**

4. *What parents are mourning the loss of their child this morning?* How many people had to suffer in their death while celebrating the future of their lives? How many were innocent victims? Nobody expects it, and most never see it coming. Each loss of life sends a tidal wave of ill effect down onto the families, relatives, and friends of the deceased. **What a way to start the birth of a new year . . . with the announcement of death at your doorstep!**

5. I awoke to a clear blue window above me. Completely consistent in color. The brightness of the sky soaked through my skin. I made no new resolutions this morning. I've been planning-and executing, my vows of resolutions since June 28ᵗʰ

of last year. Ten days after entering the prison system. Now if I could just get out of here, I would be in good shape. I'm ready to work the rest of my plan.

6.   It is Saturday. The first day of the year 2005. I wonder if I'll be visited. I longed to call everybody, but my pre-paid phone card had not been delivered yet. I'm glad. All I would have probably done was cry during the conversations with family anyway. Football blared from the TV all day. I was watching even when I didn't want to be watching. It was just there, along with my book, my cellie, my guard, and my thoughts. It was all . . . just there.

7.   It is Saturday night and my phone card has arrived. It's a dangerous thing to have when feeling so abandoned and desolate. The first thing to do is reach out to those who you think care. Or at least you try to convince yourself they do. I struggled not to call her. The temptation lingered. I resolved myself to the most obvious outcome. I knew nothing good would come from trying to mend old wounds with a 15-minute time card. I opted to call my father. He began to cough intensely. It was a violent, overly strained, dry heave of a cough. I was taken back, and for the first time, I understood the extent of his illness. We hung up the phone. *My father*: a man of courage, struggling to do the best he can, while battling to stay alive. I must get out . . . before it's too late!

8.   I'm afraid to begin to believe that this chapter in my life will end soon. I've been let down so many times now. I've heard the word "*Rco1, ATW, and pack your shit*" enough times to know that all it may mean is a transfer in another tour toward another bunk in another place called hell. It's all the same. A different side of hell with the same burning stench to bring tears to your eyes.

9.   I know I'm ready to face the world as a mature adult now. Regretfully, I've had to venture into the darkest of places to find out what needed to be done. But I've got myself together now. *I'm ready to be a law-abiding citizen now*. Truly, this is a major requirement of being a successful person in the free world. I never said anything about respecting the law, or it's guards. But I will obey it.

10.   **None of this would have been possible without God on my side. The promise of His word has entered my life. It is an open abundant, available resource that opened the door for me to take responsibility for my life.**

11.   I spoke with my sister. We talked about work and breaking free from the patterns that mark my life. I knew, in fact, I had already broken free from that circle of destruction a long time ago. I have been preparing for my near future with the long term in mind for quite some time now. I know now; **I'm worth more on the outside, than in here.**

Sun. Jan. 2nd, 2005

1. I'm thinking of my mother and family. Not once has she faltered in her relentless pursuit of trying to get me out. Nor did she ever leave my side. I've cost her retirement money and added years to her life. Still, she remains. *Thanks mom*! I hope I can show you it will be worth it. I will show you by adhering to the right decisions . . . every day of my life! Looking back on it, I realize that if it wasn't for her, I could have easily left this earth. I would have given up all together. I would have found a way to stop the pain. The loneliness and despair were many times too great. It was during the deepest darkest depths of despair, I hung onto the love of my family. And at the same time, a deceiving wife was tearing at me. I've had to fight two entities of evil while being here; what I see and what I feel. Isn't that what being alive is all about? Being loved.

2. I'm thinking about my wife leaving me. Just knowing now, that she had been leading me on with any support of companionship is enough to pour liquored salt on my already open wounds. My money, my vehicle, my business, and all life as I knew it, is gone. Probably the best thing that could have happened to me. I just don't know it yet.

3. Through it all, my anger and bitterness continues to subside. I'm trying not to think about it as much, but the pain still lingers. I remember back to how devastated I had felt. It hurt so terribly bad. **My strength in my faith of God has been strained to its limit, many times over. But who am I to say what suffering meant in terms of the Almighty's shadow. Nothing I have experienced compares to his sacrifice.**

4. It doesn't help to dwell on it. I am forced to move on. Imagine that! I have spent these past 6 months putting my life back together, while she spent my last pennies tearing it apart. A love lost . . . a life realized. The hints are obvious, but of course, love is blind. I guess I should have figured it out years ago, after seeing the same bills getting paid three times.

5. I've been tested so many times since my release from the state facility. Never knowing when it will end has been the hardest part. I know, this too, will come to pass. I've had to say that many times.

6.   Is this the mercy of Christ; to put me here? Was this the ingredient necessary to save my life? Is it that unbeknown to me, I just added an additional twenty years to my life? Could it be now, I'll finally be able to live a frugal, productive life. Will I continue to endure through life's challenges? Can I utilize these very sound business practices presented to me?

Mon. Jan. 3rd, 2005

1. I am here today, because of a false accusation against me. I have been accused of domestic violence, assault with bodily injury. I have sat in this crowded dorm of angry and loud men for days on end considering the facts. It all comes down to the fact that she spoke first. And because of that, I had to be publicly displayed for all the community to see. I had to defend myself from the lying words of a cheating wife.

2. I remember that early evening way back. She had come up to my loft unexpectedly. I was still sleeping. So was everybody else. People that shouldn't have still been there. I couldn't open the door. She began to knock and bang at the door and walls. I was told that if I didn't open the door she would start *"crying wolf"*. And she did just that. The police came a knocking. I really didn't think I had to worry about her going as far as she did. She had scraped her hands up against the rough cement walls. When I saw it later that week, I instantly knew she had staged the marks. Clearly, it had been from a self-inflicted act. I could see where she had banged on the walls and door trying to get me to open the door.

3. The guilt ran deep in her veins. She had immediately tried to reverse the charge. Can't do that anymore. The state took over and decided to prosecute. She swore she'd never show. She never did. I realize now the arresting officer must have been so pissed from the words that I had exchanged with him. He feels for a crying whore who couldn't get her way. She *"thought"* other people were upstairs in my loft. There was no way of knowing until right now as I speak these words. Half the people are her friends still. But they'll never tell. Neither will I.

4. So it comes to pass, I am still in this God forsaken place. Through the New Years weekend celebration, I could hear the party down below in the streets. These used to be my streets. Now it is my imprisonment.

5. We had made amends since that day. I knew I had to get it together for the summer of '04, and had starting paying attention to her and the boy. It had been going well for the 2 months up to that fateful night in June. And now it is January '05 and I'm here because she's not letting up in her attempts to now keep me here. I've already paid a bond on this charge but nobody is letting me out. *Why?* Because now all

230

my customers have placed charges of theft on me. Customers that she could take care of over six months ago. Customers who have had their checks cashed through her bank so she could keep any kind of lifestyle. Customers who only wanted to hear they were to be reimbursed. But no, she couldn't come forward just for the moment and relieve them of their anger by responding. She chose to ignore it all together. She chose to ignore my parent's pleas to get the required info. Now there is another hold on me. So even when I leave here, I will transfer up north . . . . way up north!

6. I cannot leave here just yet. I've been told by my court appointed attorney that the prosecution is seeking another six months in prison for this assault charge that's still looming over me. *Do I want to stay here another day?* Not on your life! If I plead not guilty, they will set a court day a long time away. Then I'll have to sit here for all this time. I can't. I've got to get out. Not even she can get these charges dismissed now. She realizes her mistake. This boils down to being at the wrong place when a woman of anger spills her revengeful spit out on to the street.

7. *I appeal to you, as my reader: It does not matter how far away you are at any given moment, if she cries "wolf" and your name happens to be on that bill . . . you're done! I never opened the door for her and this infliction has been placed upon me. This is your fair warning. If you feel it coming to an eruption, get out and get away.*

8. She accused me of a crime because of *"what she thought she knew"*. She didn't know the half of it. They never do. She was hurt that day because I didn't go to her friends wedding. For what? So she begins her revengeful ways to seek retribution. Just to feel better about putting me down. I've got to just feel sorry for that kind of person who can lash out at someone they love for feeling rejected.

9. If I plea *"guilty"*, I can leave on time served. Absolutely! Do I even give a rat's ass what my criminal record looks like from where I'm standing? Nope! I want to go home. I'm trying to get mom to post a bond in the other city so I don't have to go to another prison. Mom is telling me to ride it out. She's telling me to just stay in prison until they decide to transfer me. *I can't do it.*

10. I'm almost forty years young now. I want my family back. She should have waited to see all the good. Has she really moved on with someone else? Does she love him? Breaking the family up would be so much bigger than what I have done. The rewards of keeping the family together are great. The consequences would be worse, 10 times over, and for the rest of our lives. I know that one part of her is so angry. She is torn. **Can she not see that the worst things that happened to me have actually become the best thing that happened to me?**

I'm putting together the pieces of this *I'm working on this . . . whatever*. It describes a man stripped to the bone. There is nothing left to take. He is at the beginning of what's left of his life. Now, he knows everything that is important . . . but nobody's listening.

This man, put to the proof, falls apart
Standing alone, the wind becomes his only audience
The cries of his shame are scattered in the dark
Meaningful words become howls of echoes
Faded briskly to a whistle
A tiresome groan warms the air
It lasts only as quickly as it cools
    Nothing is heard
    Emptiness fills the night occupying everything that is lost
    The remainder of this man has become only, but a rock
    Steadfast, immoveable, and resistant
    I have become unttemptable

    Peter, the rock

11. **I want my family back!**
12. *I don't understand after all these years; I can't get you to forgive me the way I have with you. I've had to learn it! You must know the checks and balances in our lives would never allow for this to happen again. Don't you want to see all the good that has come from this terrible chapter in our lives? You fell in love with half the man that I am today. Nothing compares to the character I possess today. You were so easy when I was so casual. It seem you have much pleasure in revisiting the bar scene. Do it, if you must to satisfy your sense of needing that kind of attention. You asked me to do my time and get it together for the long run, for us, for the kids! Don't break up the family! It's bigger than what I've done. Don't you know the consequences for the kids-and us, can be far worse for our lives if we don't at least consider our fortune together. People are given chances . . . 2nd chances! I have given you a daily run down of my commitment to a healthy, productive life. Everything is different now! I can forgive for most things. How can I forgive your decision to turn your kid into a bastard child? Take the time to know me again. If you can do it for another man, surely you can do it for me, and for your child. Ask me to come back into your life! Tell me to do this. Make it right. Demand me to make it right! Always and forever.*
13. *Now, read this . . . then wrap your mind around it! I know one part of you is so angry. I could tell you that I deserve it. But I don't! What I deserve, and should be granted, is your commitment to stand by your man! What you deserve is to know all of it. The complete truth. And after, what you should do is wrap your arms around me and kiss me passionately. Tell me you know this could never happen again. Tell me you know this is true to your heart. I am paying this debt for both of us. If the world knew the truth, you'd be right in here with me.*

14. *Do you need seduce someone I know to feel even? Do you need to get even? Have you already? Your past says this is the way to make things right. Will your past continue to indicate your future? Will the two wrongs make a right for you? If that's what it takes, then do it and get it over with. Then come back to me.*

Tues. Jan. 4ᵗʰ, 2005

1. Johnny Ray tells me, "*Time is the healer. Don't push it on her*". This is so she can heal from what's been told to her. Johnny and I are having sensible conversations. He speaks with the wisdom of a true cellie doing his time. He's got the golden rule down. "*Give it some time, and abide by your time*". He says, "All this running to the phone is going to push her away". I must let it come to pass.

Wed. Jan. 5th, 2005

1. The woman pressed play to the Lord's song. It echoed through K block. We wept openly. Grown men giving their hearts and souls to the Lord. I stood back in silent celebration of my love for God.

2. **Come with me to church. Come to the house of the Lord. Sit with me. Talk to me. Listen to me. Fellowship with me in the name of God and His glory upon you. Let him guide us. Let us put him first in our lives. Worship Him, with me. He is almighty powerful to our lives. He will grant peace to our angry souls. Come to me. Let us pray to Him. I've waited so long for this. This has not happened over night. It has been cultivating within me for many months since coming here. At first I was resistant. Mostly rebellious. I have come to a crossroads in my life so many times. Each negative outcome has been directly proportional to the distance of my faith in God. The further I was away from His message, the more chaotic my life became.**

3. *I wanted my time with you as a free man to salvage the family. I wanted to come forth with what you deserve to know. You will not be disappointed with my character. Just let me live to be a free man to tell you. You said you are happy in your life without me; your job, school, friends, lovers, child, home, and family. Why couldn't my name be included in your happiness? I am in disbelief to live one more day without you.*

4. *I have been so angry in here for the many times you have abandoned me. You did this long before you knew. Weeks on end. So many heartbroken nights of trying to justify your neglect of my life given to you. Anger and bitterness have prevailed. Confusion has halted any worthiness within my weary mind. It has come to pass that the Lord has healed much of my torment. The pain still lingers. I continue to hold vigilance to your love coming back to me. You constantly share that we are truly soul mates. Why can't you see into my soul now? You continue to reject me with every visit. Why do you continue to come here everyday. Your smiling face holds contempt. Do not make one more excuse of why you cannot write me.*

5. *I am standing in the middle of the street. I can see you. Yes, I see you waiting for me to get you. There you are, coming up the street to meet me . . . to greet me, with*

a smile. Because you are happy to see me, and so am I. We kiss and embrace for a love shared. Hello is understood. "Let's eat" you say. So we do. And we have fun . . . because we are fun. We are extraordinary.

6. **I am weeping now. The pain crushes my chest. The lump has become lodged in my throat. My tears flow freely to the floor. There is barely a pause between splashes. It is never ending.**

7. *So now we get the little one because he's waiting. He's waiting to take his walk. He's waiting and crying because he misses us. He's misses us. He's crying on the floor. He sees us and now he's happy. He's happy now because we're going for a walk. Together, we are going to walk and talk. We are talking and listening to the little one. He is pointing at all the things along the walk; the bushes, the grass. We can see the ants, and he's laughing. Now he's happy and he's laughing because we are there. So we are still walking. Can we walk some more together? As we walk, will you let me hold you? Can we hold each other? Can we group hug? Could you be happy with that? To hold me. Your head in my chest, and my arms around you. Can I keep you secure? Can you pretend? I know I can wait all my life to feel the warmth of your embrace upon my skin just one more time. It has been 53 days since I have felt such a pleasure from you. I will wait 53 years more.*

8. *__To forgive is to become unburdened with details.__ I will satisfy your wishes, no matter what your intent may be thereafter. I pray for our outcome. I want your motivations to be honorable with me. Have you received a love as deep and as meaningful as mine? Can we cherish the companionship we held so close to our hearts. Remember the fun you keep reminding me about? Imagine the fulfillment of my attention to you now, that those burdens of sin are gone. They are, in fact, so far from my life. __The best of everything has come into my life because of the worst things that could have happened to me.__ I know you know this. It must occupy your heart, mind, and soul. I know it.*

9. *I wonder if you are capable of taking responsibility for you're past the way I have with mine? Should we just leave it there . . . in the past? Or will you continue to drag it with you. Mine is over now. I've come to terms with it. Your decisions will haunt you for all times if you choose the path you're on. I will keep the memories. The wonderful memories of us, and the kids. Can't we walk together in the present? Can't we look to the future and prepare for what's to come? Can you include me in your happiness? Eternally, me*

Sat. Jan. 8th, 2005

1. Yesterday, I pleaded guilty to still, another case of crime. I remain in jail today. If only someone could have paid a simple $200 dollars of $2000 on a required bond. I would be home today, but I'm not. Hopefully, I'll only be waiting on one more city to come and get me. It is for the crime of theft; deliveries not made due to irresponsibility's and business practices. It makes no difference. Theft is theft. To take money and not deliver is stealing, no matter what the circumstances. She sure got to enjoy their money. I should have moved away from her long before this trap of *"wanting to be accepted at all costs"* set into my life.

2. So far, it's been dope, driving while license suspended, child support, assault, and now, theft. When will it end?

3. So here and now, I'm waiting for the train . . . I mean the chain. Yea, that's it, the chain gang is coming to take me away from my family, my wife, and my life. We've been talking in the mornings. She comes to see me before going to work and school. She's listening. She has conscience to my pleas. She's available to try. She wants to see how it's going to be. It's a start to a new beginning. Is it false hope? *Lie to me and tell me it's for real.* She's been seeing him, but now he's gone. Maybe he was never there. How am I to know? Maybe, he won't ever be there again. Will there be another? Maybe, it wills my turn now.

4. She has told me so much about him. I didn't know it went that deep. It's been going on for a while. She's buffering. People only tell half-truths to keep the lies from surfacing in the worst ways. It's not working. I know her. She did this to the guy before me while I sat by and listened. And now it *is I*! I never knew she had this guy on her cuff.

5. *All this time, I've been rebuilding my life to better myself for you, for me . . . for us. You have left me long ago. I never knew. Why did you lead this on? How come you couldn't have just let go? Now, I've come to my senses and re-established myself as a responsible person. Yet, I find myself begging for your return. Wanting you back in my life has been the motivating force to better myself in every facet of existence. It made me try that much harder to better myself and appreciate you even more.* **It is here, in the sorrow of abandonment, I find myself unable to let go of what**

could have been a wonderful life together. Even as all hope is lost, I've used the imagination of a better life with you as my true source of excellence. Your scent was the fuel that encouraged my diligence. Your smile reversed my sadness. Your touch lifted my spirit. Your voice brought forth warmth to my heart in a place that's always frigid. This is passion. It is my greatest incentive to receive your love.

Sun. Jan. 9th, 2005

1.   It is Sunday. To wake to another day . . . with one less tooth. They are falling out now. I began brushing with normal toothbrush just days ago. For the last 7 months, I've been shoving my fist into my mouth with a two-inch piece of brittle brush that never really gets the job done. I never reach all the right places. And of course, now that I've got the brush, commissary is without toothpaste. So it becomes a dry brush.

2.   I'm sick of football. I long to see a movie. Maybe, dinner and a movie with my sons and wife.

3.   The sun is shining brightly through my window above my bunk. The Galveston warmth, the beach, and the Strand were yards so close, but so many thousands of moments away. As told, I would have to endure yet another transfer. Hundreds of miles away from my home, my wife, my children, and my life. Or what's left of it. I am to be uprooted again for the *"umpteenth time"*. How many more times will my bunk become my world? **Hell has so many homes for me. Each is different, yet remains the same in its characteristics of filth, danger, disease, noise, and death.**

4.   They argue just to hear their own voice. Most fights are of nonsensical virtues, or about statistics that can't be proven by the numbers anyway. Arguments carry on through the wee hours of the night . . . every night. Most are too insignificant to give the time of day. I don't even care what day it is anymore.

Mon. Jan. 10th, 2005

1. *I constantly want to talk to you. Always wanting to set your mind at ease.* I like the conversations she and I are having. We are being polite and respectful with each other. For the first time in a very long time, I am given the opportunity to speak like a gentleman. It's not possible to do in here. My heart and soul are soaring high above the stench and misery of this cellblock. My mind is alive with hope.

2. Hope should never have false ideals. **Hope is the giver of life; an antidote to survive.** Am I giving in to false hope again? My shadows are dancing on the walls. She dances with me. I don't what to loose this hope. *Please . . . make it real for me Lord*! Will she come in the morning? I will be encourageable. It will be good.

Tues. Jan. 11ᵗʰ, 2005

1. *It's like this: you come here day after day to retrieve info from me regarding my past. Each time, you strip away a little more of my dignity. It leaves me wondering whether or not I'll ever see you again. And then you go away feeling that much more in contempt. And all the while, never once have you offered me anything of regret or sorrow for enacting those terrible deeds against me . . . Not once! If you'll notice, I've never pushed you to reveal what could only leave me in despair and anger. So you can't find your own faults within your acts of adultery and revenge. I'm suffering the consequences of your actions and all you're doing is justifying whatever it is that you do. I never want to be put in the position of having to explain my actions to anyone. I'll be free soon. You will remain to be chained to your conscience, and your past. I'll see to it.*

2. *You come to me in prison only to boast of your infidelity. My skin crawls at the thought of another man slipping inside of you. It rips me into a rage of turmoil. It cast evil shadows on the wall. It erodes my health and dances on my stress. It continues to pound me against a cruelly created time zone of infinitely small intervals. I cannot move through the numbness. We are supposedly able to control one thing in this world. It's the only thing that we are able to mold and bend. Why am I loosing this battle to control my own thoughts? My mind bends in ways I cannot control. I'm out of control. I'm living in my head in absolute solitude. Where is the peace and harmony I have prepared for all this time? Why do you continue to reveal unwanted acts of betrayal to me? Stop coming here.*

3. I exercised outside in the caged parking lot this morning. The sun's heat blazed down on us. I welcomed it. It warmed my face and for the first time in many days, I felt the sweat pouring down my body. It cleansed my soul. I looked out of a crack in the hull of this death ship. Across the street, I found the old style, colonial homes. I could see the grass in the yards and the flowers surrounding the homes. Would I ever get to feel the coolness of grass between my toes again? Would I ever get to feel her toes against my skin? Will I ever feel the warmth of our love together as one?

Wed. Jan. 12th, 2005

1.   **What am I searching for with this time?** A chance . . . a long, since wanted chance, to better myself. This has been a time of reflection and a chance to escape the deadness of my life. All has been laid to the test. Everything I've ever known to do, and be, has been replaced with a different agenda. And for all reasonably expected results, I have arrived. But the thing is, she didn't stick around to catch it. She left the station long before my train was to pull in. I am vainly trying to call her back. The confusion of wanting to win her back or to go on without her constantly evolves in my head. At the same time, she spends her time pulling me in, and pushing me out during her visits. I had long since, made the decision to move on. I had promised myself to be unwavering in my temptation to change. Why then, am I balancing on my big toe upon this pillar of commitment? The debate for fight or flight is burdensome. I have become weary of each battle, and tired of this war of nemesis. There is a constant insecurity of needing to draw her into my world even though I know full well she is paying attention, in detail, to another agenda. I am drowning in it. It must stop! This emotional outcry must end today . . . tonight!

2.   I have educated her with my letters. I have shown her what the greatest capacities of love can be to another. I have revealed the spawning of infinite passion and love to an uninterested recipient. It has shed my skin. Exposed to all, is my undying desire of being accepted. **All of my pain has come from the desire to be desired. This is my true imprisonment.** It is how I feel today. It is how I will always feel. My skin ripples, and my body shudders, as I try to hide the agonizing sound within silent screams. My mouth is gaped open in suspension. Nothing enters or leaves as I struggle to breathe. When will my heart cease to burn with each passing beat? How can life still be pulsating through such a lifeless mass of flesh? I'm looking out to the sun as it crawls into darkness. Once again, I will venture into another long night ahead.

3.   **The color of my skin fades into its chameleon. Invisibility reveals my nothingness. The uncertainty of never knowing my fate-date adds years to each passing moment with no end in sight. With no flight in sight, I remain to be unspoken for within these walls. Will I too, become lost in the cracks of a**

faceless institution? In the end, will all that remains, be only my scrubs scattered thinly under the sheets. An unsorted number to be shuffled back into the pile. A constant crisis within my head beckons the question of when will my number come up. Is it stalemate or stay put? Will I transfer, or God willing, will I be released back to life?

4. Everything remains to be a contradiction. The fight to remain brings nothing but discontentment. Why do I continue to live in fear?

Thurs. Jan. 13th, 2005

1. She came to see me this morning and ended 7 months of deliberation in my life. I will never forget this episode of complete disregard for human suffering. Over the last days and weeks, I've been welcomed with each visit and left holding my cut out heart. *Today, she leaves with the finality of life without me.*

2. I crumbled, as she dug her boots deep into my sides, revealing her disgust in me and the unwillingness to ever give love a chance. She doesn't even want to ever look at me again! I can hear all the sentences spew from her lips, but I am in disbelief to realize the truth of what I'm hearing. I slid up to my bunk and buried myself into my tomb for hours. I skipped dinner for the first time in months. I prayed for death to take me. I struggled to find the strength to end my life with each breath. I cannot bare this torment. I have to rid myself of this captivity.

3. I finally arose sometime in the wee hours to take a shower. It felt like coming up from the dead. I flashed to a sight unseen in too long. It was a vision of my own life and how easily I had forgotten my own goals. It was uplifting. The shower cleansed my soul . . . and my ass! Thoughts of a better life seeped through my skin. The warmth of the shower brought comfort and security. It was going to turn good for me. Things had to turn around for the better. A departure of myself from the wicked ways of this woman is the necessary ingredient. Out of sight . . . out of mind! Conform myself back into society. Strive for success. Belong to no one. Self-acclaimed achievement is the lust that I longed for. I shaved and groomed. I felt better. Got a bite to eat and began to write. I will wish her the best in her own life . . . *but not as much as my own life!*

4. I have achieved so much in my quest to better everything about myself. Not once did it depend on her praise or encouragement. And not once will I look for it, or accept it into my heart. I did it for me. Finally, I've done something of substance for my own well-being. I thought it would have appealed to her. But it looks like I'll be running solo again.

Fri. Jan. 14ᵗʰ, 2005

1. Just when I've given up entirely and resolved myself to spending the rest of my days alone, I get a visit . . . again. Now what I'm getting this morning from her is *"I love you and we should move away together as a family"*. And as for me? All the love, commitment, and dedication of bringing this family back together comes flooding in. It is an outpour of *"whatever it takes"*. It's the right thing to do and we don't even have to work at it. We are that good together. To keep this tragedy together.

2. *You've read this next part before, at the beginning of the book. This is the place where and when I actually wrote it. Read it again to remind yourself of where you don't want to be today.*

3. **The point of discovery is both an end and a beginning: the end of false justification and the beginning of regretful truth. A place where the past, present, and future are simultaneously blended into one constant time zone. Within this presence, the present situation of being arrested, all future regrets are occurring from a multitude of bad decisions. The feeling is mind bending. The sensation triggers numbness. The steal around your wrists collapses all instances of being able to retrace your steps. The domino effect sets in, as the events of the moment leave behind the reasons you didn't think of, or of what you chose to ignore. It's too late! You're going to jail today. There is no *'rewind'* to press, or *'stop'* button to leave time enough to escape. Now, your only option is to continue on with *'play'*, and that means playing the role of inmate. And it's always in the SLP baby; that's the *'slow long play'* mode. There is no *'fast forward'* here. The intervals crawl, and more often than not, *'pause'* seems to have permanence. You've been caught in the snare!**

4. And so now you've got a different life to contend to. It's a life of your own mistakes. Or maybe it's not. Whatever it is, you must continue with the problem of human behavior. Now, you have no freedom to rid yourself of the present company. That company being all the guards, inmates, and yourself. There is no escape from any of these people while in prison.

5.   What's happening in here has nothing to do with family. I am alone in here. I should deal with it alone. But instead, I've become a *"rake"* dragging everyone back into my own pathetic life.

6.   It has been about 5 days since giving in to see the nurse for boils on my body. I shower twice a day in here, but there is no escape from other's lack of hygiene. For whatever reasons, I've got them. One is on my knee. It is pressing against my kneecap. The pressure has fluid leaking down my leg. There are large ones on my scalp and ass. I cannot bend, sit, or lay flat down on them. All requests have been ignored to get me down there. I've gone through 4 guards and 6 request slips.

Sun. Jan. 16th, 2005

1. *1. It is difficult to remain seated in this roller coaster ride of your emotions. This lack of consistency, and constant betrayal of my heart felt dedication of my for love you and this family, has even me questioning my ability to hold vigilance to its purpose. And that purpose is being able to save a family . . . this family! Why have you, once again, turned an about face to our friendship?*

2. *First, you come here and, without remorse, express your lack of desire to maintain any integrity to our marriage. At the same time, I must endure your expressions of likeness to your lover. So here I sit listening to your adulterous affairs. What else can I do but accept it and wish you and your son good luck and farewell? Still, within this fuck festival of yours, you continue to encourage my commitment to you . . . all the while enjoying my torment through your rejection.*

3. Then it happens all over again. My consistency and endless love pays off. You say, *"Yes, I love you. Let's move away together".* I cannot believe what I'm hearing. And now I'm ready to share all the wonderful things that I can bring to this family table.

4. However, it is short lived, because now my calls are not being answered or accepted. Rather, they are being rejected because you are hanging up on me. *You are in the company of friends. I can hear them laughing in the background. Laugh, as you want. I had hoped you would have had more prudence in your capacity to offend me. Once again, I am wrong. As usual, I will participate in your rejection. With this, I have become a fool for your love: footstool for you to stand. It overshadows my love for you.*

5. *I had truly wanted to believe that you longed for me. I thought you loved me. Don't you know that between us, this is something worthwhile? I have loved you always. Impatiently, I wait for a letter of love that never comes. So instead, I take out the old ones and wear down the pages reading and re-reading every word. How I miss you. I love you till it hurts and I feel that I will always be lonesome for you. Even when I'm free. I have so much to share. We have so much more to experience. I thought you might have moved through this the way I have. Why are you hanging up on me and ignoring my phone calls after expressing your love for me. This is*

not reasonable dialogue between people in love. Where is the concern for me . . . for us . . . for the family?

6. *Please, now is the time to tell me. Shall I just stop this nonsense? Is this effort endless in its quest to bring us into something more? This turmoil has sidetracked me from a very straight and narrow path of success. I have long ago succumbed to your abandonment and adulterous ways while I've been incarcerated. I've held on because of the belief of what we have is bigger and more than everlastingly important. It seems our souls have gone from these two mates. The fire to maintain any source of connected energy has died. The central element is gone.*

7. *I cannot believe what I'm hearing at this time!*

8. "Attention inmate customers, would inmate number ####### please pack his shit for ATW." *Whooooosh!* The flush sweeps over my body, sending chills down my spine. It is followed by a wave of sweat across my brow. I am sitting in my bunk writing my sorrowful and pitiless life away. It is about 10 pm on a Sunday night. Who could possibly want to come for my transfer tonight? Oh no! Please don't tell me I've got to sit down in the holding cells for the rest of the night. Why the fuck am I being moved tonight? Why can't I sleep in my bunk tonight? Why must I go down to the holding cells with all the incoming drunks, druggies, and wastoids. I don't even want to be surrounded by the temporary complainers in these cells. Nag . . . Nag . . . Nag. That's all the holding cell is good for; telling stories of why you shouldn't be in here. Anyway, I knew the call was for real because the guard even used my name. But still, I knew it was just another transfer. One more step closer to home . . . wherever that may be in the future. I'm wondering whom it is this time that's coming to take me away. I can think of two more locations. Inside, my heart pounded with the anticipation of escaping. I'm so close to her, but yet so far away.

9. I'm sitting on the tables with my shit packed on the floor. My mat is on the floor and all that I own is at the bottom of a sheet role. I looked over at my buddy Johnny Ray. He's a good man. He's been good to me in the ways of helping me pass the time. To this day, I've never met another who can tell a story like him. *"Thanks, Johnny"*! It is rack time. The wait slows to a crawl while waiting to go anywhere within these prison walls. I sat there in front of all to see. I sat in the waiting area as all other inmates were *"racked up"* in their bunks.

10. I am glad to leave this place. This place especially. I find it hard to accept her visits anymore. They are the torturous sessions of my day. I prayed that my name wouldn't be recalled back to my bunk. The guard got on the phone. I heard my name. Damn it! I knew it. He was going to tell me to go back to my bunk. I remember last week it had happened to another inmate. He had been all packed up and ready to go with mattress in hand when the guards called him back. What a feeling. The guard looked concerned. My heart sank as he approached with that sympathetic look on his face.

11. Boom! It came. *"Inmate, show me your razor, towel, spoon, and sheet. Ok, let's go!"* Wow, it's happening. The way out is beginning. The end of this place is near. The start of another will begin in the morning. Who will it be? Where will I go?

12. **"God Bless Ya'll, and fuck you for the noise, rudeness, and endless, mindless arguments of nothingness. "Down the shoot baby!"**

13. I am sitting in the holding cell waiting for *"whatever"* to come my way. I have been given a women's pair of jeans and a pair of sneakers two sizes too small. That's funny. I wore prison issued slippers three sizes too big in the state facility for months. Now my shoes are too small. What is this . . . momma bear, papa bear? I am wearing my thermal shirt and nothing more. I've got my fish net bag of goodies. It is nothing more than notebook paper, and a few hygiene products. It is all that I possess. *It contains what you are reading right now. I am writing it now as I wait in the holding cell where I first entered 222 days ago.* That fateful Friday night so long ago. As a free man, it would have passed in a blink of an eye. Forgotten with each passing day. I cannot say that for these 222 days of eternity. Everyday passed into a lifetime of regret, remorse, and remembrance.

    This holding cell is the place where everybody is initially brought in for booking. Booking is always just a zoo of everything you are trying to avoid. That's unless you are being transferred to solitary for 20 years. It's actually a good place to be if you are going to solitary confinement because within a very short period of time while sitting here, you will be tired of the human race in general. It's loud and the stench is of the nastiest of flavors. There is no avoiding it's toxic waste from seeping into your skin.

14. So here it is. I have come back to the point of entry. I am watching all the people being brought in from the street. Nothing more than old warrants, petty drug arrests, and public drunkenness. I am listening to civilians (now prisoners) complaining of being here for the next hour or so till their bond money arrives. I remember sitting here wondering how long I too, would be sitting here when I first came in. Seven and a half months later, I'm still sitting here wondering that same question. Still, I have no answer. I wish I were invisible, so I could just stand up and walk past the guard as he opens the door to the outside to let people come into this nightmare. Yep, I could stand and walk over to the door and wait for it to open. I'd have to go ahead and knock the teeth out of the guard's mouth as I ventured past. Actually, I wouldn't want to be invisible for that one. I need him to remember the face . . . my face; just about the time he's hitting the ground.

15. I'm looking at the door to the outside. The place where prisoners are brought in from the street. Here comes this black chick. She is all dressed up in tight designer jeans and a nice top. High heel pumps give her that *"come fuck me look"*. She is crying as she pleads with the intake officer. She is weeping uncontrollably as she continues to lay blame on everything but herself. She cannot believe this is happening to her. She keeps telling the officer to call her boss and everything will be okay. *She is A Correctional Officer*. She is under arrest for dope and outstanding warrants. *She is in jail today*. She is not in uniform. She is not getting paid for being in jail. *She is paying for her crimes in jail today*. There is no escape for her. She can't believe this is happening. She is in absolute denial of all charges against her. Her boyfriend

walked. He was not arrested today and for that, she is pissed. **Her car has been impounded for the transport of dope. She is reeling a lifetime of regret. She begs for release. She cannot talk sensibility. She is not coherent. She refuses to look at the other inmates. She is about to become one for a long time. She is afraid someone will recognize her. She has become what she covets. She cannot bear to see what she has become. She is an inmate. She will be treated as such. She looks for mercy. She will not get it. She begs for compassion from the guards. She is not getting what she thinks she deserves. She would love to press the "stop" button and play time into "reverse". But that's not going to happen. She must move forward. I am watching her fall apart.**

16. I'm looking around at the other prisoners. I can tell who's done time and who's riding in their "*first rodeo*". I can see who's scared and who's bored. I know in an instance by looking at them who will be staying, and who's going. We are looking at the arrested guard. We are in silent celebration of what our eyes are seeing and hearing. A guard has been put in the position of demanding empathy. She has been forced to put herself in our shoes. She must live "*a day in the life of a prisoner*" to know her job should never be taken for granted again. Neither should her lack of concern for people, whether they are inmates or civilians. I say it that way because when you become an inmate of any kind, you no longer are considered a civilian anymore. That's a fact.

17. The nurse is interviewing her. She cannot speak. She is crying too hard. Her head is buried in her arms. The nurse is telling her to get it together. She keeps getting up to talk to the guard. He is yelling at her to sit down with the nurse. And now he is yelling at me to get up and approach the counter. "*Fuck him*" is what I'm thinking. He can blow a lung out screaming at me for all I care. I'd watch him gasped for his last breath and walk off. He can blow that windpipe all he wants. Nothing he does to me will be anything that hasn't been done before. So he is yelling and I'm approaching him. I whispered something to the arrested guard as I walked by. "Get ready for a ride,into the worst nightmare *that you can't imagine*". She began screaming at me. I just laughed. I had to just laugh. This is her christening to prison life and I am the star witness. I feel nothing of sympathy for her. I can only hope she experiences the worst a person can suffer in a place like this. This way she'll never have to inflict that kind of unwanted drama on any other inmate. Maybe her actions will emulate to other guards. But I doubt it.

18. The guard is handing me papers to sign. It is a bond. My mother has hired an attorney to come down here and pay my bond for a hold that has been placed on me from another city. The attorney is on the other side of the glass across the office. I can see her writing stuff. She will not look at me. I don't know what to do. I'm looking around for an officer from another city. I am not seeing one. Did I just come down here to sign this crap and go back up? What's happening? He tells me I'm leaving. I've been hoping for that, but I was afraid to ask so the wait has lasted a lifetime. Are they making a mistake? I won't bother to ask. *I see the whore that used to*

please me. She is in a holding tank with the other female prisoners. The arrested guard will soon be there with them. The whore will eat her up for lunch and spit her out.

19. **The guard is giving me my commissary check as he is opening the big cell door to the civilian lobby. I am walking into a lobby with no guards or other inmates. I have passed through to a place where there are no bars. I can hear the door slam behind me but it's different this time. The door closes to keep me out of the worst of conditions a human has to suffer. It is behind me and freedom is in front of me! There are the glass doors to the street. I am in a daze! I can see the officers standing outside the door. They are looking at me. I will try to walk by them.**

20. I'm on the curb looking back at the building. It looks nice from the outside. Almost like any other office-building complex. The only difference is, it is littered with evil on the inside. Most coming from the people that work in there.

21. Left alone, inmates are peaceful. Saturate their environment with nasty speaking, control freaking, guards, and they will turn on a dime to give you the beating of your life. I saw a couple of guards get what they deserved while in prison. They did only what I dream about. Occasionally, an inmate would kick a guard's ass to give the rest of us a wonderful memory of seeing it happen. His punishment would be like *"taking one for the team"*.

22. I'm waiting for one of the officers to tackle me down. I'm waiting for them to tell me it's a joke or they made a mistake. But it's not. **I am a free man . . . right now, at this moment. Quicker than I came in, I have been released.** There is no one waiting for me. I see no body that I recognize. It is dark. *Am I dreaming this?* I am unfamiliar with what way to go. I know what used to be my home is just blocks away, but I cannot find the familiarity of it. I begin to walk toward the dark shadows of the street. I want to disappear as quickly as I can into the night. The tennis shoes they have given me are two sizes too small. It is hard to walk and I want to be running already. I take them off and run down the street into the night. It is difficult to run. I realize I have no heel muscles. I've spent the last 7 months running on the spot for exercise using only the front balls and toes of my feet. My back heel is weak. I can't help myself. I keep looking back to see if they are coming after me. I keep looking to see that I'm not being followed. The cool night air is overwhelming. My lungs cling to the freshness of the grass and trees. I am running to somewhere, but don't know where to go. I must try to find my way.

23. **How did I arrive at today? How will I reach tomorrow? How do I gather up the momentum to move forward after everything of nothing has been stripped from my life. Who do I turn to? Where will I go? How will I get there?**

24. The streets are quiet, as I walk through the shadows of the night. I have fought so hard to get back to the place I thought I missed so much. I have struggled with every moment of every second to get back to the people I love and long to be with. But now, I find myself walking toward, what I am afraid, will be nothing more than

disappointment for me. All my worries, fears, and predictions, have been nothing more than hearsay up until now. Will I finally face the reality of what my eyes are about to see? How will I be received?

25. **I have to protect who I am now. And if you don't want to go to jail today, you should consider doing the same.**
26. **Practice living your life . . . every moment of it!**

Written by Peter Hall

This book is dedicated first to my mother.

Mom, you have given me a life of love and compassion. I cannot begin to express the patience, endurance, and unconditional love you have provided for me. Since I can remember, your understanding and good-natured wellness has brought much of what is good to my life. Your soft-spoken guidance always provided me with the *"alternate"* answer to my troubling questions. Thank you Mom for being there each and every step of the way.

Dad, your sense of knowledge carries with it a looking glass of wisdom. If only I would've, could've, and should've listened to your message. I am truly sorry to have shamed your name with this terrible misfortune in my life. Thank you dad for hanging in there and not giving up. Your visits will never be forgotten: to sit across from one another and share stories of life and tragedy will remain with me for all my life. Your life is a life of greatness in my eyes. Your accomplishments are only dreams to others . . . and to me. I know you gave me every opportunity to succeed in achieving great advances in my life. If only . . .

And for this I can only ask both of ya'll to accept my greatest apology for dragging you down into the center of hell's fiery pit. It was only then, in the confinement of incarceration I began to add up all the times that my life was anchored safely to prevent me from sliding toward the drop off in troubled times. What happened next, became "out of your hands". And then it became time to serve my debt to society.

In this time, I have learned how to serve many splendid dishes of new responsibility. I made a commitment to ya'll about my own life many times while begging for my life to be saved. I will continue to adhere to those desperate words of *"never again"* while I live my life as a free man. As you say: *"It was a multitude of bad decisions"* spread out over the course of years that finally landed me in prison. Mom and dad, I will spend my life making sure it never happens again. I love you both dearly.

And now on to my son, *Nicholas.* For what your eyes have seen, and your ears have heard. And still, you remain to be a loving son to your father's life. Shining brightly with hysterically funny stories and events that fill up the day. You have given me the opportunity to relive my youthful years through your own eyes. For this, I am forever thankful. You have brought purpose to my life and I would truly be lost without you. Gone are the days of longing for you.

We are in the present and we are loving life . . . every minute of it!

An Offering to You

If you are reading this while residing in jail today, I can only offer you this:

Cause no harm to yourself, or to others . . . unless you are protecting yourself. Ignore the guards and never allow them to seep into your life. Never react negatively to their aggressiveness or foulness of character. It is not yours to encourage, it is theirs to live with. Never give reason for the wrong kind of attention. If you breed hatred toward them, you'll only end up begging for attention in matters of importance later.

Do your time . . . long or short. It is still, only a temporary sanctuary from the law-abiding society that you failed to uphold. Be strong minded and true to yourself.

If your family is supportive, then be the best you can be to show them how important it is for you to return to them. Let nothing in here keep you from getting back out there.

If you have been abandoned, then stand tall by yourself. Create a standard in your life that allows nothing or no one to compromise that promise and commitment to yourself. Begin your life skills training, so that when you leave here, you will not have spent this time in vain. It's better to be prepared . . . than to complain.

If you are not ever leaving, learn to master the system, rather than fight it. Earn every privilege allowed in this system that will enable you to enjoy the fruits of accomplishment. Your time here on earth will come to pass. How you get there, is what living is about. This is the journey.

I lost everything while in prison. I begged for death many times before my release. But yet, at the same time, the human instinct to survive, *and succeed,* became my best friend. I lived with it, spoke to it, listened to it, and learned from it. It will get better if you can believe in yourself.

I had to re-build the foundations of integrity, health, and stability from within. I did this while residing in a place where the sole purpose of the conditions and events, were breaking me down. It took some time to develop strong attributes, but I eventually became addicted to improving myself. Make it a way of life. *Make it your life!*

Owe nothing to anyone and if offered, give thanks. Give to those in need, with no expectations of anything in return. It will come back to you . . . *ten fold*.

Eat right, exercise regularly, read what you can, and write whatever comes to mind.

Enjoy your memories and think of the best times of your life. Use it as a motivating source to remind you of how precious your freedom means to you.

Take this time to reflect on all the events that put you here. Tell yourself, *it can never happen again*. It *can* change . . . *for the better*. Create new opportunities for yourself and a better world will draw in around you. Surround yourself with positive people and you will become part of a more productive mission: Your mission in life is to succeed. It's better than just surviving.

Take advantage of this time to learn new skills. Learn to communicate properly . . . with your arms at your side! Prepare now . . . in your mind and with your hands.

In a world full of uncertainty, you will find comfort in knowing that nobody, *but nobody* can take away what you've learned. If it's good . . . share it! You have complete control of one thing in this world . . . *It is your thoughts.*

Remember this cardinal rule:
Your actions are a direct result of your thoughts
How you think, will determine how you act out your life.
Make the best of them.

Hope to see you *in the free*!
Peter Hall

Peter Hall can be reached for questions, comments, and public appearances. He frequently offers motivational sessions to high school and college forums.

Peterocks212@yahoo.com

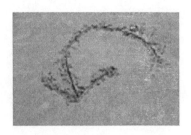

A WRONG TURN . . . AND A BAD DECISION.

Do you really want to lose your freedom?
Do you want to lose your family?
Are you prepared to lose your home?
Are you willing to give up your children?
Do you value your job?
Do you want to be told what to eat?
When to sleep? When to talk?
Can you live without the warmth of the sun?
Will you miss the rain?
Can you stand the abuse?
Will you tolerate the noise?
Can you smell the stench?
Do you want to live in a cage?
Can you feel the truthful pain of what I'm telling you?

Do You Really Want To Go To Jail today?

Peter Hall